YES, THERE IS HELL,
YES, THERE IS DEVIL,
YES, THERE IS KARMA

Samael Aun Weor

March
2021

info@ageac.org

www.ageac.org · www.samael.org
www.vopus.org · www.radiomaitreya.org

WARNING

PROLOGUE

Going down into the Infernal Worlds, Planetary Infra-Dimensions or Tenebrous Abysses mentioned in all religious texts of antiquity, always constituted an impressive task with which ancient Heroes, Titans, Gods or Demi-gods, would gain their right to abandon the earthly world and its misery, to exalt themselves in the spheres of the Infinite and the Eternal.

Already the Great Initiate from Florentine Italy, Dante Alighieri, evoked in his *Divine Comedy* the terrible designs awaiting the lost souls condemned to the disintegration of their psychic material in the Arcades or Circles of the Underworld, or "Tartarus" according to the metaphysical Greeks.

Similar adventure awaited, hundreds of centuries before, in the esoteric Crete, that Greek Hierophant named Theseus upon descending into the cursed labyrinth where awaited quietly and maliciously the disgusting Minotaur, which deprived many bold ones of their lives, devouring them without mercy. However, Theseus, intelligent and obedient to the guardian Gods, descended aided by the divine Ariadne, who gave him one of her hairs, serving as guide to enter and exist that den, without the risk of remaining trapped in those enigmatic depths. Finally, armed with a symbolical sword and

endless courage, the noble hero beheads the Minotaur and strips him off the sacred jewelry that, for millennia, has been in the hands of that monster.

All these accounts, dear reader, bear the seal of hermetic symbolism and, without the help of Gnosis –divine Knowledge– it is impossible to decipher the high contents of these journeys to the domains of darkness. To excogitate, investigate, aspire to the supreme knowledge that encloses these accounts, is, besides a legitimate right, a duty that every human being must fulfil, if he wants to find the roots of his existence and the background it holds.

Hermes Trismegistus already said it: "Before going up, it is necessary to go down", and V.M. Samael Aun Weor as loyal interpreter of the occultist tradition, solemnly affirms: "Before any exaltation comes a frightful humiliation." Jesus Christ himself, before ascending to the Father of all Lights –the Kabbalistic Kether of each one of us–, descended into the Infernos, and on the third allegorical day, he ascended to Heavens to remain at the right of the Omni-Merciful.

From all of the above, it is easy to deduce that every true aspirant to the Supreme Light has to fulfil similar tasks within their own Atomic Infernos, to uproot from Darkness that Light that once shone in the heart of man and which, after humanity fell into animal generation, remained trapped into demonic entities that we gnostically define as "I's" or "undesirable Psychological Aggregates".

Yes, blessed reader, the Light is the daughter of terrible "voluntary sufferings" and "conscious sacrifices", done in our occult psychic or spiritual anatomy. This is the great mystery of Sophia –the Soul– engulfed in chaos and calling upon Heaven for her soon release, while different enemies of the Light fight feverishly to submerge her more and more in the abyss of her own perdition.

This treatise, illustrious reader, reveals one of the master books of hermetic literature: *The Divine Comedy*; and it does so by using a very valuable tool called "direct mystic experience". Only by means of the most elevated qualities of the awakened Consciousness, is it possible to realize all the meticulous investigations that are described in this book and which, apart from all dialectic or historic materialists, offer testimony that "YES, THERE IS HELL, YES, THERE IS DEVIL, YES, THERE IS KARMA".

Pseudo-esotericism negated many times, lacking the rigorous methods of investigation, the existence of the Devil of all religions, the Infernal Dwellings and the punishment or Karma to which are subjected the souls. However, in this treatise, all this subject-matter is scientifically developed with the help of a transcendent and transcendental logic.

The Law of Action and Consequence has always manifested throughout eternity, and ignoring it is typical of the short-sighted individuals who try to bury their head in the sand. Now, it is not enough to know that we are flagged by a Cosmic Justice; the important thing is to get to know the practical formulas to escape the persecution of the Archons of Destiny, and this, esteemed reader, is one of the parameters that guides the reading of these sacred pages.

Some atheists or enemies of the eternal have once said: *"Hell does not exist, it is here, in this world and that is all."* We reply with Mr. Emmanuel Kant –the great philosopher of Königsberg– *"The exterior is a reflection of the interior"*; and to tell the truth, the world nowadays has turned into a living hell, however, the causes of this global anomaly must be sought inside of us, here and now.

The cultivated materialists ignore that beyond the three-dimensional life, we continue existing in other dimensions already presumed by contemporary physics and where, upon reaching our time of death, our own energetic determinants –psychological "I's" fighting among themselves– will take us based on vibrational affinity, to dimensional spheres similar to all those that have already been described by majestic theological treatises of different people of antiquity, and where *only the weeping and gnashing of teeth are heard.*

Positivist materialists must understand that in the universal mechanics, there is not only Evolution, but also its twin sister, Involution, and these two Laws share all the physical and metaphysical phenomena. Thus, speaking like the Great Avatar Krishna in his *Doctrine of Transmigration of the Souls*, it is not surprising to know that a Soul which does not incarnate his divine energetic principles and has uselessly

wasted his cycles of cosmic manifestation, he will have fortified within himself everything that is contrary to the Light, to the Truth, to the Being and therefore, will involute in the Atomic Infernos of nature in order to liberate, by means of painful processes, that which is essential and which must re-bind one day with the Eternal.

All these introductions about the pilgrimages of the Soul from Abyss to Abyss, are masterfully explained throughout this magnificent book, so that the words of Hermes Thot are fulfilled, who, foretelling the return of true natural-born occultism, exclaimed: *"After comes what was before, and before was what will be now."* John, the great seer of Patmos, said it like this: *"From the times of the Prophets, the Heaven is taken by assault and only the brave ones have taken it."* Gnosis has done its duty of getting close to your portal; now it is up to you, kind reader, "to give seed to the one who wants to sow and does not have and give advice to the one who wants to learn and does not know."

Thelema be your blazon.

Kwen Khan Khu

1

HELL

Q uestion: In this day and age we can no longer accept that the Hell of fire and flames of which the Catholic religion speaks to us about is anything other than religious superstition, according to scientists. Is this true, Master?

Answer: Distinguished gentleman, allow me to inform you that any Hell of a religious type is exclusively symbolic.

It is not superfluous in these moments to recall the Glacial Inferno of the Nordics, the Chinese Hell with all of its yellow torments, the Buddhist Hell, the Mohammedan Hell or the Infernal Island of the ancient inhabitants of the country of Marapleicie, whose civilization is today found hidden within the sands of the Gobi desert...

Unquestionably, these various traditional Hells emphatically allegorize the Submerged Mineral Kingdom.

Remember, good friend, that Dante found his *"infernus"* within the living entrails of the Earth – namely, *The Divine Comedy.*

Question: Master, you speak to us about the Submerged Mineral World, nonetheless, all of the drilling into the crust of the Earth by the mining, oil and other types of companies have not revealed signs of a living world even in the first interior layer of the Earth. Where is that Submerged Mineral World?

Answer: Great friend, allow me to inform you that the tridimensional world of Euclid is not everything...

Clearly, above this world of three dimensions –length, width and height– there are various superior dimensions. Obviously, in accordance with the Law of Contrasts, below this tridimensional zone various infra-dimensions of submerged mineral type also exist.

It is indubitable that the mentioned Dantean types of Hells correspond to these infra-dimensions.

Question: Forgive me for insisting, Master, but in all the books that I have scrutinized, driven by my longings, I do not remember any writing or document that even talks about these infra-dimensions, or that at least indicate how to discover them. Therefore, I ask you: what is the purpose of talking about the infra-dimensions which as far as I have been able to verify no human being has seen or touched.

Answer: Distinguished gentleman, I find your question interesting; it is however worthwhile to clarify that the International Gnostic Movement has systems, methods of direct experience, by means of which we can verify the harsh reality of the infra-dimensions of nature and of the cosmos.

We can and should locate the Nine Dantean Circles precisely below the epidermis of the Earth, within the interior of the planetary organism in which we live.

Obviously, the cited nine circles intelligently correspond with nine natural infra-dimensions.

It is clear and manifest that the *"Nine Heavens"* of Dante's *Divine Comedy* are nine dimensions of a superior type, intimately correlated with the nine of an inferior type.

Anyone who has ever studied *The Divine Comedy* from an esoteric point of view cannot ignore the reality of the Infernal Worlds...

Question: Master, what is the basic difference between the Hells of Catholicism and those considered by the Gnostic Movement?

Answer: Good friend, the difference between the symbolic Hells of one religion or another is that which can exist between one flag and another of different nations. Each country allegorizes its existence with a national flag; likewise, each religion symbolizes the Infernal Worlds with an allegory of an infernal type.

However, all Christian, Chinese, or Buddhist Hells, etc., etc., are really nothing else but different emblems that correspond to the harsh reality of the Atomic Hells of nature and of the cosmos.

Question: Why do people have nightmares, as we commonly call them? What happens in this case? Do they travel to those Infra-dimensional Worlds?

Answer: I will very gladly answer this interesting question from the audience... Ladies and gentlemen, I want you to comprehend what nightmares truly are.

Occult Anatomy teaches us that in our lower abdomen there are seven infernal doors, seven inhuman chakras or negative vortices of sinister forces.

It can happen that someone with indigestion caused by some heavy meal may activate these infernal chakras due to this disorder. Then these abysmal doors open, as is clearly taught by the religion of Mohammed, and that night the individual penetrates the Infernal Worlds.

This is possible by means of the projection of the personality. It is not difficult for the Ego to penetrate into the Abode of Pluto.

The monsters of nightmares really exist. They originally de-scend from archaic times; they normally inhabit the infra-dimen-sions of the Submerged Mineral World.

Question: Venerable Master, does this mean that not only those who die without having saved their Soul enter into Hell?

Answer: It is evident, clear, and manifest that those who are alive also penetrate into the Infernal Worlds, as demonstrated by nightmares. Obviously, the human infra-conscious is infernal in nature; it could be stated with complete crystal clarity that all abysmal horrors are within the Atomic Infernos of man. In other words, we emphasize the following: the infernal abysses are in no way divorced from our own subconscious and infra-conscious.

Now the audience will understand why it is so easy for any-one to penetrate into the Nine Dantean Circles, at any time.

Question: Beloved Master, I do not really understand why you first said that the Infernal Worlds are found in the infra-di-mensions of the Earth, and thereafter you mention that those Atomic Abysses are found within oneself. Would you be so kind so as to clarify this to me?

Answer: I find your question magnificent. Whoever wants to discover the Laws of Nature must find them within himself. Who-ever does not find within himself what he seeks, will never find it outside of himself. The ancients stated: *"Man, know thyself and you will know the universe and the Gods."* We must find within our interior everything that exists in nature and in the cosmos. There-fore, the Nine infernal Dantean Circles are within us, here and now.

Question: Master, I have had nightmares in which I have seen a world of darkness and many monsters. Could it be that I have entered into those Infra-dimensional or Infernal Worlds?

Answer: Your question is quite important. It is necessary for the audience to comprehend that those infra-dimensions are found within the submerged depths of our own nature. Obviously, I repeat, during nightmares the seven doors of the Atomic Infernos of the lower abdomen are opened and then we descend into the Submerged Worlds...

Rare are those persons who have not at some point in their life visited the Kingdom of Pluto. Nevertheless, it is good, ladies and gentlemen, that while studying this subject matter, we think about the crude natural reality of those worlds that are situated in the infra-dimensions of the planet in which we live. Let us think, for a moment, about worlds that mutually penetrate and interpenetrate each other, in densely inhabited regions etc., etc. that do not lose themselves in one another.

By no means should we interpret religious allegories literally; let us seek "the Spirit that vivifies and gives life." The Hells of the diverse religions allegorize crudely natural realities; we must not confuse symbols with cosmic phenomena in themselves.

Question: Master, I would like you to explain to me a little bit more about these Infernal Worlds, since in the nightmares that I have had, I have never seen light or beautiful faces. Could you tell me why?

Answer: I will gladly answer this question. Infernal Darkness is another type of Light; it certainly corresponds to the infrared spectrum.

The inhabitants of such subterranean realms perceive the diverse color variations that correspond to that zone of the solar spectrum.

I want for you, my friends, to comprehend that all the colors that exist in the ultraviolet are also found in the infrared.

That a yellow exists in the ultraviolet? This is something very notable, but yellow also exists in the infrared in a different manner, and this also happens with the rest of the colors. Therefore, I emphatically repeat the following: Darkness is another type of Light.

Unquestionably, the inhabitants of the Submerged Mineral Kingdom are found too far away from the Sacred Absolute Sun, and for that reason they indeed become terribly malignant and frightfully ugly.

Question: I understand, Master, that in the Submerged Worlds of the Earth there are all kinds of monsters, and that they live there —but how is it possible that within myself, who is so small in comparison to the planet, I can find those very worlds?

Answer: My good friend, allow me to tell you that any molecule of starch, or of iron, copper, etc., etc. is a complete solar system in miniature. A disciple of Marconi imagined our solar system precisely like a great cosmic molecule.

Whoever does not discover the movement of the planets around the Sun within a simple molecule is indeed very far from comprehending Astronomy.

Nothing is unlinked in this universe; there really is no effect without cause, or cause without effect. Likewise, within each one of us there are forces and atoms that correlate either with the Celestial Spheres or with the Infernal Spheres.

It is good to know that within our organism there are psychic centers that put us in touch with the nine superior dimensions of the cosmos, or with the nine inferior dimensions.

I have already clearly stated that this tridimensional world in which we live is not everything, since above us we have the superior dimensions and below us the inferior ones.

Unquestionably, all these heavenly or infernal dimensions are related with the distinct zones of our own psyche, and therefore, if we do not discover them within ourselves, we will not discover them anywhere else.

Question: Master, you frequently mention the words "Atomic Abysses". Why "Atomic"?

Answer: I find this question extraordinary and I will very gladly answer it. First of all, I want you to know that every atom is a trio of Matter, Energy, and Consciousness.

Now, let us think for a moment about "Atomic Intelligences"; obviously, there are solar and lunar ones; there are also terribly perverse "Malignant Atomic Intelligences".

The atoms of the Secret Enemy within our organism are controlled by a certain malignant atom located exactly in the coccygeal bone.

These types of atoms cause illnesses and give origin to distinct manifestations of perversity within us.

Let us expand this information a little bit more and let us think for a moment on all the malignant atoms of the planet Earth. Obviously, the heaviest ones, the most demonic ones, inhabit the Abode of Pluto; that is, the infra-dimensions of the world in which we live.

Now you will comprehend the reason why we talk about "Atomic Abysses," about "Atomic Infernos," etc.

Question: I think that the majority of us, when we think in terms of "the atom," we imagine something infinitely small. Therefore, when we are told that all the suns and planets of the cosmos constitute an atom, this somewhat confounds our reasoning process. Master, is this coherent?

Answer: Distinguished gentleman and friend, it has never occurred to me to think of reducing the entire Universe –or the universes– to a simple atom. Allow me to tell you that worlds, suns, satellites, etc., are constituted by sums of atoms, and this is different, right? If in any part of my speech I compared the solar system to a big molecule, I did it based upon the Law of Philosophical Analogies; I never meant to reduce that system to a simple atom.

2

THE THREE ASPECTS
OF THE INTERIOR OF THE EARTH

Question: Master, based on what you have previously explained to us, should we understand that beneath the interior layers of the Earth there are only infra-dimensions, since the supra-dimensions –that correspond to the Heavens– are only found above the terrestrial layer?

Answer: Distinguished gentleman, I find your question quite interesting and I hasten to answer.

It is good for all of you to understand that this planetary organism in which we live has three clearly defined aspects in its interior:

1st Mineral Region – merely physical.

2nd Supra-dimensional Zone.

3rd Infra-dimensional Zone.

Question: Supposing that these three aspects of the interior of the Earth that you are speaking to us about were to exist —and I clarify that as far as I am concerned I accept it hypothetically— we would have to come to the conclusion that the Nine Celestial Spheres co-exist with the Hells that correspond to the infra-dimensions. Is it perhaps coherent that the Heavens are to be found in the same location as the Hells?

Answer: Esteemed gentleman, it is urgent to comprehend in an integral manner that everything in nature and in the cosmos is reduced to the additions and subtractions of the dimensions that mutually penetrate and interpenetrate each other without losing themselves in one another.

There is a hermetic postulate that states: "As above, so below." Apply this postulate to the subject matter in question.

It is clear that within the interior of our planetary organism the Nine Heavens have their correlations in accordance with the Law of Correspondences and Analogies.

Within the interior of the planetary organism in which we live, these Nine Heavens correlate intelligently with the nine deep zones of planet Earth.

However, I still have not explained this subject-matter in depth; what really happens is that these Nine Heavens have a Center of Atomic Gravitation that is located exactly in the center of the planet Earth.

In other words, I want to tell you, and all of you, ladies and gentlemen, that the Nine Heavens gravitate around the central atom of planet Earth, extending far beyond the entire solar system. This same process is repeated in each of the planets of the solar system of Ors.

Question: Venerable Master, I find your explanation very beautiful and it fills the gaps of my understanding perfectly; notwithstanding, I must admit that according to the precepts of logic, the explanation that you have given us cannot be clearly demonstrated. Therefore, how can we verify your affirmation in this regard?

Answer: Esteemed gentleman, your question is troubling. Unquestionably, formal logic leads us to error. It is not by means of such logic that we can reach the experience of what is Real; we need a Superior Logic, which fortunately exists. Ouspensky has already written *Tertium Organum*, "*The Third Canon of Thought...*"

It is clear that there exists a sense of unity in the mystical experience of many transcended individuals. Such men, through the development of certain cognitive faculties, have been able to verify for their own selves and in a direct manner, the reality of the Infernal Worlds in the interior of the planet in which we live.

What is interesting about all of this is that the information enunciated by one Adept after the other is similar, in spite of the fact that these men live in different places on Earth.

Question: Then Master, are you telling us that only a certain and very limited number of Adepts –who have had the fortune of being endowed with those cognitive powers– are able to verify the infra-dimensions and the supra-dimensions of the planets and the cosmos, as well as those within man himself?

Answer: In the field of direct experimentation, in the field of practical Metaphysics, there is a great diversity of individuals with psychic faculties that are developed to a greater or lesser degree.

It is obvious that there are disciples and Masters. The former can give us more or less incipient information; the latter, the Adepts or Masters, have faculties at their disposal that are immensely superior, which enable them to perform in-depth investigations and therefore allow them to speak in a clearer, more precise and detailed manner.

Question: If you, Master, have taught us that we must verify through our own experience what the Adepts and Enlightened affirm; is it then possible for us, the profane, to verify the reality of the Infernal Worlds through our own experiences, apart from the –experiences of a simple nightmare caused by stomach indigestion?

Answer: Esteemed gentleman, it is obvious that direct experimentation in the field of Metaphysics is accessible only to the individuals who have developed the faculties that are latent within man.

However, I want to tell you with complete clarity that every person can superficially experience the crude reality of these Atomic Infernos when they have one of those disgusting nightmares.

Undoubtedly, by this I do not mean to say that the aforementioned nightmares allow for the complete verification of the crude reality of the infra-dimensions of nature.

Whoever really wants to experience that which is below the tridimensional world of Euclid must develop certain faculties and very special psychic powers.

Question: Is it possible for all of us to develop these faculties?

Answer: Distinguished gentleman, allow me to inform you that the International Gnostic Movement possesses methods and systems by which every human being can develop their psychic powers in a conscious and positive manner.

Question: Master, could you tell us what we should understand in regards to the Devil that lives in some Infernos that have flames of fire and a terrible smell of sulfur, where the beings who have behaved badly in this life are punished?

Answer: I am going to reply to the gentleman's question...

Unquestionably, within the submerged regions of the Mineral Kingdom, beneath the very epidermis of planet Earth, different zones exist...

Let us briefly remember the Igneous Zone; its existence is clearly demonstrated by volcanic eruptions.

Let us now mention the Aqueous Zone; no one can deny that there is water in the interior of this planetary organism.

Let us think for a moment in the Element Air: although it seems incredible, within our planet Earth there are also air currents, special zones. It has even been said with absolute clarity that within the interior of this world there is a certain vast region that is entirely hollow —we would say "aerial."

In no way can we deny the reality of stones, sand, rocks, metals, etc., etc., etc.

When thinking about the concept of "demon" or "demons," let us also reflect upon the lost Souls; this is truly interesting...

Many inhabitants of the Infernal Worlds dwell in the Region of Fire, others in the Regions of Air, and finally others inhabit the Aquatic Regions and the Mineral Zones.

It is obvious that the inhabitants of the Earth's interior are greatly connected with sulfur since it is an integral part of volcanoes; however, it is evident that only the dwellers of fire can be specifically associated with sulfur.

Therefore, distinguished gentleman, honorable public, respected ladies and gentlemen, I want for you to comprehend Hell or the "infernus" in a crudely natural way, without artifices of any type.

Question: Could you tell me, Master, why is the region of the lower abdomen —associated with the Infernal Worlds— located in the region of the Silver Cord? Does this mean that the aforementioned Cord is in constant communication with our Infernal Worlds?

Answer: Honorable gentleman, I want to respond to you with perfect clarity... Much has been said about the Silver Cord; it is indubitable that each Soul is connected to the physical body through this magnetic thread. We have been told that an offshoot of this cord, or Thread of Life, is connected to the heart, and another to the brain.

Various authors emphasize the idea that seven of these offshoots derived from the Silver Cord are connected with seven specific centers of the human organism.

In any case, this Thread of Life, this cord that you are speaking about, that represents the very basis of your question, is in no way connected to the seven chakras of the lower abdomen.

It is interesting to know that during the hours of sleep, the Essence, the Soul, escapes from the physical body in order to travel to different places of the Earth or the cosmos; at that time, the magnetic thread of our existence is set free, it extends infinitely; thereafter, it draws us back to the physical body at the moment we awaken in bed.

Question: Master, can you expand on what you have just said with respect to the seven chakras that are found in the lower abdomen, since we have been told in other lectures and even in your own books that the seven chakras are located in different parts of our organism?

Answer: Honorable gentleman, I have listened to your question and I hasten to answer with great pleasure.

I see that you, sir, have confused the seven chakras of the lower abdomen with the Seven Churches of the *Book of Revelation* of St. John, which are located on the spinal column.

Undoubtedly, nowhere in this lecture that we are delivering here tonight in Mexico City, have I made any allusion to such magnetic centers or vortices of force located on the Staff of Brahma or spinal cord.

We have only cited, mentioned, the seven infernal doors of hell, which the religion of Mohammed talks about, the seven specific centers or chakras that are located in the lower abdomen and related to the Infernal Worlds; that is all!; understood?

Question: Venerable Master, based on everything that has been stated so far, can we infer that the physical aspect of the center of the Earth belongs to the tridimensional world, and that the supra-dimensional and infra-dimensional aspects are located in those subterranean regions of the planet, where the tridimensional intellectual and sensorial perceptions of the rational animal do no reach?

Answer: Distinguished gentleman, allow me to inform you and the entire audience in general that is listening to me, that our five senses perceive only the tridimensional aspects of existence; however, they are incapable of perceiving the supra-dimensional or infra-dimensional aspects of the Earth and of the cosmos.

It is obvious that the subterranean regions of our world have three fundamental aspects. Yet again, the ordinary senses only perceive what is physical, tridimensional in a superficial manner.

If we want to know the superior and inferior dimensions of the interior of the Earth we must develop other faculties of perception that are latent in the human race.

Question: Beloved Master, should we understand that living beings inhabit the supra-dimensions as well as the infra-dimensions?

Answer: My friends, it is unquestionable that the three Zones of the interior of our world are inhabited.

While the infra-dimensions are inhabited by lost souls, in the supra-dimensions of the planetary interior dwell many Devas, Elementals of a superior order, Gods, Masters, etc. who work intensely with the intelligent forces of this Great Nature.

We could talk very extensively about the populations of the central or supra-dimensional or infra-dimensional zones of the interior of our world; however, we will address this topic in future lectures, for now I bid you farewell and wish you a very good evening.

3

THE SEVEN COSMOS

Well friends, we are gathered here again with the purpose of studying the Ray of Creation.

It is urgent, indispensable and unpostponable to clearly and precisely know the place that we occupy within the very much alive Ray of Creation.

First of all, esteemed gentlemen, distinguished ladies, I kindly ask you to follow my lecture with infinite patience.

I want you to know that there are seven cosmos, namely:

1st: Protocosmos

2nd: Hagiocosmos

3rd: Macrocosmos

4th: Deuterocosmos

5th: Mesocosmos

6th: Microcosmos

7th: Tritocosmos

Unquestionably, the first one is formed by multiple, transcendental, divine, Spiritual Suns...

Much has been said about the Sacred Absolute Sun, and it is obvious that each solar system is governed by one of these Spiritual Suns. This means that our planetary system possesses its own Sacred Absolute Sun, just like all the other solar systems of the unalterable infinite.

The Second Order of Worlds is actually formed by all the millions of suns and planets that travel throughout space.

The Third System of Worlds is formed by our galaxy, by this great Milky Way that has the sun Sirius as its central cosmic capital.

The Fourth Order is represented by our solar system Ors.

The Fifth Order corresponds to the planet Earth.

The Sixth Order is Microcosmos-Man.

The Seventh Order is in the Infernal Worlds.

Let us expand this explanation a bit more... I want you, ladies and gentlemen, to understand with total clarity what the First Order of Worlds really is: extraordinary Spiritual Suns that sparkle with infinite splendors in space. Radiant spheres that astronomers would never be able to perceive through their telescopes.

Think now of the billions and trillions of worlds and stars that inhabit the infinite space. Now, consider the galaxies: when looked at separately, anyone of them is certainly a Macrocosmos, and our galaxy, the Milky Way, is not an exception.

What would we say about the Deuterocosmos? Unquestionably, every solar system —regardless of which galaxy it belongs to, whether it is made of matter or antimatter— is obviously a Deuterocosmos.

In space, Earths are as numerous as the sands of the immense sea. Indubitably, any of these, any planet, regardless of its center of cosmic gravity, is in itself a Mesocosmos.

Much has been said about Microcosmos-Man. We emphasize the transcendental idea that each one of us is an authentic and legitimate Microcosmos. Nevertheless, we are not the only inhabitants of the infinite. It is clear that many inhabited worlds exist. Any inhabitant of the cosmos or of the cosmoses is an authentic Microcosmos.

Finally, it is useful to know that within each planet there is a submerged Mineral Kingdom, with its own Atomic Infernos. The latter are always situated within the interior of any planetary mass and within the infra-dimensions of nature, beneath the tridimensional zone of Euclid.

Thus, ladies and gentlemen, may it be understood that the First Order of Worlds is completely different from the Second, and that each cosmos is absolutely dissimilar and radically distinct...

The First Order of Worlds is infinitely divine and ineffable; not a single mechanical principle exists within it; it is governed by the Unique Law.

The Second Order is unquestionably controlled by the Three Primary Forces, which regulate and direct every cosmic Creation.

The Third Order of Worlds, our galaxy or any galaxy of sacred space, is indubitably governed by 6 Laws.

The Fourth Order of Worlds, our solar system or any solar system of infinite space, is always governed by 12 Laws.

The Fifth Order, our Earth or any planet similar to ours, orbiting around any sun, is absolutely governed by 24 Laws.

The Sixth Cosmic Order, any human organism, is definitely governed by 48 Laws. We can see that this is totally proven in the human germinal cell which is known to contain 48 chromosomes.[*]

*. *The V.M. Samael analyzed the topic on chromosomes during the time when the scientific community claimed that human beings possessed 48 chromosomes, just like the apes. The fact that there are 46 chromosomes became widespread in the second half of the 20th century. In spite of this, it is useful to know that one pair of those 46 chromosomes, specifically number 2, is the result of the fusion of two ancestral chromosomes. Therefore, human chromosomes can be considered as really being 48 pairs.*

Lastly, the Seventh Order of Worlds is under the total control of 96 Laws.

I want you to know, in a precise manner, that the number of Laws in the abyssal regions multiplies scandalously.

It is evident that the First Dantean Circle is always under the control of 96 Laws; however, this number doubles in the Second, producing 192 Laws. In the Third it triples; in the Fourth it quadruples; thus, the number 96 can be multiplied x 2, x 3, x 4, x 5, x 6, x 7, x 8, x 9. So then, in the Ninth Circle, when multiplying 96 x 9, we get 864 Laws...

If you reflect profoundly on the First Cosmos, you will see that the most absolute freedom exists there, the most absolute happiness, since everything is governed by the Unique Law.

Complete happiness still exists in the Second Cosmos, due to the fact that it is completely controlled by the Three Primary Laws of entire Creation.

However, in the Third Cosmos, a mechanical factor already introduces itself, because upon dividing themselves, these primeval, divine Three Laws become six. Obviously, a certain cosmic automatism is already in place. No longer are the Three Forces working alone for upon dividing themselves, they have given rise to the mechanical interplay of any galaxy.

See then what a solar system is. It is clear that in it, the 6 Laws have once again divided themselves, becoming 12, thus increasing mechanicalness, automatism, complication, etc., etc.

Let us now focus on any planet of the infinite, and especially on our terrestrial world. Obviously, it is more heterogeneous and complicated due to the fact that in it the 12 Laws of the system have become 24 laws...

Let us now frankly look at Microcosmos-Man; let us examine the germinal cell and we will find the 48 chromosomes, which are the living representation of the 48 Laws that control our entire body.

Obviously, when these 48 Laws divide themselves, in and by themselves, they originate the 96 of the First Dantean Circle.

I want you then, ladies and gentlemen, to comprehend the place that we occupy in the Ray of Creation.

Someone said that Inferno comes from the word "infernus" which in Latin means "inferior region". He thus emphasized the idea that the place we occupy in the tridimensional region of Euclid is the Inferno, since, according to him, it is the inferior place of the cosmos…

Regrettably, the one who made such an unusual affirmation in fact did not know the Ray of Creation. If he would have had more information, if he would have studied the Seven Cosmoses, he would have clearly realized that that inferior place is not this physical world in which we live, but the Seventh Cosmos, which is situated exactly within the interior of the planet Earth, within the natural infra-dimensions, beneath the tridimensional zone of Euclid.

Question: Venerable Master, after having listened with attention and patience to the scientific exposition on the Ray of Creation, I have observed that when you refer to the First Order of Worlds —that is, the Protocosmos— you mentioned that movement, life, corresponds to the First Law where absolute freedom reigns… We were told, according to the words of the great Kabir Jesus: "Find the truth, and the truth shall make you free." *By following the Law of Analogies and Correspondences, should we understand that since we, the men who move and have our Being in the Sixth Order of Worlds —that is, the Microcosmos— in order for us to experience the Truth and thus to be completely free, we must strive to become inhabitants of those worlds governed by the Unique Law?*

Answer: I will most gladly answer the question of the gentleman… Distinguished ladies and gentlemen, it is indispensable to comprehend that the greater the number of Laws, the greater the degree of mechanicalness and pain; the lesser the number of Laws, the lesser the degree of mechanicalness and pain.

Unquestionably, in the Sacred Solar Absolute, in the Central Spiritual Sun of this system in which we live, move, and have our Being, there is no mechanicalness of any type, and therefore, it is obvious that the most absolute bliss reigns there.

Clearly, we must fight in an inexhaustible manner in order to free ourselves from the 48, 24, 12, 6, and 3 Laws, so as to return to the Sacred Absolute Sun of our system.

Question: Master, based on what you have formerly explained, we can deduce that worlds with a greater number of Laws are more mechanical and therefore, by logic, denser and more material. Does this mean that the Infra-dimensional or Infernal Worlds will cause greater suffering, and this is why they are called the Region of Penalties and Punishments?

Answer: I find this question from the audience quite interesting, and of course I hasten to answer it with great pleasure.

Distinguished gentleman, I want you and everybody to know and understand that the greater the number of Laws, the greater the degree of mechanicalness and pain.

The 96 Laws of the First Infernal Zone are terribly painful; however, as this number of Laws are multiplied in each of the infra-dimensional zones, pain, mechanicalness, materiality and weeping also multiply.

Question: Venerable Master, we have observed that previously you spoke to us about the Nine Concentric Circles in the Region of the Infra-dimensions, which correspond to the Nine Circles of the Supra-dimensions of the Cosmos; however, when referring to the Ray of Creation, you only enumerate and explain Seven Cosmoses. Is there not some inconsistency in that?

Answer: Honorable sir, it is indispensable for you to make a clear differentiation between the Seven Cosmoses, the Nine Heavens, and the Nine Dantean Circles of the natural infra-dimensions.

Obviously, the Nine Heavens are related, as we have already explained, with the nine submerged regions below the epidermis of the Earth. This is what Enoch saw while in a state of ecstasy upon mount Moriah; a place where he later built a subterranean temple with nine interior levels in order to allegorize the transcendental reality of his vision....

It is unquestionable that the Nine Heavens are fully concretized in the Spheres of the Moon, Mercury, Venus, Sun, Mars, Jupiter, Saturn, Uranus, and Neptune. It is clear that all of these Nine Heavens correspond to the Deuterocosmos.

So, is it clear in your mind that the Seven Cosmoses are not the Nine Heavens?

Question: Master, you explained to us that, as we descend to an increasing number of Laws from the First Cosmos towards the Infernal Regions, mechanicalness, automatism, materiality progressively increase. This makes me think that as we move away from the Three Primary Laws, we separate ourselves from the direct will of the Father at the same time, thus being left to our own miserable fate. Is this the case?

Answer: Distinguished gentleman, honorable ladies who listen to me in this auditorium, I want you to know in a clear and precise manner that the Sacred Solar Absolute, gloriously shines beyond this system of worlds that form our solar system.

It is indubitable that the unalterable happiness of the eternal living God exists in the Central Spiritual Sun, which is governed by the Unique Law. Unfortunately, as we move farther and farther away from the Sacred Absolute Sun, we then penetrate into worlds that are increasingly more complicated, where automatism, mechanicalness, and pain are introduced...

Obviously, the bliss within the Cosmos of 3 Laws is incomparable, because the materiality is less. In that region, any atom possesses within its interior nature only 3 atoms of the Absolute.

Yet, how different is the Third Cosmos! There, materiality increases because each of its atoms possesses within its interior 6 atoms of the Absolute.

Let us penetrate into the Fourth Cosmos. There, we find denser matter due to the concrete fact that each of its atoms possesses, within itself, 12 atoms of the Absolute.

Let us be little more specific; if we carefully examine the planet Earth, we will see that each of its atoms possesses within its inner nature 24 atoms of the Absolute.

Carefully specifying, let us study in detail any atom of the human organism, and by means of divine clairvoyance, we will perceive inside it 48 atoms of the Absolute.

Let us descend a little more and let us enter into the Kingdom of the most crude materiality, into the Infernal Worlds, below the crust of the planet on which we live, and we shall discover that in the First Infra-dimensional Zone, density has increased terrifyingly because each inhuman atom possesses within its inner nature 96 atoms of the Absolute.

In the Second Infernal Zone every atom possesses 192 atoms; in the Third every atom possesses within its interior 288 atoms of the Absolute, etc., etc., thus increasing materiality in a dreadful and terrifying manner...

Upon submerging ourselves within Laws that are increasingly more complex, we obviously become progressively more independent from the will of the Absolute, and fall into the mechanical complication of all of this Great Nature. If we want to re-conquer freedom, we must free ourselves from so much mechanicalness and so many Laws and return to the Father.

Question: Beloved Master, if divine will is not fulfilled within Microcosmos-Man, then why is it stated that not a single leaf of a tree moves without the will of God?

Answer: Distinguished gentleman, as we have already stated, only the Unique Law governs in the Sacred Solar Absolute; in the

Cosmos of 3 Laws the will of the Father is still fulfilled because everything is governed by the 3 Fundamental Laws. However, in the world of 6 Laws, a mechanicalness is without any doubt already in place, which in a certain sense makes it independent from the Will of the Absolute.

Now, consider the worlds of 24, 48, and 96 Laws. It is obvious that within such orders of worlds, mechanicalness multiplies independent of the Sacred Solar Absolute. This, of course, would possibly lead us to conclude that the Father is excluded from all Creation; however, it is good for everyone to know that all mechanicalness is previously calculated by the Sacred Absolute Sun, since the different orders of Laws and the diverse mechanical processes could not exist if this had not been previously arranged by the Father.

This universe is a totality within the intelligence of the Sacred Solar Absolute, and these phenomena crystallize progressively in a successive manner, little by little; understood?

Question: Venerable Master, could you tell us why you relate the number Seven with the Laws of Creation, the human organism, and the worlds? Is this a tradition or is it really a Law?

Answer: The question that the gentleman is asking deserves an immediate answer. I want all of you, ladies and gentlemen, to comprehend with complete crystal clarity what the Laws of Three and Seven are. It is urgent for you to know that at the Dawn of Creation, the Cosmocrators, the creators of this universe in which we live, move, and have our Being, each one of them worked under the direction of their individual Cosmic Divine Mother Kundalini, developing in space the Laws of Three and Seven, so that everything would have abundant life. This was the only way our world could come to exist.

It is, therefore, not strange that every natural cosmic process unfolds in accordance with the Laws of Three and Seven. By no means should it seem incredible that such Laws are correlated in the infinitely small as well as in the infinitely large, in the Microcosmos and in the Macrocosmos, to everything that is, to everything that has been, and to everything that will be.

Let us think for a moment about the seven chakras of the dorsal spine, about the seven principal worlds of the solar system, about the seven Rounds which the ancient and modern Theosophy refers to, about the seven human Races, etc., etc., etc.

All these gigantic septenary processes, every septuple manifestation of life, always has as its foundation the Three Primary Forces: Positive, Negative, and Neutral; understood?

Question: Master, why is it that when you talk about the creation of worlds, beings, or galaxies, you express yourself using terms such as: "it is clear," "it is indubitable," "it is obvious," "it is natural" etc.? What do you base yourself on to say it with such certainty?

Answer: I see that someone among the audience has asked a quite interesting question, and I am glad to answer it.

Ladies and gentlemen, I want you to know in a concrete, clear, and definite manner, that two types of reasoning exist: the first we shall denominate as "subjective"; the second we shall qualify it as "objective".

Unquestionably, the first one has as its foundation, external, sensory perceptions. The second one is different, and is only processed in accordance with the intimate experiences of the Consciousness.

It is obvious that behind the terms quoted by the gentleman are really the various functionalisms of my own Consciousness. I utilize such terms of speech as specific vehicles for my concepts of content.

In other words, I am placing certain emphasis in order to say to the gentleman and the honorable audience listening to me the following: I would never use the words quoted by the gentleman if I had not previously verified with my conscious powers, with my transcendental cognoscible faculties, the truth of everything that I am affirming. I like to use precise terms with the purpose of making exact ideas known. That is all!

Question: Venerable Master, in your previous exposition you mentioned the Dawn of Creation. Could you explain to us in which epoch it occurred and whose work it was?

Answer: Distinguished gentleman, in Eternity time does not exist. I want all of you who have attended our lecture this evening to perfectly understand that time does not have a real basis, an authentic, legitimate origin.

Certainly, and in the name of truth, I must tell you that time is something merely subjective, that it does not possess an objective, concrete and exact reality.

What really exists is the succession of phenomena. The Sun rises and we exclaim "It is 6 in the morning!" It sets and we say "It is 6 in the evening 12 hours have elapsed!" Yet, in which part of the cosmos can we find those hours, that time? Can we perhaps hold that time in our hand, place it on the table of a laboratory? What color does that time have? Of what metal or substance is it made? Let us reflect, ladies and gentlemen, let us reflect a little. It is the mind that invents time, since, indeed, what truly exists in an objective manner is the succession of natural phenomena; unfortunately, we make the mistake of assigning time to every cosmic movement.

We put our beloved hours between the rising and the setting of the Sun; we invent them; we associate them with the movement of the stars; nevertheless, these are fantasies of the mind.

Cosmic phenomena succeed one another within the eternal instant of the Great Life in its movement. Our universe exists as an integral, unitotal, and complete whole within the Sacred Absolute Sun. Within it, all cosmic changes process themselves within an eternal moment, within an instant that has no limits.

It is evident and manifest that when the different successive phenomena of this universe crystallize, then, unfortunately, the

concept of time comes to our mind. Such a subjective concept is always placed between phenomenon and phenomenon.

In truth, the Solar Logos, the Demiurge Architect of the Universe, is the true author of all of this Creation. Nevertheless, we cannot assign a date to his work, to his Cosmogenesis, because time is an illusion of the mind and this goes far beyond everything that is merely intellective. The Inferno, or the Infernal Worlds, have existed for all of eternity. Let us remember the phrase of Dante in his *Divine Comedy*:

> *Through Me Pass into the Painful City;*
>
> *Through Me pass into Eternal Grief;*
>
> *Through Me Pass among the Lost People.*
>
> *Justice Moved My Master-Builder;*
>
> *Heavenly Power First Fashioned Me*
>
> *With Highest Wisdom and with Primal Love.*
>
> *Before Me Nothing was Created That*
>
> *Was Not Eternal, and I Last Eternally.*
>
> *All Hope Abandon, You who Enter Here.*

Question: Venerable Master, to the best of my understanding, Master G. assigns the world of 96 Laws to the Moon, however you state that this region is found below the epidermis of the planetary organism in which we live. Could you explain the reason for this divergence of concepts?

Answer: Respectable sir, I hasten to answer your question.

Certainly, Master G. thinks that the Ray of Creation ends with the Moon, and I emphatically affirm that it ends in the Submerged Worlds, in the Inferno.

Distinguished gentlemen, the Moon is something different; it belongs to a past Day of Creation, it is a dead world, it is a corpse.

The voyages of the astronauts to our satellite have come to demonstrate in a conclusive and definitive manner, the irrefutable fact that the Moon is a dead world. I do not know how Master G. made this mistake in his calculations. Any moon of infinite space is always a corpse. Unfortunately, Master G. firmly believed that in our system the Moon was a new world that was being born, that was surging from within the chaos.

In a previous Cosmic Day, the Moon had abundant life, it was a marvelous planet of space, however now it is dead, and in the future it will have to be totally disintegrate; that is all!

Question: Beloved Master, according to Master G., our satellite, the Moon, originated from a detachment of terrestrial matter due to tremendous magnetic forces of attraction within the laws of gravity, thus forming a new world where, with certainty, the lost souls enter in order to suffer within these Infra-dimensional Regions of Avernus. Master Samael, does this mean that Master G. arrived at this conclusion because his cognoscible faculties were poor?

Answer: I am listening to the question from the gentleman and it is clear that I am glad to answer. By no means do I want to underestimate Master G.'s psychic faculties; obviously, he fulfilled a marvelous mission and his work is splendid. Nevertheless, man has the right to make mistakes; it is possible that he took such information with regards to Selene from some legend, from some source, from some allegory, etc., etc., etc. In any case, we emphatically affirm what we know, what we have been able to directly verify for ourselves, without undervaluing the work of any other Master.

That the Moon was the outcome of a collision between the Earth and another planet, or that it emerged from the Pacific Ocean, as another respectable Master stated, are concepts that we respect but that we have not practically evidenced...

I affirm in a conclusive manner and with certain emphasis, and I limit myself to exclusively reveal with my Objective Reasoning, what I have been able to see, hear, touch, and feel for myself.

Never in the entire cosmos have we come to know of any moon becoming an inhabitable world. Any well-awakened Initiate knows by means of direct experience that the worlds, like men, plants and everything that exists, are born, grow, age, and die.

It is clear that any planet that dies, in fact and by its own right, becomes a corpse, a moon. Our planet Earth will not be an exception and you can be sure, ladies and gentlemen, that after the Seventh human Race, our Earth will also become a new moon.

Therefore, let us be exact. I am mathematical in investigation and demanding in expression. We have methods, systems and procedures by means of which we can and must come in contact with those Infernal Worlds; then we will recognize the reality of *The Divine Comedy* of Dante, who situates the Inferno beneath the epidermis of the planet Earth.

4

MONADS AND ESSENCES

Beloved friends, once again we are gathered here, in this place, to talk in depth about the different causes that lead intellectual humanoids along the descending, involutive path towards the Infernal Regions.

Unquestionably in these moments millions of involutive, descending creatures are crossing the Acheron in order to enter the Avernus.

After having completed their cycle of existences in the physical tridimensional world of Euclid, waves of humanoids cease to incarnate in human bodies in order to definitely submerge themselves into the Mineral Kingdom.

It is certain that the evil of the world, no matter how monstrous it may be, has a barrier, a defined limit.

What would become of the universe if there was no insurmountable obstacle to evil? Obviously, the latter would develop infinitely until reigning sovereign in all of the spheres.

It is worthwhile to mention here, with complete crystal clarity, the tremendous reality of the 108 existences that are assigned to each living Essence, to every divine animic principle.

This reminds us of the 108 beads of Buddha's necklace, as well as the 108 times that the Hindu Brahman turns around the Sacred Cow. It is indubitable that with the last turn he finishes his daily rite, he then introduces the tail's end of the well-known allegorical animal into the cup of water that he is going to drink.

Having understood all of this, we can proceed: it is obvious that the Divine Mother Kundalini, the Igneous Serpent of our Magical Powers, attempts to achieve our Intimate Self-Realization during the course of the 108 existences that are assigned to each one of us. Evidently, within that cycle of successive lives, we have innumerable opportunities for Self-Realization; to take advantage of them is appropriate. Unfortunately, we incessantly slip back into errors, and the final result is usually failure.

It is obvious and evident that not all human beings want to tread the Path that will lead them to Final Liberation.

The different Messengers that come from above, Prophets, Avatars, great Apostles..., have always wanted to show us precisely the Rocky Path that leads to authentic and legitimate happiness.

Regrettably, people want nothing to do with Divine Wisdom. They have imprisoned Masters, assassinated Avatars, have bathed themselves in the blood of the righteous, they mortally hate anything that has a taste of divinity.

Nevertheless, all of them, like Pilate, wash their hands; they believe themselves to be saints, and presume that they are on the Path of Perfection.

We cannot deny the emphatic and definitive fact that millions of sincere but mistaken people exist, who very honestly boast of being virtuous, thus thinking the best about themselves.

All kinds of anchorites live within the Tartarus; mistaken mystics, sublime fakirs, priests of many cults, penitents of all types, who would accept everything, except the tremendous truth that they are lost and that they walk on the path of evil.

This is why the Great Kabir Jesus stated in his own right: *Of a thousand who seek me, one finds me; of a thousand who find me, one follows me; of a thousand who follow me, one is mine.*

The Bhagavad-Gita textually says the following: *Among thousands of men, one perchance strives for perfection; even among those who strive for perfection, one perchance attains perfection; and amongst the perfect, only one perchance knows me in truth.*

Jesus, the Great Kabir, emphasizes the difficulty of entering the Kingdom:

But woe unto you, scribes and Pharisees, hypocrites! For ye shut up the kingdom of heaven against men: for ye neither go in yourselves, neither suffer ye them that are entering to go in. Woe unto you, scribes and Pharisees, hypocrites! For ye devour widows' houses, and for a pretense make long prayer: therefore, ye shall receive the greater damnation.

When the great Kabir Jesus refers to those many false apostles who wander about going everywhere founding diverse sects that never lead to Final Liberation, he says:

Woe unto you, scribes and Pharisees, hypocrites! For ye compass sea and land to make one proselyte, and when he is made, ye make him twofold more the child of hell than yourselves.

Distinguished friends, noble brothers, respectable ladies, what is serious here is that those who are lost, the sincere but mistaken ones, always think that they are doing very well.

How to make these people comprehend that they are going astray? How to make them understand that the path that leads to the Abyss is paved with good intentions? In what manner could I demonstrate to the people with a sleeping Consciousness that the sect to which they belong, or the tenebrous school to which they are affiliated with, will lead them to the Abyss and to the Second Death?

It is unquestionable that no one thinks the worst of his own sect; all of them are convinced by the words of the blind leading the blind...

Certainly, and in the name of truth, we must say with great frankness that only by awakening the Consciousness can we see the narrow, strait, and difficult Path that leads to the Light.

How could those who sleep, see the Path? Could the mind perhaps discover the Truth?

In the Great Book of Universal Life it is written in words of gold that the mind cannot recognize what it has never known.

Do you perhaps believe that the mind has once known that which is Real, what Truth is?

It is obvious that understanding goes from the known to the unknown. It moves within a vicious circle, and it so happens that Truth is what is unknown from moment to moment.

I beg you, dear brothers, noble friends and distinguished ladies, to reflect a little.

The mind can accept or reject whatever it pleases, it may believe or doubt, etc., etc., etc., but it can never know what is Real.

Observe carefully what happens in the different corners of the world. It is clear that sacred books circulate everywhere and they serve as a basis for many religious cults.

Nevertheless, who understands the concepts contained within those books? Who has complete Consciousness of what is written in each verse? The masses only limit themselves to believing or denying, and that is all.

As proof of what I am affirming, see how many sects have been formed with the marvelous verses of the Four Christian Gospels.

If the Christian devotees had full Consciousness of the Christic Gospel preached by the Great Kabir Jesus, it is obvious that so many sects would not exist; truly, only one Christic religion of a universal cosmic type would exist.

However, believers are not able to reach an agreement amongst themselves because they have their Consciousness asleep; they know nothing, nothing is evident to them, they have never personally talked with an Angel, they have never consciously and positively entered into the Heavenly Regions; they walk because others walk; they eat because others eat, they say what others say and in this manner, with blindfolded eyes, they go from the cradle to the sepulcher.

Unfortunately, time passes with terrifying swiftness, the cycle of human existences finishes, and finally, the devotees, convinced that they walk on the Upright Path, enter the horrible Abode of Pluto, where only weeping and gnashing of teeth are heard...

The descent of waves of humans into the interior of the planetary organism is made by descending through the stages of animal and plant, until definitely entering into the mineral state in the very center of the planet Earth.

I want you to know, I want you to comprehend, that it is precisely in the very center of this planet where millions of humanoids pass through that Second Death spoken of in the *Book of Revelation* of St. John.

It is evident that the destruction of the Myself, the annihilation of the Ego, the dissolution of the Myself within the Submerged Regions of the Avernus, is absolutely indispensable for the destruction of evil within each and every one of us.

Obviously, it is only through the death of the Ego that the liberation of the Essence is made possible; then the latter resurges, emerges up to the planetary surface, to the light of the sun, in order to begin again a new evolving process within the painful Wheel of Samsara.

The re-ascension always takes place by passing through the mineral, plant and animal stages until reconquering the humanoid state that was formerly lost.

It is clear that when we reenter into this state, 108 existences are once again assigned to us, which —if we do not take proper advantage of them– will eventually lead us on the descending path back to the Avernus. In any case, dear brothers, noble ladies that are listening to me, it is good for you to know that 3,000 of these cycles of cosmic manifestation are always assigned to each Essence, to each Soul.

Those who definitely fail, those who do not know how to take advantage of the innumerable opportunities that these 3,000 periods confer upon us, grant unto us, will remain forever excluded from Mastery.

In this latter case, that Immortal Spark that we all have within, our sublime Monad, collects its Essence –that is, its spiritual principles– it absorbs it into itself, and thereafter submerges itself forever into the Universal Spirit of Life.

Thus, Monads without Mastery, those that did not achieve it or who did not want it, remain definitely excluded from any hierarchical rank. I clarify: not all immortal Sparks, not all sublime Monads, want Mastery.

Yet, when any Monad, when any divine Spark truly wants to reach the sublime state of Master-Monad, it is indubitable that it then works on its Essence, on its Soul, awakening in this Soul infinite desires for transcendental spirituality.

Question: Beloved Master, based on what you have just explained, it seems to me, if I am not mistaken, that this is precisely what Lord Krishna wanted to say when he spoke about the Transmigration of Souls, as well as Master Pythagoras when referring to Metempsychosis. Is this so?

Answer: I hear the words of the gentleman who asked the question and of course I hasten to answer it...

Friends, ladies, indeed what I am affirming tonight has documentation in India and in Greece. The first within the marvelous Doctrine presented by that ancient Hindu Avatar called Krishna, and the second within the Doctrine of Pythagoras.

Obviously, the Metempsychosis of the great Greek philosopher and the Doctrine of the Transmigration of Souls taught by the Hindu Avatar, are identical in their structure and in their depth. Unfortunately, people misrepresent the Teachings and, finally, reject it in an arbitrary manner.

Question: Illustrious Master, what I do not understand is why distinguished personalities, recognized as Masters, such as Lady H.P.B. and Charles Leadbeater, as well as Annie Besant, founders of the Theosophical Society, who were people with faculties of clairvoyance, clairaudience and other powers, never became aware of the facts that the Great Kabir Jesus, as well as Krishna, Pythagoras and you, Master Samael, have taught us. On the contrary, they have proclaimed in each one of their treatises —which are greatly renowned in the world of pseudo-esoteric schools— that man inexorably walks on the ascending path of evolution until one day, with the passage of time; he attains perfection and becomes one with the Father. Can you explain such incongruence?

Answer: I hear a gentleman who is asking a very important question, thus unquestionably I hasten to answer in the best possible manner.

Certainly, the Laws of Evolution and Involution work harmoniously and in a coordinated manner in all of nature.

It is indubitable that every rise is followed by a fall; every ascent is followed by a descent; therefore, it would be absurd to assume that the Law of Evolution were to be something different.

If we climb a mountain, we will undoubtedly arrive at its summit; afterwards, we would need to descend. Thus, that is how the Laws of Evolution and Involution work, my dear brothers...

These two great Laws constitute the mechanical axis of all nature; if either of these two Laws would cease to function for even just a moment, then all the natural mechanisms would in fact become paralyzed.

There is evolution in the grain that germinates, grows and develops; involution exists in the plant when it withers and dies.

There is evolution in the baby that develops within the maternal womb, in the child that is born, in an adolescent, in a young person; involution exists in the one who ages and dies.

The evolutionary and involutionary processes are completely organized within this Great Creation.

Regrettably, those who have bottled themselves up within the Dogma of Evolution are no longer capable of comprehending the infinite destructive and decadent processes of everything that is, of everything that has been, and of everything that will be.

Neither evolution nor involution can ever take us to the Intimate Self-Realization of the Being.

If we truly want to liberate ourselves, if we seriously long for authentic happiness, we need to, in an urgent and unpostponable manner, enter the Path of the Revolution of Consciousness.

It is not superfluous to emphasize the transcendental and transcending idea that it is not possible to reach Great Reality as long as we turn incessantly in the Wheel of Samsara.

Of what use is it, ladies and gentlemen, to return incessantly to this valley of tears, to evolve and involute constantly, and to descend again and again into the Infernal Worlds?

It is our duty to awaken the Consciousness to see the path that will lead us with absolute precision to Final Liberation...

Unquestionably, many illustrious intelligences of occult knowledge transmitted to humanity a simple, elementary teaching at the end of the last century and at the beginning of the present one.[*]

It is clear that such persons only aimed at publicly teaching the first letters of the Secret Doctrine. Therefore, they did not spend too much time on the analysis of the Evolutive and Involutive Laws.

---

*. It is understood that the last century is the nineteenth and the present one would be the twentieth, during which Master Samael delivered his teachings.

Rudolf Steiner already affirmed in 1912 that they, the Initiates of that epoch, had only delivered an incipient, elementary teaching, but that later, a superior esoteric doctrine of a transcendental order would be given to humanity.

Now, we are delivering this type of superior esoteric doctrine.

It is therefore indispensable not to condemn or criticize those who in the past worked in some way for humanity. They did what they could; now we must elucidate and clarify...

Question: Master, you stated that some Monads are interested in self-realizing and others not, despite that all of them emanate from the Absolute. I thought that all of them had the duty to seek their Self-Realization. Could you explain this a little more?

Answer: I hear the words of a young man and I will gladly answer. Friends, before anything else, I want you to comprehend that what is divine, God, the Universal Spirit of Life, is not dictatorial.

If that which is Real, if that which is Truth, if that which is not of time, were to be dictatorial, what fate could we expect?

Friends, God respects his own freedom as well. With this I want to say to you that, within the bosom of the divine, there are no dictatorships. Every virginal Spark, every Monad, has the complete liberty of accepting or rejecting Mastery, understood?

Question: Master, based on what you have just explained, could we say that the Monad is responsible for the Essence going to Hell?

Answer: I see amidst the audience a lady who with full sincerity has asked this question, and it is evident that I will gladly answer... Ladies and gentlemen, when a divine Monad wants Mastery, it is obvious that it achieves it by working incessantly on its Essence from within, from the deepest part.

It is clear and evident that, if the Monad is not interested in Mastery, it will never awaken any intimate aspiration within the incarnated Essence. Obviously, in this case, the Essence, deprived of any aspiration and bottled up within the Ego, embedded within the Myself, will enter into the Infernal Worlds. Therefore, I emphatically answer: yes, the Monad is at fault for the failure of every Essence...

If the Monad would truly, profoundly work its Essence, it is unquestionable that the latter would never descend as a failure into the "Tartarus".

> *Question: Master, it terrifies me to think that my Essence would have to suffer for 108 lives multiplied by 3,000, that is 324,000 human existences, so that in final analysis it would end up living within the Absolute as a failed Monad, in other words, without Self-Realization. Under these circumstances, it is worthwhile making all possible efforts and sacrifices in order to achieve Self-Realization, no matter how much suffering this might imply, since it is absolutely nothing in comparison to that which nature will impose on me if I choose the path of failure. Don't you think so?*

Answer: Distinguished gentleman, great friend, allow me to emphatically tell you that every divine Spark, every Monad, can choose the path.

It is indubitable that there are trillions of absolutely innocent Monads, beyond good and evil, in infinite space.

Many of them attempted to attain Mastery; unfortunately, they failed. Millions of others never wanted Mastery. Now, submerged within the bosom of the Universal Spirit of Life they enjoy authentic divine happiness because they are flashes of the divinity; unfortunately they do not possess Mastery.

It is clear that the gentleman who asks this question has enormous longings. This is due to his inner Monad motivating and working him incessantly. His duty is therefore to proceed firmly on the Path of the Razor's Edge until achieving the Intimate Self-Realization of the Being.

Question: Master, is it because of this that many people to whom we talk about the Gnostic Teachings, even when they grasp perfectly what we are explaining to them, do not choose to follow the Path of the Revolution of Consciousness? Does this mean that their Monad does not work on them for them to follow the Path of Self-Realization?

Answer: I am going to respond to the young man who asks this question...

We need profound reflection in order to focus on this matter from different angles. It so happens that many Monads like to go slowly with the risk of their Essences failing in each cycle of human existences; others prefer to work on their Essences in an intermittent manner, from time to time; and, lastly, we have Monads that definitely do not ever work on their Essence.

Therefore, this is the reason why not all the persons who listen to the Teachings actually accept them. Nevertheless, it is good to know that someone, for example, who in this present existence did not accept the Gospel of the New Age of Aquarius, could accept it in subsequent lives, as long as he has not yet reached the 108th.

Question: Master, do these Monads that are never interested in working on their Essence belong only to the planet Earth or do they also exist in other planets?

Answer: Young friend, remember the Law of Philosophical Analogies, the Law of Correspondences, and of Numerology: "As above, so below..."

Earth is not the only inhabited planet in starry space; the plurality of inhabited worlds is a tremendous reality. This invites us to comprehend that the Monads from other planets also enjoy complete freedom in order to accept or reject Mastery.

The personality is different. With this I want to emphatically say the following: not all of the human personalities existing in other inhabited worlds of infinite space have fallen as low as we, the inhabitants of the Earth.

Friends, in the diverse spheres of the infinite there are marvelous planetary humanities who march in accordance with the Great Cosmic Laws; however, I repeat, not all Monads want Mastery.

Infernos exist in all the worlds, in all the galaxies, however not all the planetary Hells are inhabited.

The Sun, for instance, is a marvelous star whose light illuminates all of the planets of the solar system of Ors. It is interesting to know that the Infernal Worlds of the king star are completely clean. Obviously, on this brilliant Sun it is not possible to find cosmic failures; none of its inhabitants go through submerged involution; the creatures that live on the king star are completely divine, they are Solar Spirits.

It is good not to forget that any cosmic unit that emerges into life inevitably possesses a Submerged Mineral Kingdom within the natural infra-dimensions.

There are worlds whose Submerged Mineral Kingdom is densely populated, among them is our planet Earth; this indicates and points at the failure of many Monads.

However, we need to delve a little more into this matter and understand with complete clarity that the descent of any Essence into the horrible Abode of Pluto does not always mean definite failure.

It is clear that the final failure is only for the Essences, for the Monads, that did not achieve Intimate Self-Realization in the 3,000 cycles or periods of existences, better said, in the 3,000 turns of the Wheel of Samsara, since when arriving at the last of these cycles, as I have stated so many times, the doors are shut...

5

THE FIRST DANTEAN CIRCLE

THE SUBMERGED SPHERE OF THE MOON

My friends, today, we are gathered here once again, and we are going to study the First Dantean Circle of the Infernal Worlds.

It is indubitable that this First Submerged Region corresponds to the "Limbo", the Orcus of the classics mentioned by Virgil, the poet of Mantua.

We have been told with complete clarity that this mineral zone is vividly represented by all of the caverns of the world, which united astrally, end up complementing the First Submerged Region.

Dante, the Florentine elder, states that in this region he found all of those innocents who died without having received the waters of baptism —all of this should be understood in a strictly symbolic manner.

If we carefully study *The Ramayana*, the sacred book of the Hindustanis, we can evidence with mystical astonishment the conclusive and definitive fact that the Sacrament of Baptism goes way back before the Christian era.

In *The Ramayana* we can verify the remarkable case of Rama, who indeed was baptized by his Guru.

Unquestionably, in ancient times, no one received the baptismal water without first having been fully instructed in the Mysteries of Sex. The Sacrament of Baptism is therefore a pact of Sexual Magic.

It turns out to be extraordinary that, when entering any School of Mysteries, the first thing one received was the Sacrament of Baptism.

It is indispensable, it is urgent, to transmute the Pure Waters of Life into the Wine of Light of the alchemist; only thus is it possible to achieve the Intimate Self-Realization of the Being.

In the Orcus of the classics, in the Limbo, we find many learned men who died without having received the waters of baptism.

They were sincere but mistaken, filled with magnificent intentions, but mistaken; people who believed that Liberation was possible without the need for Sexual Magic.

Thus, the cold and sepulchral dead dwell in the First Sub-Lunar Region, below the epidermis of this planet on which we live.

One feels true sadness, supreme pain, when contemplating so many millions of disembodied people wandering in the Region of the Dead with their Consciousness asleep.

Behold them there, like cold shadows, with their Consciousness profoundly asleep, like specters of the night!

The shadows of the dead come and go everywhere in the First Dantean Circle, they attend to the same activities as in the physical life that passed, they dream of the memories of yesterday, they live totally in the past...

Question: Master, you have explained to us that the souls of those who have not been baptized dwell in the First Subterranean Sub-Lunar Region called the Limbo, Baptism being understood as a pact of Sexual Magic, which induces me to ask the following question: do perhaps all beings who have not practiced Sexual Magic automatically enter into this region when they disembody?

Answer: Distinguished friend, your question is quite interesting and I hasten to answer...

I want you to comprehend that the First Submerged Region is like the antechamber of Hell. Obviously, the shadows of our loved ones, millions of human beings who never transmuted the Seminal Waters into the Wine of Light of Alchemy, dwell there.

Few are those Essences, those Souls who, after death, really attain some vacation in the Superior Worlds.

It is indubitable that most human beings return immediately into a new human organism, spending some time in the Limbo before re-incorporating themselves once again.

However, due to the critical state in which we currently live, innumerable deceased definitely submerge themselves into the Infernal Worlds, passing through the tenebrous spheres of the Moon, Mercury, Venus, the Sun, Mars, Jupiter, Saturn, Uranus, and Neptune.

The last of these regions is definitive. There, the lost ones go through the final disintegration, the Second Death, which is so indispensable.

Thanks to this horrifying annihilation, the Essence, the Soul, is able to liberate itself from the regions of "Tartarus", to ascend to the planetary surface and initiate a new evolution that inevitably has to begin from the Mineral Kingdom.

Question: Venerable Master how should one understand what is said in the language of the Roman Church, that the innocent children enter the Limbo?

Answer: Distinguished friend, this matter about innocent children must be understood in a symbolic and allegoric manner.

The word "innocent" must be interpreted, not in its pristine original form, but as radical ignorance. Indeed, he who ignores the

Mysteries of Sex is ignorant, even if he boasts of being wise and possesses vast erudition.

Remember that there are many learned ignoramuses who not only ignore, but who also ignore that they ignore, understood?

Question: Master, are you saying that the person who has not created his Solar Bodies has not been baptized?

Answer: Distinguished young man, your question, which gives us a basis for a beautiful explanation, pleases me...

The Sacred Scriptures speak clearly about the "wedding garment of the Soul," the To-Soma-Heliakon, the Body of Gold of the Solar Man, the living representation of the Supra-sensitive Bodies that every human creature must elaborate.

In our previous books, we already spoke clearly about the work related with the creation of the Existential Bodies of the Being, and therefore I believe that our Gnostic students can now understand us.

It is indubitable that the intellectual animal mistakenly called man does not possess such vehicles, and therefore, he must create them by working in the Lit Forge of Vulcan; sex.

In these moments, it comes to my memory the case of a friend who passed away some years ago. He was a convinced Gnostic, however, he was not able to create his Existential Bodies of the Being; I was able to verify this in the Region of the Dead, in the Limbo.

While being out of my physical body, I found him: he had a gigantic appearance, and his spectral face was really of the graveyard or the cemetery.

I walked around with him to different places, down different streets of a city, unquestionably beneath the tridimensional region of Euclid, in the Limbo...

"You are dead." I told him.

"What? Impossible! I am alive!"

That was his answer.

As we passed near a sumptuous mansion, I took him inside with the intention of making him look at himself in a mirror. He obeyed my instructions, I then saw him very much astounded...

"Try to float," I continued telling him, "jump a little so that you will convince yourself that you are now dead..."

That phantom, obeying, tried to fly, but I saw him fall head down instead of rising like the birds. In those moments, he assumed different animal-like figures.

"You now have the shape of a horse, a dog, a cat, a tiger," thus I described to him his different animal aspects as they appeared.

Indeed, that phantom was made up of a host of quarrelsome and vociferous "I's" that mutually penetrated and interpenetrated one other without blending into each other. My efforts were useless; that deceased was not able to understand me; he was an inhabitant of the Region of the Dead, a sum of "I's" personifying psychological defects.

Despite the fact that this friend had known Gnosis, he had not succeeded in creating his Astral Body. All that I had before my eyes was a host of phantoms, giving the impression of a personality as a façade.

It is obvious that this individual had not received the Sacrament of Baptism. In other words, we shall say that he had not transmuted the Pure Waters of Life into the Wine of Light of the alchemists.

Question: Master, does this mean that those who inhabit the Region of the Dead, that is, the Limbo, will always have the opportunity to return to a new womb?

Answer: Distinguished friend, do not forget that God Mercury, with his Caduceus, always takes out the Souls that are submerged in the Orcus, with the purpose of reincorporating them into a new organism. Only in this way is it possible for us on any given day to be truly baptized. Understood?

Question: Beloved Master, I understand that the Essence and the "I's" of the deceased enter the Limbo, but that it is not a region of suffering. Am I correct?

Answer: Distinguished gentleman, since you speak of Essence and of "I's," it is good that we lay the cards on the table now in order to clarify concepts and to define doctrinal viewpoints.

Many believe that the Ego, the "I", the Myself, the Oneself, is something overly individual. This is what multiple authors of treatises on modern psychology erroneously suppose.

We, Gnostics, go further; we like to go in depth; we like to delve into all of these mysteries, to inquire, to investigate, etc., etc., etc.

The "I" does not possess any individuality whatsoever. It is a sum of different psychic aggregates that personify our psychological defects; a bunch of errors, passions, hatreds, fears, vendettas, jealousy, anger, lust, resentments, attachments, greed, etc., etc.

These diverse aggregates have various animal-like forms in the hyper-sensitive regions of nature.

Upon dying, this entire group of quarrelsome and vociferous "I's", this entire range of varied psychic aggregates, continue beyond the sepulcher.

Our animic Essence, the psychic material, is bottled up within those negative values.

It is therefore obvious that this animic material embedded in the Ego submerges itself in the Orcus, in the Limbo, in order to return a little later to this physical world.

Question: Master, for a perfectly ordinary and asleep person, would the Limbo be a continuation of his life?

Answer: Young friend that is asking the question, I consider it to be slightly incorrect. It is necessary to ask in a better way, in order to clarify...

There is no tomorrow for the personality of the dead. Every personality is a child of its time, it is born in its time and it dies in its time.

That which continues beyond the sepulcher is the Ego, a sum of diverse brutal, animal-like psychic aggregates.

When I contemplated my friend in my story I was able to understand with pain, that his personality had been annihilated. All that I now had before my eyes was a sum of grotesque animal-like figures, mutually penetrating and interpenetrating one another so as to give a false appearance of a sepulchral, cold and spectral personality.

What had become of my friend? Where was he? Since he had not created the Astral Body, it is obvious that he had ceased to exist. If my friend had created an Astral Body by means of sexual transmutation, if he had really practiced Sexual Magic, it is clear that yes, he would have created the Sidereal Vehicle, and then he would have continued with his astral personality in the Hyper-sensitive Regions of nature. Regrettably, this had not been the case...

To be baptized, then, implies having practiced Sexual Magic. Whoever has not proceeded in this manner, has not received the sacramental waters; he is an inhabitant of the Limbo.

Question: Master, could this false personality made up of those grotesque "I's that was once your friend, become your enemy in that region without a future?

Answer: Young friend, it is urgent for you to comprehend that the Ego is constituted by many "I's" and that some of them may be our friends or our enemies. Indubitably, some of the "I's" of that phantom that I have referred to continue to be my friends; yet others, obviously, can be enemies or simply grotesque, indifferent phantoms.

At any rate, it is the Ego that returns from the Region of the Limbo to repeat all the painful dramas of past existences in this physical world.

The personality, as I already stated, is perishable, it never returns, and this is something that you must clearly comprehend.

Know how to distinguish between the Ego and the personality. Understood?

Question: Master, should I understand that the true Sacrament of Baptism can only be received by one who becomes initiated on the Path of the Razor's Edge?

Answer: Distinguished gentleman, the authentic Sacrament of Baptism, as I already stated in this lecture, is a pact of Sexual Magic.

Regrettably, people go through the baptismal ceremony, through the rite, but they never fulfill the pact. This is why they enter the Limbo. If people were to fulfill that religious pact, they would then fully enter the Path of the Razor's Edge, that Path cited by Christ when he said: *"Because strait is the gate, and narrow is the way which leadeth unto Light, and few there be that find it."*

It is indispensable to know that the Secret Path that leads Souls to the Final Liberation is absolutely sexual.

Question: Master, does this mean that the deceased who are entitled to some vacation are those who have begun to practice Sexual Magic?

Answer: Distinguished Madam who asks the question, I invite you to understand that the Ego can never enter the Heavenly Regions. The only option for the psychic aggregates is the Abyss and Second Death, understood?

Nevertheless, let us delve deeper in order to elucidate and clarify this lecture... When the Ego is not too strong, when the psychic aggregates are very weak, then the pure Essence, the Soul, succeeds in freeing itself for some time in order to enter the Heavenly Regions and thus enjoy some vacation before returning to this valley of tears.

Regrettably, in this day and age, the animal Ego has become very strong in many people, and for that reason human souls no longer have the happiness of such vacation.

Certainly, nowadays, very rare are those souls who succeed in entering the Devachan, as the Theosophists say, or the Causal world.

I want all of you to comprehend the concrete fact that the souls, incidentally very rare nowadays, who may enjoy for a certain time some happy vacations between death and a new birth, are those who we could call in this world "very good people." Thus, because of this, the Great Law rewards them after death. Understood?

Question: Master, those souls who manage to escape from the Ego in order to enjoy some vacations, when they re-enter in another womb, do they have to become bottled up in the Ego again?

Answer: Friends, the Ego can only be destroyed, annihilated, in two ways:

1. By means of conscious work on ourselves and within ourselves, here and now.

2. In the Infernal Worlds, through submerged involution, undergoing horrible sufferings.

Unquestionably, heavenly vacations do not dissolve the Ego. Once the Essence, the Soul, exhausts the fruits of its reward, when returning to this valley of tears it will have to remain bottled up within its Ego, the "I", the Myself.

Question: Master, when after its vacations the Essence returns to a new womb bottled up in the Ego; does it not bring the longing to liberate itself in order to achieve its Self-Realization?

Answer: Distinguished Madam, your question is magnificent... I want to emphatically tell you the following: the ascent to the Superior Worlds comforts and helps us.

When the Essence returns from some vacation in the Superior Worlds of Cosmic Consciousness, it comes back fortified and with greater enthusiasm. Then it fights tirelessly to attain its Total Liberation. However, any effort would be useless if the pact of Sexual Magic contained in the Sacrament of Baptism were not to be fulfilled.

Question: Master, can you tell us what the regions of the first Dantean Circle or Moon Circle are like, what is life like there and what is done there?

Answer: I will immediately answer the gentleman who asked the question. The first sub-lunar Dantean Circle, represented by all the caverns of the Earth is quite interesting, when seen internally.

There, we find the first submerged counterpart of our cities, streets, villages, counties and regions. It is no surprise, therefore, that a life similar to the actual one is experienced; in no way should we be astonished by the fact that the deceased visit the houses where they lived, or that they wander through the same places that they knew before, busying themselves in the same trades or jobs that they used to have...

I remember the pathetic case of a wretched carrier of heavy bundles. After his death, his Ego kept on carrying a load, package or bundle, on his back. When I tried to make him comprehend his situation, when I tried to make him understand that he was already completely dead and therefore he had no reason to continue carrying heavy bundles on his body, he looked at me with a sleepwalker's eyes. His Consciousness was asleep. He was unable to understand me.

The deceased continue selling in their stores, or buying merchandise, or driving cars, etc., etc., etc., each one busy with those tasks which they had before. It is very astonishing to see those bars filled with disembodied drunkards, those brothels with prostitutes still fornicating after death, etc., etc., etc.

Question: Master, what process do those who inhabit the Limbo follow, in order to return to this tridimensional world?

Answer: Those who dwell in the Limbo must recapitulate the life they just went through, slowly re-living it. Once such a retrospective process is concluded, all of the actions of our previous life are simply reduced to mathematics. Then the Judges of Karma make us return to this valley of tears with the purpose of correcting our errors and searching for the path that shall lead us to Final Liberation. That is all!

6

THE SECOND DANTEAN CIRCLE

THE SUBMERGED SPHERE OF MERCURY

My friends, we are now going to carefully study the Second Dantean Circle. I am emphatically referring to the negative aspect –or better said, the submerged aspect– of planet Mercury.

We are not going to speak about the Heaven of Mercury. I repeat: it is indispensable that we investigate a little what is strictly related to the antithesis of that brilliant Heaven...

When we penetrate into the interior of the Earth with the Astral body, we can verify for ourselves perfectly and in a direct way what the Hell of Mercury is.

Upon penetrating into this submerged region, we feel in the depth of our Soul the perpetual boiling of those negative passionate forces that incessantly flow back and forth in this subterranean zone.

It is not superfluous to say that we feel there the hurricane wind of Mercury, a certain fatal aerial element. This subterranean zone is the place where fornicators live, those who enjoy extracting the sacred sperm from their organism.

These miserable creatures from the underworld, sunk in vice, desperately come and go, here, there and everywhere. One is astounded at seeing these lost ones incessantly cohabiting within the Atomic Infernos of nature.

Such egos blaspheme incessantly and mortally hate anything that has the flavor of chastity.

There, we find the Empress Semiramis, the terrible fornicator, who established laws that favored animal passions in her country.

In that Abode of Pluto we also find Queen Dido, who killed herself for passion after having sworn fidelity to the ashes of Sichaeus. There, we also find Paris, who was to kidnap the Beautiful Helen of ancient Troy, and Achilles, the impetuous warrior, destroyer of citadels...

Tartarus of misfortunes, abysses of iniquity, terror, horrors!

With profound grief we find in the Second Dantean Circle the fallen Bodhisattvas, those who murdered the God Mercury, unhappy souls who exchanged their birthrights for a plate of lentils.

What grief we feel in the depth of our Consciousness to discover within those Mercurial Abysses the fallen angels cited by ancient religious theogonies!

Those who exchanged their Scepter of Power for the Distaff of Omphale, come and go through the black air of that submerged region.

A region where human understanding does not function; a world of brutal instincts where lasciviousness mixes with the impetus of violence.

Behold there the Mysteries of Minos or Minna. In these frightening depths live the Black Tantrists, who have developed the Abominable Kundabuffer Organ, the cause of so much wickedness.

Alas! If only the glorious Archangel Sakaky with his sacred commission would have foreseen with mathematical exactitude the fatal outcome of that satanic tail, of that Organ of Abominations, which humanity was allowed to develop for definite planetary purposes in times of yore! How different the future of this wretched suffering humanity would have been!

It is clear that each human being is a creature that captures distinct cosmic forces in order to transform them and transmit them into the interior layers of the Earth.

In view of the fact that on the Lemurian continent, some 18 million years ago, the Earth trembled incessantly, its volcanoes spewing fire and lava; certain sacred individuals led by the Archangel Sakaky allowed the development of the Abominable Kundabuffer Organ: terribly negative Luciferian fire, projecting itself from the coccyx towards the Atomic Infernos of man.

It is not superfluous to remember that this negative Fohat covered itself with a physical tail, similar to the one we see in apes. Hence, the dwellers of the Earth had in their appearance such an appendage or projection of their spinal column.

Thus, as a result, the forces that in those times passed through human organisms underwent categorical modifications that permitted the stabilization of the terrestrial crust.

Much later in the history of the centuries, other sacred individuals, considering that there was no longer any need for the Abominable Kundabuffer Organ —Satan's tail— eliminated that appendage from the human body.

Unfortunately, the awful consequences of that Organ of Witches' Sabbaths remained in the five Cylinders of the organic machine, known as: Intellect, Emotion, Movement, Instinct, Sex.

By going deeper into this topic, we can discover for ourselves that such tenebrous consequences are perfectly defined as psychic aggregates or quarrelsome and vociferous "I's", personifying our errors and constituting the Ego, the Myself, the Oneself.

Millions of human creatures live with the Abominable Kundabuffer Organ completely developed within the Submerged Sphere of Mercury.

With this I am not saying that the physical tail of apes is presently found developed in the anatomy of the three-brained or three-centered biped.

There is certainly a very incipient osseous residue of that abominable tail in the human anatomy. Nevertheless, the psychic aspect of such an organ is found in the metaphysical appearance of millions of rational humanoids.

We can have proof of this clearly, when attired in our Astral body; we penetrate the submerged realms of Mercurial type, beneath the epidermis of the planet Earth.

Question: Beloved Master, I wish to know if the persons and facts that appear in your exposition of the Second Dantean Circle are simply mythological or real, since although Dante mentions them, we understand that his work is simply a literary work of great merit...

Answer: Noble gentleman, distinguished ladies, allow me to solemnly affirm that *The Divine Comedy* of Dante is an initiatory esoteric text that very few human beings have understood.

The mythological characters cited in this text or the dwellers of the Submerged Sphere of Mercury, symbolically represent the living animal passions in that region.

The impetuous Achilles with his terrible sexual debaucheries, the adulterous Helen, the ever-libidinous Paris.... clearly personify the inhabitants of the tenebrous zone of Mercury.

I want to say in particular that one of these characters –that Helen kidnapped by Paris and the cause of so many wrongdoings in ancient times– has other positive symbolisms, which are more beautiful, that I do not want to talk about at this instant. Let us look only at the abysmal aspect, the antithesis of the resplendent aspect, the tenebrous Mercurial phase.

Ladies and gentlemen, remember that each symbol can be interpreted in seven different ways; tonight, we are only studying this very particular abyss of Mercurial type, beneath the epidermis of the planet in which we live.

Question: Master, can you tell me if this Mercurial Circle is of a denser level and of greater suffering than the first?

Answer: Friend who is asking the question, remember what we have already said in past lectures when we studied the Ray of Creation.

It is evident that the greater the number of Laws, the greater the degree of mechanicalness and pain. The Submerged Sphere of the Moon is governed exclusively by 96 Laws; however, the tenebrous aspect of Mercury, within the planetary mass in which we live, is constituted by 192 Laws. Therefore its mechanicalness is even greater, and as a result suffering is much more intense. In addition, the atoms of this tenebrous Mercurial Sphere are much heavier, since each one of them contains 192 atoms of the Absolute in its interior.

This means that the Tenebrous Mercurial Region is even denser than the Lunar one.

Question: Master, do the Souls that enter into this Submerged Zone of Mercury not have the possibility of returning?

Answer: Distinguished lady, honorable gentlemen, do not forget that Justice is always alongside Mercy.

Within these tenebrous abysmal regions dwell some Masters of the Great White Lodge, Great Initiates, Divine Beings, who have renounced all happiness in order to help the lost ones.

When some Soul repents in the Abode of Pluto, undoubtedly it is always assisted by these saints.

Unquestionably, the mentioned beings instruct, admonish and show the Path of Light to all those who truly regret their perversities.

Now and then, although very rarely, these Divine Beings succeed in taking out a repented Soul from the Abyss of Damnation.

When this happens, those who were condemned to perdition, return, re-enter, reincorporate into a new organism.

Question: Master, why do you emphasize that the dead belong to the First Submerged Lunar Region whereas you do not state the same thing when mentioning the Second Submerged Zone of Mercury?

Answer: Very well, Sir, listen to me. Review carefully *The Divine Comedy* of Dante, investigate for yourself, learn to consciously and positively move in the Astral Body, experiment and see.

Obviously, the Orcus of the classics —the Limbo of the Christians— is only the antechamber of Hell, even though it corresponds to the First Dantean Circle.

Every initiate knows that after death, millions of us human beings live in that region.

The encounter with Minos, the Demon who is to mark with the turns of his tail the Circle where the deceased must go, is only found in the Submerged Sphere of Mercury. Hence, this is not a whim of mine. I repeat: may anyone who wants to investigate for himself do so in a direct manner, and he will corroborate my assertions.

Question: Master, I do not understand what you have just said. Why is it that the fornicator "I's", that also constitute the Myself or the "I am" live in the Underworld of Mercury, and the same thing happens in the First Dantean Circle?

Answer: Very well Sir, undoubtedly, almost all of the three-brained or three-centered bipeds, mistakenly called humans end up being more or less fornicators. Nonetheless, as I have already said in former lectures, the Great Law assigns to each Soul 108 existences in every Cycle of Cosmic Manifestation.

It is evident, clear and manifest that no one can be cast into the Abysses of Perdition without having completed their cycle of existences.

Normally, the dead reside in Limbo, which is physically represented by all of the caverns of the Earth. Only those fornicators who have already exhausted their cycle of human existences enter definitely into the Submerged Negative Region of Mercury.

Nevertheless, I beg you, to please understand me. There are sometimes on Earth truly monstrous humanoids who no longer offer any possibility of redemption; these are definitely lost cases, and even though they have not exhausted their complete cycle of 108 existences, they unquestionably enter into the Infernal Worlds.

Question: Master, we know that the Sphere of Mercury relates to fornicators. Does this mean that the "I's" are divided among the different Dantean Circles in accordance with the different psychic aggregates?

Answer: Young man who is asking the question, it is clear that the Ego is a sum of diverse psychic aggregates that personify errors. Some of these correspond specifically to a given Dantean Circle, and others are intimately tied with other more submerged Circles; however, the totality, the sum of all of these negative values as a whole plunge themselves, involuting within the Mineral Kingdom towards the center of planetary gravity.

The Consciousness of the damned must experience, in each descending Circle, in each infra-dimension of nature –beneath the tridimensional region of Euclid– its corresponding psychological defects.

Tonight, we are talking exclusively about the Second Circle; later on, after having reviewed the Nine Dantean Circles, we will study the Law of Perpetual Movement in detail. Then all of you, ladies and gentlemen, will be able to delve a little more into the topic that corresponds to the question that was asked by this young man here.

Question: Master, does it mean that in this Circle that corresponds to lust, fornication has become terribly mechanical and therefore painful and disgusting?

Answer: Well, my friend, listen to me: within that black and fatal air, lust tends to mix with violence, thus everything becomes instinctive and brutal. Understood?

Question: Venerable Master, what astounds me tremendously is that in spite of the tortures that are endured in this Circle, those who dwell there think that they are doing very well. Would you like to explain this matter to us?

Answer: Noble sir, the people from the Abyss always think the best of themselves. They firmly believe that they are treading the path of righteousness and love, and consider that those of us who walk on the Path of the Revolution of Consciousness are heading, as they say, towards our own destruction.

I want you to know that the tenebrous ones, moved by good intentions, tempt us incessantly with the purpose, as they say, of saving us. In these abysmal regions we see many anchorites, penitents, fakirs, mystics, monks, etc., etc., etc., admonishing diverse human groups and totally convinced that they are doing very well.

Question: Master, these Souls who are so convinced that they are doing very well, do they not know that they are in Hell, the Inferno?

Answer: Noble lady that asks the question, the word "inferno" is derived from the Latin *"infernus"*, which signifies "inferior region". In the interior of the Earth we find the World of Natural Elements, and it is unquestionable that the lost would never consider those Elements, or the Submerged Regions, as a place of damnation.

Normal, ordinary common people have their Consciousness asleep, but there are those who enter the abysmal regions awaken in evil and for evil. Such people have a very special psychological idiosyncrasy, a fatal logic of a different type.

Do not be surprised, do not be astounded if for the abysmal lost ones, white is black and vice-versa. To name Jesus, the great Kabir, or the Divine Mother Kundalini, in those Submerged Regions, is for these condemned people blasphemy, something unforgivable and consequently that would be equivalent to provoking their anger. We would then see them attacking us furiously.

The lost do not ignore the concrete fact that they have to pass through Second Death, but they are not afraid of it: they implore it, they ask for it. They know that it is the escape hatch for them to return to the surface of the Earth and reinitiate a new evolving ascension that will have to go from stone to man, understood?

Question: Master, a person like me, who observes absolute sexual abstention, would I perhaps be free from entering into the Second Dantean Circle?

Answer: Friends, brothers, it is indispensable, urgent and unpostponable to know that lust processes itself within the 49 regions of the subconscious.

Many saints who reached supreme chastity in the merely intellective level, failed when they were submitted to trials within the more profound regions of the subconscious.

Someone could, for example, have achieved chastity in 48 subconscious regions and fail in the 49th.

Many virtuous men and women, who self-qualified themselves as chaste and innocent, are now inhabitants of the Second Dantean Circle.

Thousands of religious people, priests of all beliefs who thought that they had attained the most absolute chastity, now live in the Inferno of Mercury.

Therefore, let no one qualify themselves as being chaste. Whoever feels confident, may he look back and take heed not to fall.

Question: Master, you have mentioned 49 regions of the subconscious, and I can say frankly that it is the first time that I hear of such a number, because all the treatises on Psychology, Parapsychology and Psychoanalysis, where the processes of the Consciousness, subconsciousness and infra-consciousness, etc. are mentioned and studied, do not mention these 49 divisions or regions that you cite. Why is this?

Answer: Distinguished gentlemen, ladies who listen to me, it is good for us to remember the septenary constitution of an authentic Man.

Since the three-brained or three-centered biped mistakenly called man has not yet awakened Consciousness, he has not created the Existential Bodies of the Being, he truly only possesses subconscious and subjective states.

Multiply the septuple aspect by itself and you will have the 49 subconscious regions of every humanoid.

Obviously, with the awakening of Consciousness these 49 states become conscious and only then would we have integral conscious objectivity.

We need to transform the subconscious into conscious, and this is only possible by disintegrating the psychic aggregates that constitute the Ego, the Myself, the Oneself.

Let us remember that the Consciousness is bottled up within those aggregates; disintegrating the latter, the Consciousness becomes awakened.

Lust, fornication in the Submerged Circle of Mercury, underneath the terrestrial crust, is indeed the very foundation, the base of the existential Ego.

Question: Master, in some of your books you explain that in order to awaken Consciousness, the "I" or psychological defect that one wishes to eliminate, has to be dissected with the intellect, and that this must be done in the 49 departments of the subconscious; but if we do not have our Consciousness awakened yet, how can we penetrate into these 49 regions with the intellect? Would you like to explain this to us?

Answer: Friends, it would not be possible to radically disintegrate the Ego in an instantaneous manner and simultaneously within all the 49 subconscious regions.

I invite you to reflect, to investigate this matter in a clear and perfect way.

When we want to annihilate any psychological defect –lust for example, or any other– we must first of all comprehend it.

However, the overall comprehension of the defect in question cannot be something that is reached immediately within the 49 subconscious regions; this means a progressive advancement on the path of understanding.

Gradually, we would begin comprehending and eliminating the "I's" of the defect in question in each of the subconscious regions. This would set a methodical, profound and orderly development of the Consciousness.

As the Consciousness awakens, comprehension becomes clearer each time, until it reaches its final stage. Then, the defect would be radically annihilated.

7

THE THIRD DANTEAN CIRCLE

THE SUBMERGED SPHERE OF VENUS

Friends who are listening to me tonight, we are going to talk about the Venusian Infernos located, as is already known, within the infra-dimensions of nature, beneath the epidermis of the Earth...

Unquestionably, this is a region which is much denser and coarser than the two former ones, since each atom of matter contains within it 288 atoms of the Absolute.

Obviously, these are much heavier atoms, and therefore the materiality is vastly greater.

Moreover, the very fact that it is governed by 288 laws turns this subterranean zone into something very complicated and frightfully difficult and painful.

Let us carefully observe bars, "cabarets", brothels, etc., etc., in our three-dimensional world of Euclid.

Unquestionably, we can find the vital shadow of all of this, the sinister aspect of great orgies and bacchanals in the Submerged Sphere of Venus.

Those who have always lived from orgy to orgy, from bar to bar, submerged in the slime of great feasts, banquets and drinking sprees, know very well what it feels like after a night on the tiles. Many of them, wanting to drown with wine the disastrous state in which they find themselves after a spree, continue on the path of vice until reaching the total devastation of their organism.

Expanding on this matter, going in depth a bit more on this topic, I can emphatically affirm to you that after pleasure comes pain. Now you can explain for yourselves how life must be or how existence must be for the lost souls in the Submerged Region of Venus.

No wonder Dante found incessant rain, frightful cold, mud, black water, rot, etc., within the submerged Abysses of the Third Infernal Circle.

However, the deceased in those regions hear with horror the frightful barking of the infernal dog Cerberus, the symbolic canine that with his three cruel fangs represents the violent, luciferian, sexual animal passions completely out of control.

Behold the pleasures of the ancient Rome of the Caesars transformed into fatal results. Behold Petronius who died in the midst of the ruckus of a feast, loved by all the women and crowned with roses and laurels. Behold the Goddess Lesbos and her lesbians; behold the poetess Sappho, who sang to all the degenerates of her era. Behold the lyre of Nero broken into pieces, and the arrogant lords of great feasts...

Grotesque abode of Heliogabalus! Famous gluttons, true peacocks shining gloriously in ancient carouses.

What happened to their goblets of fine baccarat? What became of the swords of the gentlemen, their oaths of love, the kisses of their lady, their sweet words, the applause of the guests, the compliments, the praises, the regal clothes, the ladies' perfumes, the pompous dances, the soft carpets, the shiny mirrors, the sumptuous poems, the wicked purple and the gorgeous silks?

Now there is only the pestilence of the underworld, where Ciacco prophesied to Dante the fall of the victorious party in beautiful Florence and the triumph of the oppressed, who newly defeated, were dominated in an even more tyrannical manner by the former.

Abominable zone of bitterness where this poet, disciple of Virgil, in an unaccustomed manner asked about Farinata and Tegghiaio, who were so worthy, and Jacopo Rusticucci, Arrigo and Mosca, and others who dedicated themselves to doing good and who now dwell in even more profound regions of the Infernal Worlds.

Many sincerely mistaken people who terrifyingly involute within these abysmal regions were people who livened the sumptuous rooms of the great lords with their lyre, beautiful virtuous maidens who sang poems, unhappy wine drinkers in the suburbs of the cities, etc., now live within these Infernos of the Third Dantean Circle.

Question: Dear Master, you mentioned that in this Third Dantean Circle of Venus live many sincere but mistaken people, in other words, many souls that undoubtedly did good deeds and in spite of this they suffer in those Infernos. So, I ask if perchance the sincerity of those souls does not constitute an extenuating element that saves them from such tenebrous punishment?

Answer: Friend, gentleman who asks this question, in life we can practice a lot of good, and you can rest assured that such good deeds will always be fully paid back and well beyond; the divine never keeps anything, it always pays everyone according to their deeds.

I patiently beg you to pay attention, to follow the course of this lecture... So, hear me, listen to me: whosoever has exhausted his cycle of 108 existences enters into submerged involution within the Infernal Worlds, if he has not achieved Intimate Realization of the Being.

However, it is clear that before entering into the Abode of Pluto we are first paid for our good deeds.

Now you will comprehend, ladies and gentlemen, the reason why many perverse people in their present life live in opulence, while some saints or people who are self-realizing scarcely have food, clothing and shelter.

It is unquestionable that after the good deeds have been well paid, those who are without Self-Realization enter into the subterranean Abysses.

Likewise, there are pious people with unspeakable secret crimes; what they have of good was always well paid by the Law of Karma, but what is bad takes them to the Abyss of perdition.

So, then my friend, understand what the Law of Retribution is; may all of you comprehend, please comprehend...

Question: Venerable Master, I would like for you to explain to me why fornicators inhabit the Region of Mercury, which is a zone less dense than that of Venus, whereas the gluttons and drunkards inhabit the Region of Venus, which is even denser than the previous one.

Answer: Ladies and gentlemen, distinguished gentleman who asks the question, please understand me...

We have been told emphatically that the original sin is fornication and this is the basis of the involuting waves of the Infernal Worlds.

I am not stating that only drunkards and gluttons live within the Third Infernal Circle. It is obvious that the lost one are hundred percent unredeemed fornicators. Now you will comprehend for yourselves why Dante found the dog Cerberus, living symbol of the sexual forces, barking lugubriously within the tenebrous regions.

This clearly means that the inhabitants of the Submerged Regions are never free from lust and they suffer frightfully.

However, we must specify, and the disciple of Virgil does so, and so do we: within each of the Nine Circles or Infra-Dimensional Regions of nature certain defects which we carry within stand out, and that is all.

Question: Master, we have learned when studying the Egyptian Tarot cards that the dog symbolizes the Holy Spirit because it guides us in getting out of the Infernos when we have decided to Self-Realize ourselves, but the Cerberus that Dante talks about, based on what you say, symbolizes lust. Would you like to clarify this dissertation?

Answer: Gentleman, allow me to inform you that the dog of Mercury is strictly symbolic, since it clearly allegorizes sexual potency.

Hercules took him out of the Abyss so that it would serve him as a guide, and we do the same thing when we achieve chastity. So then, by working in the Forge of the Cyclops, by practicing Sexual Magic, by transmuting our creative energies, we advance on the Path of the Razor's Edge until we reach Final Liberation.

Woe to the gentleman who abandons his dog: he will go astray from the Path and fall into the Abyss of Perdition!

Unfortunately, the intellectual animal mistakenly called man has not achieved chastity; in other words, he has not taken Cerberus out of the infernal domains.

Now you will comprehend for yourselves the reason why the deceased suffer within the Plutonian Abysses when they hear the frightful barks of Cerberus, the canine of the three hungry fangs.

It is obvious that the lost ones suffer the insatiable thirst of lust within the frightful "Tartarus".

Question: Master, could you tell us what the bacchanals and orgies of the Third Dantean Circle or Submerged Regions of Venus are like?

Answer: Ladies and gentlemen, upon hearing this question, the times of my youth come to my memory.

In those times I also participated in great feasts where amidst the ruckus and the partying shone nights of spree and orgies that only left bitterness and remorse within my Conscience, etc., etc., etc. After one of those parties, I –absolutely conscious– was taken to the Third Dantean Circle. Attired in my Astral body, I sat at the head of a fatal table at the party of Demons, the crude reality of a terrifying materialism, whose mere memory makes the innermost parts of my Soul shiver.

The table was covered with bottles of liquor and filthy food, especially made for gluttons. At the center of the table was a great tray, upon which the head of a pig stood out. Horrified by the macabre horrifying feast, I looked with pain at the place of the orgy...

All of a sudden, everything changed; my divine Real Being, the Intimate, that Angel of the *Book of Revelations* by St. John who holds the key to the Abyss in his hands, took me by the arm forcefully, snatched me out of that room as if by magic. He then threw me upon a white mortuary sheet on that muddy, loathsome floor; there, he flogged me with a great chain while saying:

"You are my Bodhisattva, my Human Soul, and I need you in order to deliver the message of the New Age of Aquarius to humanity! Are you going to serve me? Or what?"

Then I, feeling remorse in my heart, answered:

"Yes, my Lord, I will serve you! I repent! Forgive me!"

Thus, my friends, this is how I came to abhor liquors, feasts, gluttony, drinking sprees, etc., etc., etc. The only thing that comes from all that filth are tears –symbolized by the rain within that horrible region– those pestilent waters of bitterness and the horrible mud of misery.

8

THE FOURTH DANTEAN CIRCLE

THE SUBMERGED SPHERE OF THE SUN

Distinguished friends, tonight we are going to consciously study the Fourth Dantean Circle, located within the natural infra-dimensions, underneath the tridimensional region of Euclid.

We who have passed through the diverse esoteric transcendental processes within the Superior Dimensions have been able to directly verify for ourselves the crude reality of the Submerged Solar Mineral Kingdom.

Unquestionably, within the Solar Infernos of the resplendent star that gives life to our entire Solar System of Ors, we do not see the grotesque Dantean spectacles of the terrestrial Infernos.

It is obvious that the most perfect mineral purity exists within the Submerged Solar Mineral Kingdom.

It is indubitable that within that radiant star —which is the very heart of this great solar system in which we live, move and have our Being— only Solar Spirits happily dwell.

In view of the fact that there are sacred and eternal individuals, it is not possible to think of evident and definitive failures, like those within our terrestrial world.

The concrete fact is then evident, that there are no tenebrous dwellers in the natural infra-dimensions of the solar world.

The infra-dimensions of our planet Earth are a very different case.

The involutive states of the Fourth Circle underneath the geologic crust of our Earth are evident, clear and manifest to any esotericist investigator.

Since the Sun is the source of all life and the marvelous agent that sustains all existence, in accordance with the Law of Eternal Common Cosmic Trogoautoegocrat, thus, obviously, we come to really find the fatal and negative antithesis of all this in the antithetical solar aspect of the Fourth Submerged terrestrial Zone.

In that tenebrous region, in those Atomic Infernos of nature, we find two specific types of involuting people. I am emphatically referring to the squanderers and misers, two types of individuals who can never reconcile with one another and who incessantly attack each other over and over again.

By analyzing this matter in depth, we must solemnly affirm that squandering is as absurd as greed.

Within the strictly Common Cosmic Trogoautoegocratic process, we must always remain faithful to the scales. It is clear that the violation of the Law of Equilibrium brings about painful karmic consequences.

In the area of practical life we can consciously verify the disastrous consequences that come from the violation of the Law of the Scales.

It is indubitable that the prodigal, the squanderer, he who wastes his money, although deep down he feels very generous, is violating the Law.

The miser, he who does not allow money to circulate, he who selfishly retains it unduly beyond what is normal, is clearly harming the community, taking bread away from many people, impoverishing his fellowmen. For that reason, he is violating the Law of Equilibrium, the Law of the Scales.

It is logical that the squanderer, even though he is apparently doing good by making money circulate intensely, is producing imbalance not only within himself but also within the general movement of values. This eventually causes tremendous economic harm to the people.

Prodigals and misers become beggars; and this has been proven.

It is indispensable, it is urgent to cooperate with the Law of Eternal Common Cosmic Trogoautoegocrat, not to hamper economic balance, not to hurt oneself, not to harm others.

Since many ignore what the Law of Eternal Common Cosmic Trogoautoegocrat is, it is good to clarify the following: this Great Law manifests itself as reciprocal nourishment of all organisms.

If we observe carefully the entrails of the Earth, we will find copper as the center of gravity for all of the evolving and involuting processes in nature.

If we apply merely a positive force to this metal, we will see by means of objective clairvoyance extraordinary evolving developments. If we apply the negative force, we will be able to witness in a direct manner the involuting descending impulses within all of the atoms of the mentioned metal. If we apply the neutral force; we will see processes of atomic stabilization within that metal.

It is very interesting for esotericist investigators to contemplate the metallic radiations of copper within the living entrails of our planetary organism.

One is amazed to see how the emanations of the mentioned metal animate other metals, while at the same time, as compensation, it is also fed by the emanations of those other metals.

There is then, an exchange of radiations among the different metals in the interior of the Earth; there is reciprocal nourishment among the metals. Moreover, what is most amazing is the exchange of radiations between the metals in the interior of the Earth and those within the Submerged Mineral Kingdom of other planets of our solar system. This is the Law of Eternal Common Cosmic Trogoautoegocrat in full manifestation. This great Law enables coexistence among the planets.

This reciprocal nourishment between the planets, this exchange of planetary substances, gives origin to the equilibrium of the worlds around their gravitational centers.

In other words, we shall affirm the following: there is reciprocal nourishment between plants, between minerals, between all types of organisms, etc., etc., etc.

The economic and human processes, the fluctuations of currency, the financial debits and credits, the exchange of merchandise and currencies, the particular economy of each person, what each person earns and spends, etc., etc., etc., also belong to the great Law of Eternal Common Cosmic Trogoautoegocrat.

It is clear, we repeat, it is evident that in our solar system, the radiant star that illuminates us is, in fact, the administrator of this supreme cosmic Law. The functioning of such a Law would not be possible if all equilibrium is violated.

Now we can clearly explain to ourselves the fundamental reason why prodigals and misers alter the balance of payments and cause dire consequences in cosmic and human equilibrium.

Those who violate this Law in some way must receive their due. It is not surprising then to find prodigals and misers in the solar antithesis, in the Fourth Dantean Circle.

Question: Dear Master, you have given us a truly transcendental explanation about the Fourth Dantean Circle; informing us that therein dwell the prodigals as well as the misers. Would you be so kind as to explain to us what type of sufferings the beings that dwell there undergo?

Answer: My friend, I find your question quite interesting and I hasten to answer …

Since we only see consequences within the Submerged Worlds, I invite you to reflect. Ask yourself, what is greed; in which way is a miser similar to a beggar; what kind of life do the misers have, what kind of illnesses, what kind of sufferings, in what way do they die?

Let us go to the other extreme. Let us think for a moment of a person who has squandered all of his fortune. How does he end up? What fate do his children have and his family in general, etc., etc., etc.?

Many cases of suicide were known in the casino of Monte Carlo. Gamblers, who ended up in poverty, who lost their millions, committed suicide from one day to the next...

What could we say now about these two types of people? Friends, in the Infernal Worlds the only thing that exists are consequences and these are catastrophic, terrible, frightening. Within the Avernus prodigals and misers, desperate, blaspheme against the Divinity; they curse, they mutually fight each other, they sink into frightening desperation.

Question: What I do not understand, Master, is that if the Fourth Dantean Circle is much denser and materialistic than the Second, considering those guilty of lust to be the greatest sinners against the Holy Spirit —even though prodigals and misers commit so much harm— do you not think that the greater punishment should be for the former?

Answer: Gentleman, ladies and gentlemen, I now want to repeat what I emphatically and clearly affirmed in a previous lecture: the original sin is lust and this serves as a basis for all the descending involutive processes within the Nine Dantean Circles submerged within the entrails of our world. However, it is evident that within the total sum of all of the descending processes within each of the nine natural infra-dimensions, certain specific and defined defects, which are intrinsically correlated with their corresponding circle, stand out.

It is good to know, friends, ladies and young people who are listening to me, that in the Fourth Circle prodigals and misers are found perfectly defined, that is all!

Question: Master, since squandering as well as greed, from my point of view, are directly related with the hunger of people and individuals, and since the Great Law of Eternal Common Cosmic Trogoautoegocrat is related to equilibrium, it seems to me that this can lead us directly to the problem of nourishment and that surely this also has to do with the suffering that we endure within the Fourth Dantean Circle if we do not maintain a balance on the scale of our nutrition. Can you tell us something in this regard?

Answer: Distinguished gentleman who is asking that question, we already emphasized the case of gluttons in our past lecture on the Third Circle. Undoubtedly, they violate, in themselves and for themselves, the Law of Eternal Common Cosmic Trogoautoegocrat by putting inside their organisms an excess of foods and drinks. It is clear that any violation of the Law of the Scales causes imbalance and the result is pain.

Question: Master, are these beings who enter into the Fourth Circle only those who have already exhausted the cycle of 108 human existences?

Answer: Respectable lady who is asking the question, allow me to emphatically, categorically, and definitively inform you that all those who enter submerged involution in the Infernal Worlds, including the inhabitants of the Fourth Dantean Circle, have in fact already exhausted the cycle of 108 existences.

Nevertheless, I already said in a previous lecture that there were exceptions. I was then referring specifically to the definitely perverse ones, to those who, because of their excessive malignancy had to enter submerged infernal involution without having yet exhausted their cycle of existences.

Question: Based on this explanation, I reach the synthesis that in the Fourth Solar Dantean Circle dwell all those who unbalance the scales of universal economy, that is to say, from a purely economic point of view. Am I right, Master?

Answer: Gentleman, friend, your question is correct... Indeed, one cannot violate with impunity the Law of the Scales of World Economy without receiving one's due. The Law is the Law and the violation of any Law brings pain.

Question: Dear Master, when you were talking about gluttons in regards to the imbalance of the Scales, by analogy one can say the same of those who voluntarily, out of ignorance, lack adequate nutrition, especially because of their unawareness of the Law of Eternal Common Cosmic Trogoautoegocrat. Could we, then, consider that the orthodox of the religion of the kitchen, that is to say, the vegetarians, would dwell in the Circle that you are talking about in this lecture?

Answer: Distinguished gentleman who is asking the question, allow me to tell you with perfectly absolute crystal clarity that everyone is free to nourish themselves as they please. There are unbearable vegetarians who have turned food into a religion of the kitchen and there are also upon the Earth, bloodthirsty carnivores, almost cannibals, who have destroyed their organism.

It takes all kinds to make a world, and everyone sins due to imbalance, everyone violates the Law of the Scales and the outcome of any violation is not very pleasant.

However, it is worth repeating that everyone is free to nourish themselves as they please... Nevertheless, we must not forget the Law: If we destroy our bodies, we will have to endure the consequences...

It is a good idea to specify that there are also many vegetarians within the Abysses. However, none of them live there because of the transgression of eating vegetables, but because of many other causes and motives.

In matters of food, let everyone eat what they please; what is important, I repeat, is not to break the Law, that is all!

Question: Master, could you tell us if there is a procedure or a system that you could teach us in order to have perfect balance on the Scales?

Answer: Distinguished lady, it is good for you to understand that your inner Monad, your Immortal Spark, your Father who is in secret, as the Christic Gospel would put it, is the eternal regulator of the Eternal Common Cosmic Trogoautoegocratic process. He has the power to give and the power to take away from us.

If we act in accordance with the Law, if we live in harmony with the infinite, if we learn to obey the Father who is in secret, in the Heavens as well as on Earth, we shall never lack our daily bread. Remember the magnificent prayer of the Our Father, meditate profoundly on it, listen...

Question: Master, how can we do the Will of the Father if we are asleep, if we cannot see him nor hear him?

Answer: Ladies, gentlemen, friends, the Law is written. Remember the Ten Commandments of Moses. Do not break the written Commandments; live by them, respect them.

If each one of those present here, if each person of goodwill decides to live in accordance with the Law and the Prophets, he will do the will of the Father in the Heavens as well as on Earth.

The day will come when the devotee of the Real Path awakens Consciousness. Then he will be able to see his Father, receive his direct orders and consciously obey them.

First, we must respect the written Law and thereafter we will know the Commandments of the Blessed One...

Question: Master, what can you tell us about the materiality and the laws that govern the Fourth Dantean Solar Circle?

Answer: Respectable gentleman, friends, listen to me well: the Fourth Dantean Circle is constituted by atoms that are vastly denser than those that give form and structure to the three previous Circles.

It is evident that every atom of the Fourth Tenebrous Circle carries within its womb 384 atoms of the Absolute. These specific types of atoms give unto the Fourth Submerged Region a terribly coarse and material aspect, immensely heavier and more painful than that which is lived and breathed within the three previous Circles.

However, it is not surprising that one sees there, in those regions, stores, shops of all types, goods, cars..., all kinds of objects, which in the end are nothing more than simple coarse mental forms, crystallized by the minds of the deceased.

I still remember a very curious case. One night of many, in my Astral Body in that tenebrous region of the "Tartarus", before the display case of a luxurious store –a mere mental form of a submerged merchant– I had to call Bael. That dreadful Mage of Darkness, dressed in a blood-colored tunic and wearing an oriental red turban, came to me, seated in a chariot. In the rear his followers were bringing him forth, pushing his carriage. This sinister character, a fallen Angel, luminary of the firmament in ancient times, looked at me with hatred, hurled himself against me, biting my right hand... It is obvious that I conjured him, and finally that phantom vanished in the darkness of that horrible Abode of Pluto.

Oh, friends! One is astonished in those Regions upon seeing so many exploiters of bodies and souls. There we find lottery and cards players, many priests and hierarchs, mystics who insatiably covet the property of others.

One is really filled with amazement upon seeing so many prelates and anchorites, penitents and devotees who loved humanity, in spite of their greed. All of these lost ones live within the Fourth Submerged Region, still believing that they are doing very well, and what is most serious is that they would never accept the concrete fact that they are doing badly.

Question: Master, could you tell us if within this Fourth Dantean Circle there are not any Masters of the White Lodge who instruct those who live there with the purpose of making them comprehend that they are doing badly?

Answer: Hierophants of the Light, Nirmanakayas of Compassion, splendorous Kabirs, Sons of the Flame, abide everywhere, and many of them have renounced all happiness in order to live within the profundities of the Abyss with the purpose of helping those who are decidedly lost.

Unfortunately, the inhabitants of the "Tartarus" hate the Sons of the Light, they classify them as wicked, they give them the epithet of "White Demons", they curse them and they would never accept the idea that they are doing badly.

Those who are definitively lost always believe that they march on the path of righteousness, truth and justice.

Question: Master, can you tell us if within the Fourth Dantean Circle there is air, fire, water, earth —or what?

Answer: Distinguished lady, those who are very greedy are people who have metalized themselves very much. I invite you then to comprehend that the Fourth Dantean Circle is essentially metallic or of an extremely dense mineral.

Obviously, the creatures that live in water, the fish, do not see the element in which they live. Likewise, we who dwell within the Element Air do not see that element. Similarly, those who live in the mineral element will be able to see mental forms, shapes of stores, bars, taverns, banks, etc., etc., but they will not see the element in which they live; to them it will be as transparent as the air.

Now, what shall we say about the Element Water? Obviously, it is by means of this element that the Eternal Common Cosmic Trogoautoegocratic process is crystallized, making possible the reciprocal nourishment of all creatures. If the Earth was to remain without water, if the seas were to dry up, if the rivers were to disappear, all of the creatures that inhabit on the face of the Earth would die. Thus, the concrete and definitive fact that water is the agent by means of which the Law of Eternal Common Cosmic Trogoautoegocrat crystallizes is hereby completely demonstrated.

In the Fourth Dantean Circle, the waters are black and its fundamental element, I repeat, is mineral.

Do the prodigals and misers not violate the law perhaps? Do they perhaps not alter the equilibrium of the economic scales of the peoples? Do they not perchance alter the modus operandi of the Law of Eternal Common Cosmic Trogoautoegocrat? Reflect upon all of this, dear friends, ladies and gentlemen...

9

THE FIFTH DANTEAN CIRCLE

THE SUBMERGED SPHERE OF MARS

Friends, ladies and gentlemen, we are now going to talk a little bit about the Fifth Natural Infra-dimension or the Infra-dimension of Mars, located underneath the geological crust of our terrestrial world.

First and foremost, it is appropriate to emphatically clarify that we are not referring to the Submerged Mineral Kingdom of planet Mars itself. We are exclusively referring to that infra-dimensional section located underneath the epidermis of the Earth, related to a vibration of Martian type.

I am neither talking about the Heaven of Mars, nor about the said planet. What I am saying refers exclusively to the Fifth Infra-Dimension of our planet Earth, and that is all.

I like to clarify all of this with the purpose of avoiding erroneous interpretations, since the mind, as it is already known, can fall into many subtle deceptions...

In the Fifth Dantean Circle ironic, furious, arrogant, haughty and proud people unquestionably stand out.

Within the Hells of the planet Mars themselves —as we have already studied in our book entitled *The Three Mountains*— the esotericist investigator discovers awful witches' Sabbaths, frightening warlocks, tenebrous harpies, witches, hags or whatever else they are called.

Nevertheless, underneath the epidermis of our planet Earth, within the Fifth Dantean Circle which is a kind of Martian-like section, the followers of Selene with their disgusting warlocks —who frequently frightened the Trojans on the Strophades Islands of the Aegean Sea— certainly do not stand out.

Here Dante Alighieri, the old Florentine disciple of Virgil, poet of Mantua, only sees —within the turbid waters and the filthy mud— many arrogant people, who upon the face of the Earth solemnly shone amidst rich palaces and sumptuous mansions...

The most painful thing within this abominable Region is that the lost ones have to encounter their own millenary diabolical creations.

Unquestionably, the Consciousness, bottled up within all those psychic aggregates that constitute the Ego, the Myself, the Oneself, has to confront itself with all of its components.

I saw in those Submerged Regions, a lot of mud, stagnant waters and supreme pain.

I still remember with horror a certain desperate creature submerged within that mud of bitterness, who tried to hide from the sinister gaze of certain horrible monsters that in the depth of his own psyche, were "I's" personifying violence and that were parts of himself.

To flee from oneself? The "I" fleeing from the "I"? Oh dread, horror! The Consciousness facing itself, confronting the Machiavellian torment impossible to describe with words.

Those "I's" —the part of that living creature who was trying to flee from them— did not have their eyes in front like other mortals; they were nefariously placed to the right and left, like the eyes of birds...

They were psychological aggregates of violence. Armed with symbolic rifles, they wanted to attack the creature who was hiding; however, the latter and his assailants were all of them psychic aggregates, component parts of one and the same Ego; of the pluralized "I" in its totality.

To wallow within so much mud, to flee from oneself, to dread oneself, the "I" confronting the "I," parts of oneself confronting parts of oneself, is indeed the horror of horrors, the unspeakable, an indescribable terror that cannot be expressed with words. This is how the Consciousness of the deceased within the Fifth Infra-Dimension of planet Earth becomes aware of its own wickedness, its own horrors, its unbelievable violence, destructive wrath...

Question: Dear Master, I have observed that when referring to the Fifth Dantean Circle of the planet Mars, you tell us that there are witches' Sabbaths and convulsions of wrath; however, when you refer to the Fourth Dantean Solar Circle you inform us that with respect to the Sun star, it is clean of "I's" although in the process of Initiation, Mars corresponds to the next step ahead. If my question was understood, can you please clarify it?

Answer: Distinguished friend, I have said that within the Submerged Martian Mineral Kingdom, meaning, within the Infernos of the planet Mars, not in its Heaven or on its planetary surface, the esotericist investigator can certainly find the tenebrous harpies and their frightful witches' Sabbaths.

I have also said that in the Submerged Mineral Kingdom of the Sun that illuminates and gives us life, within its purely natural infra-dimensions, everything is clean; there we do not see the followers of Selene nor the horrible warlocks, nor the followers of Simon the Magician.

It would be absurd to suppose just for a moment that the Adepts of the Left Hand and the Fortune-Tellers of Python could live within the entrails of the radiant Sun. It is clear that the solar vibrations would destroy, would instantaneously annihilate, any impure creature...

I repeat what I previously said: only Solar Spirits, Ineffable Beings who are beyond good and evil can solemnly dwell within the Sun.

Question: You say that within the Fifth Infra-Dimension of the planetary organism, the "I's" confront other "I's" and that the Consciousness also confronts those "I's" which are terribly malignant because of their wrathful nature. Does this signify that the Consciousness is a third party in disagreement, a part of the Myself?

Answer: Distinguished gentleman, your question is important and with great pleasure I hasten to clarify...

First of all, it is urgent to know that the Ego, the "I", the Myself, the Oneself is not something individual. Certainly, the Ego is an ensemble of psychic aggregates; the latter can also be denominated "I's."

That "I" of ours is, well, a sum of small, quarrelsome and vociferous "I's" that we carry within. If we denominate them as Demons, we will not commit any specific definitive error. By carefully analyzing this matter, we can reach the logical conclusion that such Demon-I's clearly personify our psychological defects.

I invite you, ladies and gentlemen, to concretely comprehend that each one of these Devil-I's carry within its interior a certain well-defined percentage of our own Consciousness.

It so happens that in the Fifth natural Infra-dimension of our planet Earth, the Consciousness confronts itself, it acquires self-knowledge by looking at itself through many eyes from diverse angles, in accordance with each one of its "I's".

It is indubitable that the Consciousness tries to flee from itself, to flee from its own representative defects, from its own diabolic creations.

It is not at all pleasant for the deceased to try to flee from themselves, to be horrified by their own selves, one part trying to hide from the terrifying and frightening gaze of another part or parts of themselves.

I want to help all of those who are listening to me, in some way, by using a very exact simile...

Here in Mexico, at the entrance of the Castle of Chapultepec, we have the Hall of Mirrors; the visitors see themselves in completely different ways in each one of those mirrors.Some of those mirrors break down our image, depicting us as giants of ancient times; others depict us as insignificant dwarfs; others as having chubby figures, frighteningly obese; yet others as having elongated, deformed figures, horrifying and thin; still others deform our image depicting it with monstrous arms and legs, etc., etc.

Imagine for a moment that each one of these figures were to be one of our "I's", living personifications of our errors.

What would become of all those creatures within the multiple mirrors, parts of the Oneself, of the Myself, of the Ego that we carry within, if each one of them, horrified, wanted to independently flee from the others?

We, transformed into all of those multiple "I's", each one of our parts frightened by each one of our parts; each horror frightened by each horror. That is a torment worse than that of Tantalus; herein lays the torture of the Fifth Dantean Circle.

Indeed, ladies and gentlemen, the Ego that we carry within is made up of thousands of demons, "I's" that represent our psychological defects.

It is clear that such a swarm of Devils control our organic machine here in this physical world, and that there is no agreement among them whatsoever.

All of them fight for supremacy; all of them want to control the main centers of the organic machine. When one of them governs for a moment, he then feels as if he is the master, the boss, the only one. However, he is dethroned afterwards and another one becomes the boss.

Now ladies and gentlemen you will understand for yourselves the reason why all human beings are filled with inner contradictions. If we could see ourselves in a full length mirror the way we really are, we would be horrified of ourselves.

This is a concrete fact in the Fifth natural Infra-Dimension of planet Earth. Nevertheless, in the cited Tenebrous Region, the fear is even cruder, more realistic, to the point that each one of the terrified parts flees without respite, terrified, trying to hide from each one of the other parts...

The Consciousness divided into multiple pieces, horror of the Avernus, mystery, terrible things of the Darkness of Minos. Woe! Woe! Woe!

Question: Although it is evident that this Fifth natural Infra-Dimension of our planet Earth is much denser and material than the previous ones, can you explain to us what elements are characteristic of its density?

Answer: Gentleman, friends... Indeed, the Fifth Dantean Circle is denser than the four previous ones due to its atomic composition.

It is understood that each atom of the Fifth Submerged Region carries in its womb 480 atoms of the Sacred Absolute Sun.

It is therefore evident that the Fifth Submerged Region is much coarser than the previous ones; consequently, the suffering within it is greater.

Millions of condemned inhabit this zone of the Earth, people who hurt one another, blasphemers that curse the Eternal living God, persons full of hatred and of vengeance; arrogant, irate, impetuous people, assassins and villains.

All of these people believe that they are doing very well. None of them suppose even for an instant that they walk on the path of darkness and horror, and that they are doing badly. All of them feel holy and virtuous. Some of them have self-pity, describing themselves as victims of injustice. All of them, in general, boast of being just ...

Question: Regarding the Nine Labors that are carried out in the Second Mountain of Resurrection, would you be so kind as to tell us the difference between the work within the Fifth Infra-Dimension of the planet Mars and that of the Fifth Dantean Circle of the planet Earth?

Answer: Friends, friends, I invite you to comprehend what the work of the dissolution of the Ego is. Undoubtedly, when we submerge ourselves by means of meditation into our own Atomic Infernos with the purpose of comprehending these or those psychological defects, it is unquestionable that we establish contact with this or that natural Infra-dimension.

Since the Fifth Submerged Region is the fundamental section of wrath, obviously, when we are trying to comprehend the diverse processes of anger, rage, violence, arrogance, etc., etc., in an integral manner we establish contact with the cited Fifth Dantean Circle.

It is indispensable to make a clear differentiation between those inhumane elements that are related to the Nine Dantean Circles of the planet Earth, located underneath the epidermis of this afflicted world and the infra-conscious elements that within our psyche, maintain intimate relations with the Infernos of the Moon, Mercury, Venus, the Sun, Mars, Jupiter, Saturn, Uranus and Neptune.

But listen to me well, ladies and gentlemen, so that there are no confusions: distinguish between Heavens and Hells. The Heaven of each one of the cited planets is totally different from the Hell of each one of them.

Learn to always situate any planetary Inferno within the Submerged Mineral Kingdom of the same.

Heaven is different. It is a region of light, harmony, happiness... We would not be able to enter into any of these planetary

Heavens without first having worked within their corresponding Infernos.

Look at things from this angle: it is clear that we could never enter into the Heaven of Mars without first having worked within the Martian Inferno, within the living entrails of its own Submerged Mineral Kingdom.

Within the Inferno of Mars, within its natural infra-dimensions, we must eliminate certain witch-like, infra-conscious and inhumane psychic states.

These kinds of works are only possible for those sacred individuals known as Powers and who are preparing themselves to attain the state of Virtues within the Heaven of Mars.

However, any work within the entrails of the other worlds of the solar system maintains a certain psychic relationship with its corresponding infernal sections of the planet Earth.

Do not forget, ladies and gentlemen, the Laws of Correspondences, Analogies and Numerology.

In any case, it is urgent to know that even if in the Infernos of planet Mars, we must eliminate witch-like and infra-conscious psychic states, within the corresponding Fifth infernal Section of our planet Earth, we only limit ourselves to eliminating the processes of anger, arrogance, etc., etc.

10

THE SIXTH DANTEAN CIRCLE

THE SUBMERGED SPHERE OF JUPITER

Distinguished friends, today we are going to study with complete clarity the Sixth Dantean Circle, or that of Jupiter, submerged underneath the epidermis of the planet Earth.

Unquestionably, this infra-dimensional region is much denser than the five previous ones due to its atomic constitution.

It is good to know that each atom of the Sixth Dantean Circle carries in its womb 576 atoms of the Sacred Absolute Sun.

Undoubtedly, such extremely heavy atoms are the *causa causarum* of a tremendous materiality.

The people who live submerged in this Infernal Region are obviously controlled by 576 Laws, which make their existences all too complicated and difficult.

In this Region, time turns frightfully slow; each minute seems like centuries and therefore, life becomes tedious and intolerable.

If we carefully analyze the Jupiterian vibration in its transcendental planetary aspect, we discover that mysterious force which grants the Scepter to the Kings and the Miter to the Hierarchs of diverse confessional religions.

Therefore, the planet Jupiter within infinite space is extraordinarily mystical, regal and sublime.

Its antithesis, in the submerged infra-dimension, underneath the geological crust of our world, is in fact turned into the abode of materialist atheists, enemies of the Eternal.

Blasphemers also live in this Region, those who hate everything that has the taste of Divinity, and the heretics, those who cultivate the dogma of separateness.

Like Dante, one is filled with pain when contemplating so many mitered skeptics and atheists, plunged in the sepulcher of their own passions, hatreds and limitations...

When we think about the great legislators, sovereigns and lords who rule social conglomerations, we obviously discover tyrants and petty-tyrants that cause complications and pain here, there, and everywhere. The outcome of such nefarious proceedings corresponds exactly to the Sixth Dantean Circle.

It is not surprising then that in this tenebrous Region of the Abode of Pluto, the esotericist investigator finds all those hierarchs who abused their power; it is clear that such people hence suffer the unspeakable.

Jupiter, as a paternal friend, always generous, has its ominous antithesis in those terrible heads of households that, having plenty of wealth, deny food, shelter and clothing to their children. Undoubtedly, it is in the ominous Sixth abysmal Region where those sinning shadows find their dwelling place after death.

The Consciousness of the investigator is moved when contemplating those very cruel heads of households in the Submerged tenebrous Jupiterian Region; however, what is very curious is that here in this world under the light of the Sun, they always believed themselves to be virtuous, just and kind. Some of them were even profoundly religious.

In this sinister abode there are also heads of family who aspired to the Intimate Self-Realization of the Being. Despite all of their cruelties, their contemporaries believed them to be very good. It is clear that their conduct was apparently upright outside of their homes, but in their household there was weeping and affliction.

Extraordinary pietists, feigning meekness and poses of play-actors, unbearable vegetarians who turn food into a religion of the kitchen...

I would say to them: "hypocrites, Pharisees, whitened sepulchers!" to speak in the tone of the Great Kabir Jesus. However, their followers or those who would have seen them in beautiful halls of pseudo-esoteric or pseudo-occultist type would never say this.

It is also not strange to find in the Sixth Submerged Infra-Dimensional Region heads of family, very honest and sincere but terribly mistaken: what they should have done they did not do, and what they should not have done, they did.

Some of these gentlemen were extraordinarily fanatical in the world where they lived and with sticks and lashings, they taught religion to their children, as if this could be learned with whippings; ominous individuals who darkened homes, embittering the lives of their children.

Jupiter, generous as always, benevolent and altruistic, has to have its contrast beneath the epidermis of the Earth, in the Sixth Submerged Infra-Dimension.

What would be the antithesis of generosity? Egoism, usury, peculation; that is obvious...

It is not surprising then to find in this mentioned infrahuman Region the one who monopolizes all the goods on Earth for himself, such as Sanagabril and his followers. Therefore, every religious antithesis, every Jupiterian contrast, is inevitably to be found in the Sixth Infernal Circle beneath the epidermis of the Earth.

Question: Dear Master, I have observed that you mention that time is tremendously long, that minutes seem like centuries due to the great density of this Submerged Jupiterian Region. Is time long because of the sufferings or are the sufferings long because of time?

Answer: Distinguished gentleman who is asking the question, allow me to inform you that time only exists from a merely subjective point of view, because it certainly does not have objective reality.

Starting from this basic principle, we reach the logical conclusion that time is a submerged subconscious creation.

Unquestionably time in each infra-conscious zone, or better said, in what is inhuman in each one of us, goes progressively slower in the most profound depths of materiality.

In other words, I will say the following: at the purely intellectual level, time is not as slow as in the deeper subconscious levels; that is: the more subconscious the region of the universe where we live is, the slower time will be and it will take on a greater appearance of reality.

Here in this physical world where we live, on the surface of the Earth and under the light of the sun, there are minutes that seem like centuries and there are centuries that seem like minutes; everything depends on the mood that we are in.

It is clear that in complete happiness, twelve hours seem like a minute; it is obvious that an instant of supreme pain seems like centuries.

Let us now think about the Abyss, about the Submerged Abysmal Regions, about the City of Dis, the cursed city located at the bottom of the tenebrous "Tartarus"; there, the lost ones feel that each minute turns into centuries of abominable bitterness...

I think that the gentleman who has asked the question will now understand my answer in depth.

Question: That is exactly so, Master, however, since you mention states of Consciousness, namely, subconsciousness, unconsciousness and infra-consciousness, does this mean to say that when we are speaking about infra-dimensions, these also refer to states of Consciousness?

Answer: The infra-dimensions of nature and of the cosmos exist not only on planet Earth but also in any cosmic unity of infinite space: suns, moons, planets, galaxies, stars, anti-stars, anti-galaxies of anti-matter, etc., etc., etc.

These natural infra-dimensions are not then exclusive products of the subconsciousness or infra-consciousness of intellectual humanoids, but the result of mathematical Laws that have their origin in every Ray of Existential Creation.

Question: Master, does this mean that when we refer to the Consciousness itself, we must think that it is free of time?

Answer: Gentleman, ladies and gentlemen, I want to emphatically say to you that in the Sacred Absolute Sun, time is 49 times faster than here on Earth.

On analyzing this statement, we judiciously say: time being a mere subjective creation of the intellectual humanoid, it is obvious that it is 49 times slower than in the Sacred Absolute Sun.

In other words, I clarify that the mind of the humanoid possesses 49 subconscious levels and that for this reason we say that time here amongst the tri-brained or tri-centered bipeds mistakenly called men is 49 times slower than in the Sacred Absolute Sun.

Using now the inductive process taught by Aristotle in his divine Entelechy, we shall conclude: if time in the Sacred Absolute Sun is 49 times more rapid than at the intellectual level of the humanoid, obviously this means that in the Sacred Sun time does not exist. Everything there is an eternal moment, an eternal "now".

Looking now at what we call Consciousness, studying it judiciously, we will discover the original, paradisiacal, virginal Being, free from every subconscious process, beyond time.

That is to say, the Consciousness in itself is not a product of time.

Question: I beg your pardon Master, if I seem a little insistent, but I have grasped the following concept: as we awaken Consciousness, the infra-conscious and subconscious states cease to exist because they become Conscious. Is this wrong?

Answer: Sir, your question is quite interesting... Evidently, the submerged states of Pluto, let us call them infra-consciousness, unconsciousness, subconsciousness, are radically eliminated when the Consciousness awakens.

In the Sixth Submerged Dimension time seems too long to us, due to the clear and evident fact of the subconscious, unconscious and infra-conscious states; however in the Nirvana time does not exist due to the compelling and definite fact that the Ego nor the subconscious or the aforementioned abysmal states exist in that divine Region.

Question: Based on this explanation that frankly surprises me, because I had never before related time with states of subconsciousness, I reach the conclusion that the unconscious, the infra-conscious and the subconscious that psychologists speak so much about are in reality negative and satanic states, and that they are the obstacles to men's self-realization. Am I right, Master?

Answer: We have been solemnly told that we need to transform the subconscious into conscious. We also include the infra-conscious and unconscious states within these transformative concepts.

To awaken Consciousness is radical. It is only in this manner that we will be able to see the path that will lead us to final Liberation.

Obviously, the concept of time, which embitters life so much within the Sixth Submerged Dimension and within the different Dantean Circles of the "Tartarus", is definitely eliminated when the Consciousness awakens.

Question: You tell us that the Sixth Submerged Region of Jupiter is the antithesis of the planet Jupiter that orbits around the Sun. I observe, Master, that when you spoke about the other Dantean Circles you did not refer to them as the antitheses of the planets to which they correspond. Would you like to clarify this to us?

Answer: Gentleman, ladies and gentlemen, obviously, the Nine Infernal Circles are always the negative antithetical aspect of the Spheres of the Moon, Mercury, Venus, the Sun, Mars, Jupiter, Saturn, Uranus and Neptune. I believe that I have already said something about this topic in past lectures, and we have formulated the relationship between those worlds and the nine zones submerged below the epidermis of our planet Earth. Now, when looking for a simile to all of this, you see that every person under the light of the sun projects his shadow everywhere; you will find something similar with each of these nine planets of the solar system and their corresponding shadows or obscure, tenebrous zones within the entrails of the planet in which we live. Understood?

Question: Master, could you tell us if the Submerged Zone of the planet Jupiter is inhabited?

Answer: Distinguished lady, allow me to inform you and to inform all the people listening to me that within the natural infra-dimensions of the Submerged Mineral Kingdom of the planet Jupiter there are terribly perverse demons, involuting creatures, people heading towards Second Death. I clarify, I am not talking about the Heaven of Jupiter; I limit myself exclusively to mentioning the Submerged Mineral Kingdom of that planet.

Question: Master, can we consider that in spite of the fact that there are terribly involuting malignant beings in the Infernos of Jupiter, that these Infernos are antithetical to the Infernos of the Sixth Dantean Circle of planet Earth?

Answer: Friends, the tenebrous corresponds with the tenebrous. There is no antithesis whatsoever between the Jupiterian Infernos and the Sixth Dantean Circle submerged below the geological cortex of our world Earth.

We must look for antitheses exclusively between the luminous and obscure aspects of Jupiter.

Indubitably, the Jupiterian splendors have their opposites, their shadows, not only in the entrails of that radiant planet, but also underneath the crust of our afflicted world.

Question: Master, could you tell us which materials or elements make up this tenebrous zone of the Sixth Submerged Dimension of our planetary organism?

Answer: Friends, we have already said in past lectures that the inhabitants of this or that natural element never perceive the element in which they live.

The fish never see the water. We, the inhabitants of this tridimensional world of Euclid, never perceive the air that we breathe; we do not see it. The Salamanders do not see the fire; likewise, those who dwell within the petrous, rocky element never see such an element; they only perceive objects, persons, events, etc., etc., etc.

Obviously, the petrous density of the Sixth Abode of Pluto turns out to be unbearable, terribly dense. Now we will understand the reason why Dante saw so many condemned in their sepulchers.

These are not sepulchersin the literal sense of the word; what is meant by this is sepulchral states, very narrow limited conditions of the subconsciousness and infra-consciousness, etc., etc., etc. These are the painful conditions of life within the Sixth Abysmal Region.

11

THE SEVENTH DANTEAN CIRCLE

THE SUBMERGED SPHERE OF SATURN

Friends, gathered here once again, we shall talk profoundly about the Submerged Sphere of Saturn.

Certainly, we are not talking about eternal damnation or endless punishments.

Unquestionably, eternal damnation in itself does not exist and every punishment, regardless of how serious it might be, has to have a limit beyond which happiness reigns.

We differ then, radically in that sense, with clerical orthodoxy.

Undoubtedly, the involuting processes of life, carried out in the entrails of the Earth, in the submerged infra-dimensions, beneath the geological crust of our world, conclude with Second Death. After this, once the Essence is liberated and the pristine purity of the psychic material is restored, new processes of a completely evolutive type inevitably have to reinitiate.

Therefore, our opposition to the dogma of an absolutely eternal damnation is obvious and evident.

Our way of comprehending the expiation of faults appears in plain sight. We could never conceive that any expiatory debt, as serious as it might be, would not finally come to an end.

It is clear that Divine Justice would never fail. Every fault, as serious as it might be, has its exact mathematical expiatory equivalent; it is not possible to pay for more than what is owed, and if Divinity collected more than what is owed, it would obviously not be just.

I started our talk of today in this way, dear friends, as a preamble before entering into the Submerged Sphere of Saturn, with the ineludible purpose that you comprehend our esoteric-occultist point of view, which is radically opposed to all sectarian dogmatism. Let us now delve a little bit more into this question related to the Submerged Spheres.

In our past talk we studied in detail the Sixth Dantean Circle, and it is a good idea that today we boldly penetrate into the Seventh, or that of Saturn.

If we carefully read *The Divine Comedy* of *Dante*, we will find this region converted into an ocean of blood and fire.

Allow us the liberty to say that this point of view is completely allegorical, or symbolic. This is referring to the concrete and definite fact that in the stated Saturnine Region, a certain reddish, bloody color, which distinctly characterizes violent animal passion, definitely prevails.

When we speak about colors, we must know that above the solar spectrum, in the superior dimensions of nature and of the cosmos, shines the entire ultraviolet range and that below the solar spectrum, the infrared range fatally shines. The latter is characteristic of the infra-dimensions of nature, underneath the geological crust of our world.

Therefore, such a passionate, blood-red color of the submerged Saturnine Region could not be displayed in our tridimensional world of Euclid.

This color finds its opposite in a similar one in the ultraviolet range, above the cited tridimensional region.

It proves interesting to know that all those who enter the Seventh Dantean Circle display in their radiant aura this abominable blood color, which indeed puts them in affinity with that submerged zone of our planet Earth.

The Seventh Dantean Circle is, therefore, the dwelling of the violent against nature, the violent against art, the fraudulent, the violent against God, the violent against themselves, against their own property or against the property of others.

Moving in my Astral Body in a positive and conscious manner in this submerged Region, I was able to witness the reigning violence in such a frightening place of bitterness.

I still remember two very notable Demons whom I approached diplomatically, with the purpose of not hurting their susceptibilities or provoking unnecessary psychological reactions. They pronounced themselves against the Cosmic Christ, they denied him emphatically, feeling perversely satisfied with their miserable satanic condition.

Violence reigned everywhere; unnecessary destructions, frightening blows against things, against people, against everything, were seen here, there and everywhere within that bloody, submerged atmosphere.

I felt as if the saturnine influence with its definitely centrifugal forces aimed at disintegrating everything in that region, to reduce to cosmic dust, people, furniture, doors, etc., etc., etc.

I was very surprised to find there a very respectable creature,whose eyes still reflect the soft light of day.

It was the case of a very famous doctor, a true Samaritan, who in life has only aimed to heal the sick with true love and without any exploitation...

What I am saying might cause bewilderment. Many could object, telling me: "How is it possible that one being good can end up in the region of the evil?" The matter of life and death could also be debated: the good man in question is obviously still alive, he is still breathing under the sun; why then is he living in the Seventh Dantean Circle?

It is necessary to answer these enigmas, to clarify, to probe with precision, to inquire, to investigate.

If we think about the multiplicity of the "I", it is not surprising for any of these psychic aggregates related with the crime of violence against nature to be living in its corresponding submerged region, even when the personality is still living upon the face of the Earth.

Obviously, if this doctor does not dissolve the pluralized "I," he will have to descend with the involutive wave in the entrails of the world to especially stand out in the Seventh Dantean Circle; there is a great deal of virtue in the evil and there is a great deal of evil in the virtuous.

Once the cycle of 108 existences that is assigned to every Soul upon the face of the Earth has concluded, it is unquestionable that one descends with the involutive wave, even when one has beautiful virtues.

It is worthwhile for us to now remember Brunetto Latini, that noble gentleman who with so much love taught the Florentine Dante the path that leads to the immortality of man. A noble creature submerged in that Abyss due to the crime of violation against nature.

Question: Master, could you explain to us when is it that we commit the crime of Violence against Nature?

Answer: With the greatest pleasure I hasten to respond to the lady who has asked the question...

There is Violence against Nature when we do violence to the sexual organs.

Such a crime exists when a man forces his wife to have intercourse, when she is not in the disposition to do so.

Such a crime exists when a woman forces her husband to have intercourse, when he is not in the disposition to do so.

Such a crime exists when the man forces himself, doing violence to his own self in order to engage in coitus, when his organism is not in the adequate conditions to do so.

Such a crime exists when the woman forces herself to engage in coitus when her organism is not really in favorable conditions.

Such a crime exists in those who commit the crime of rape, taking possession of another person against their will.

Since crime also hides in the cadence of the verse, it is therefore not surprising that Violence against Nature is committed when the phallus is forced to get an erection, when the latter is not really in favorable conditions for intercourse.

Violence against Nature exists when —with the pretext of practicing Sexual Magic or even with the best of intentions of attaining self-realization— the male forces himself to perform the chemical copulation, or forces his wife with this purpose, when the creative organs are not in the precise amorous moment and in the favorable harmonious conditions, indispensable for intercourse.

Violence against Nature exists in those ladies who, in the need of Intimate Self-Realization, do violence to their own nature by pitilessly obliging themselves to have intercourse when they are certainly not in the required conditions to do so.

Violence against Nature exists in masturbators or in those who perform the chemical copulation when the woman is menstruating.

Violence against Nature exists when spouses engage in sexual union when the woman is pregnant.

Violence against Nature exists when the strong type of the Vajroli Mudra is practiced several times a day or during the night, when the sexual organs are not really in favorable and harmonious conditions.

Violence against Nature exists when Sexual Magic is practiced two times in a row, violating the laws of the creative magnetic pause.

Question: Master, in the case when the spouse does not have complete potency and he is practicing Sexual Magic, is violence to nature also being committed in this manner?

Answer: With the greatest pleasure I hasten to reply to the gentleman who asks the question. What happens is that an organ that is not used atrophies; if someone, if any man were to remain abstinent in a radical and absolute manner, it is clear that he would harm himself, because he would become impotent.

Obviously, if this man wanted to heal himself from that dire condition, he could very well achieve it by practicing Sexual Magic: the connection of the phallus and the uterus without ejaculating the semen.

It is clear that in the beginning the connection would prove almost impossible, due precisely to the lack of erection of the phallus. However, when attempting it by approaching the phallus to the uterus, with the mutual exchange of caresses, there is no Violation against Nature, but rather an erotic medical therapy, indispensable in order to achieve such healing.

In the beginning, these types of patients can use some type of clinical medical treatment based on the advice of their physician, with the specific purpose of achieving the first sexual connections.

It is clear that if the couple withdraws before the orgasm in order to avoid the ejaculation of the semen, the latter will be reabsorbed within the organism, thus fortifying the sexual system extraordinarily and the outcome will precisely be the healing.

In this entire process, I repeat, there is no Violation against Nature.

Question: Master, when you talk about Violence against Nature, are you referring exclusively to the violence of the human organism?

Answer: Distinguished friend, I want you to know in a clear and definitive manner that when we talk about Violence against Nature, we are emphatically referring to all types of sexual violence, clearly specifying, the one referring to the sexual organs of human beings.

I do not mean with this that there are no other types of Violence against Nature. If someone were to force the inferior creatures of nature to perform unnatural copulations, in this way violating their free will, there would be Violence against Nature; if someone were to artificially inseminate animals, as is the custom in this day and age, there would be Violence against Nature.

There is Violence against Nature when we commit adultery, or when we adulterate vegetables and fruits with the infamous grafts that have been invented by the know-it-alls of this Black Age of Kali Yuga.

There is Violence against Nature when we castrate ourselves or when we have animals castrated.

Therefore, there are innumerable crime that fall into this category of Violence against Nature.

Oh, friends!, ladies and gentlemen that are listening to me, people that are receiving this Christmas Message of 1973-1974, remember that: crime also hides amidst the incense of the temples; amidst the beautiful paintings that the painter sets on his canvas, crime also hides; crime also hides in the most delectable harmonies with which the musician delights us here on this planet Earth; amidst the perfume of prayers that delightfully whisper in the temples, crime also hides.

Crime dresses itself as saint, as a martyr, as an apostle, and even though it seems incredible, it disguises itself with priestly garments and officiates at the altars.

Remember friends, ladies and gentlemen, Guido Guerra cited by Dante, the grandson of the chaste Gualdrada, the nobleman that during his lifetime achieved so much with his talent and with his sword.

Remember also Tegghiaio Aldobrandi, whose voice in the world should be appreciated; noble men that now live in this Seventh Infernal Circle because of the crime of Violence against Nature.

Question: Master, if we disintegrate the "I" of Violence against Nature, or almost all the "I's" that have our essence bottled up, but if we still have some left, will we also fall into any of these Dantean Circles?

Answer: Distinguished lady, I am glad to hear your question, which is quite opportune...

Someone could eliminate from his psyche those psychic aggregates related with the crime of Violence against Nature, and nevertheless still fall into any of the other Dantean Circles. As long as the animal Ego exists within us, it is obvious that we are sure candidates for the Abyss and Second Death.

Question: Master, if we have already reached the last of the 108 existences that are assigned to every human being, and we are working on the Path of the Razor's Edge, would we be given another opportunity to finish our work?

Answer: Noble lady, I am very pleased to listen to you... You must know with complete clarity that the Laws of Nature are not governed by tyrants but by just and perfect Beings.

If someone –despite having finished his cycle of 108 existences– enters the Path of the Razor's Edge and disincarnates while on the Royal Path, obviously he will be helped. New existences will be assigned to him with the purpose of attaining his Intimate Self-Realization, however, if he were to stray from the Secret Path, if he were to complain, if he were not to dissolve the Ego, and relapsed into his same crime, then he would inevitably fall into the Abyss of Perdition.

Question: Based on what has previously been stated during the course of this lecture, I reach the conclusion that once we involute within the Atomic Abysses of nature, we are indeed inhabitants of all of the Dantean Circles of our planetary organism. Am I right, Master?

Answer: I want to tell the gentleman that is asking the question that he is certainly right. When someone enters into the submerged involution of nature, with time he slowly descends from circle to circle, most notably standing out in that zone where his worst crime is specifically found.

Question: Master, what can you tell us of homosexuals and lesbians? Do they commit Violence against Nature?

Answer: Distinguished gentleman, I find your question quite interesting...

It is urgent to comprehend that homosexuals and lesbians inevitably submerge into the Seventh Dantean Circle of Saturn, precisely because of the crime of Violence against Nature.

I want you to comprehend that this type of degenerates, enemies of the Third Logos, are indeed lost cases, seeds that do not germinate.

Question: Master, do lesbians and homosexuals come into the world that way due to Karmic Law, or does the engendering of such children have some relation with heredity? Which of these two factors predominates?

Answer: I hear the question that an International Gnostic Missionary is asking, here at the Patriarchal Headquarters of the Gnostic Movement in Mexico City... Ladies, gentlemen, it is useful to know that those humanoids who in former lives violently precipitated themselves on the path of sexual degeneration, obviously involuting from existence to existence, finally become homosexuals or lesbians, before entering into the Infernal Worlds.

Lesbianism and homosexuality are, then, the result of degeneration in previous lives; a fatal karmic consequence... That is all!

Question: Master, if a lesbian or a homosexual had for a moment, awareness of their punishment, the karma of their degeneration, and asked the Law for help, could it concede them the grace of returning to their normal state, or would they not have sufficient strength to ask for such benefit?

Answer: Ladies, gentlemen, there is a proverb that says, "God helps those who help themselves". Divine Mercy is side by side to Justice, but "Actions speak louder than words."

If any of these degenerates of infra-sexuality were to truly repent, let them demonstrate it with concrete, clear and definite deeds; may they immediately marry someone of the opposite sex, and may they truly enter the path of authentic and legitimate sexual regeneration...

That these types of delinquents cry out, pray and beg is correct; but let them demonstrate their repentance with deeds. Only in this manner is salvation possible for these types of creatures.

Nevertheless, it is very difficult for homosexuals and lesbians to have the courage, true longing for self-improvement.

Undoubtedly, this has to do with completely degenerated people, in which certain areas of the brain are no longer working; rotten seeds, where it is almost impossible to find a longing for regeneration.

Some individuals of this kind have turned their crime into mysticism disguised with the garments of sanctity; these latter exponents of human corruption are even worse and more dangerous.

We must not, therefore, forge illusions with regards to these persons; they are lost cases, abortions of nature, definite failures.

Question: Master, according to this, is every hope for Realization lost for those who reject the opposite sex, or does any door remain open?

Answer: Distinguished friend, listen: infra-sexuality is symbolized in ancient Kabbalah by Adam's two wives: Lilith and Nahemah.

Lilith in herself frankly allegorizes what is most monstrous in sexual degeneration.

Within the Sphere of Lilith we find many hermits, anchorites, cloistered monks and nuns who mortally hate sex.

We also find in this sphere all those women who take abortifacients and who murder their newly born babies—true hyenas of perversity.

Another aspect of the Sphere of Lilith corresponds to pederasts, homosexuals and lesbians.

Unquestionably, those who violently reject sex as well as those who abuse it, falling into homosexuality and lesbianism, are lost cases, terribly malignant creatures. For these types of beings all doors are closed, except one: that of repentance.

The Sphere of Nahemah is represented by another type of Violent against Nature: the irredeemable fornicators, the fornicators of abomination, etc., people who find themselves very well defined as Don Juan Tenorio or Casanova types and even the Devil type, which is the worst of the worst.

Ladies and gentlemen, let us now continue talking a little bit about the Violence against God...

Reaching this point of our talk, I would like to recall Capaneus, the ancient of Crete, one of the seven kings who laid siege to Thebes, and who now lives in the Seventh Submerged Zone of Saturn, beneath the geological crust of our Earth.

In his *Divine Comedy,* the Florentine Dante, disciple of Virgil, the great poet of Mantua, cites this terrible case related with this particular theme.

That shadow cried out:

What I was alive, I am the same dead! Though Jupiter wear out the smith from whom He seized in wrath the sharpened thunderbolt Which on my last day was to strike me down, Though he wear out the others, one by one, Serving at Mongibello's soot-black forge, As he bellows, 'Good Vulcan, help me! help me!' The way he did on the battlefield at Phlegra, Though with his whole force he flash out at me, Yet he will never have his fond revenge.

The arrogance and pride of the Violent against the Divine is the worst torture in the Seventh Submerged Infra-dimension.

There is Violence against the Divinity when we do not obey superior orders, when we attempt against our own life, when we wrathfully blaspheme.

There are many subtle modes of Violence against the Divine. Undoubtedly, the one who is Violent against God is the one who does not want anything to do with mystical or spiritual matters, who supposes he can exist without Divine Mercy, and who in the depth of his Soul rebels against everything that has the aroma of Divinity...

There is Violence against God in that self-sufficient individual who smiles stupidly in a skeptical manner when listening to matters that in some way have to do with the spiritual aspects of life.

There is Violence against God within those scoundrels of the intellect, in those know-it-alls who deny man any spiritual possibility, in those who believe that they have monopolized Universal Knowledge, in those "paragons of wisdom," in those learned ignoramuses who not only ignore, but moreover ignore that they ignore, in those iconoclasts who make a clean sweep when they analyze religious principles but who leave their followers without any new spiritual base.

There is Violence against God in the Marxist-Leninists, pseudo-sapients who have taken away the spiritual values from humanity.

In these moments there comes to memory an encounter with Karl Marx in the Submerged Worlds...

I found him in those tenebrous Regions. That individual had awakened in evil and for evil, nonetheless, he was a fallen Bodhisattva.

Lenin followed him like an ominous shadow, unconscious and profoundly asleep.

I questioned Marx with the following words:

"It has been many years since you disincarnated, your body became dust in the tomb and nevertheless, I find you here, alive in these regions. What remains, then, of your Dialectical Materialism?"

That individual, looking at his wristwatch, did not dare give me an answer whatsoever, he turned around and left, but a few meters away he burst into a sarcastic and horrifying cackle...

Through intuition I succeeded in catching the living essence of that cackle. In it was the answer that we could summarize with the following phrase: "That dialectic was nothing but a farce, a dish to fool the gullible..."

It is curious to know that when Karl Marx disincarnated, he received the religious funerary honors of a Great Rabbi.

In the first International Communist, Karl Marx took the floor, saying: "Gentlemen, I am not a Marxist." There was then astonishment among the audience, shouts, screams and from this instance many political sects were born: Bolsheviks, Mensheviks, Anarchists, Anarchist-Unionists, etc., etc. It is therefore quite interesting to know that the first enemy of Marxism was Karl Marx.

In a magazine from Paris, we can read the following: *"Through the triumph of the world proletariat, we will create the Universal Soviet Socialist Republic with its capital in Jerusalem, and we will take possession of all the riches of the nations, so that the prophecies of our Holy Prophets of Talmud be fulfilled."*

Certainly these couldn't be phrases of a materialist or of any atheist; Marx was a Jewish religious fanatic.

I do not want to criticize political matters, now, in this talk; I am emphatically referring to essentially occultist matters.

Karl Marx, moved precisely by religious fanaticism, invented a destructive weapon in order to reduce all the religions of the world to cosmic dust. That weapon is without a doubt a jargon that would never withstand an in-depth analysis. I am referring to the Dialectical Materialism.

The rascals of the intellect know very well that Karl Marx availed himself of the Dialectic Metaphysics of Hegel in order to elaborate such deceitful dish, such a farce.

Obviously, he stripped this work of all the metaphysical principles given to it by its author, and with it he elaborated his dish. It is worth repeating in this talk that Marx, as the author of such a lie, of such a farce, of such communistoid dialectic, never believed in it, and therefore he did not have any inconvenience in confessing his feelings in full assembly when exclaiming: "Gentlemen, I am not a Marxist."

Undoubtedly, this gentleman only fulfilled one of the Protocols of the Elders of Zion that says: *"It does not matter if we have to fill the world with materialism and repugnant atheism; the day when we triumph, we will teach the religion of Moses universally, coded and in a dialectical manner, and we shall not allow any other religion in the world..."*

With this, I do not want to condemn any race in particular. I am frankly alluding to some Semitic characters with Machiavellian plans. They are the Marxs, the Lenins, the Stalins, etc., etc., etc.

From a rigorously occultist point of view, I was able to witness that the cited fallen Bodhisattva struggled for Divinity in his own way, using a clever weapon in order to destroy the other religions.

Marx was a priest, a rabbi of the Jewish religion, a faithful devotee of the doctrine of his ancestors.

What is really astonishing is the credulity of the fools who believing themselves to be erudite, fall into the skeptical trap set by Karl Marx.

These simple-minded one of Marxist-Leninist Dialectical Materialism obviously become Violent against Divinity, and for this reason they enter into the Seventh Dantean Circle.

Question: Venerable Master, in the Masonic Order to which I belong, it is said that religion helps man to die well and that Masonry helps man to live well; hence, I believe that the majority of Masons that I know do not know what religion is,

*and confuse it with something totally negative. Since we are
dealing with Violence against God, would you like to give us
the correct concept of what "religion" means?*

Answer: Good friend who asks the question, esteemed gentleman, people who are listening to me, religion derives from the Latin word "religare," which means "to bind again" the Soul to God.

Strictly speaking, Masonry is not a religion; it is rather a Fraternity of a universal type. Nevertheless, it would be very advisable that such a meritorious institution study the Science of Religion.

By no means are we suggesting that one should affiliate to this or that school; everybody is free to think as they please. We only limit ourselves to recommending the study of the Science of Religion.

The latter is precisely Gnosticism in its purest form, Wisdom of a divine type, profound analytical Esotericism, transcendental Occultism.

*Question: Allow me to insist, dear Master, since I have heard
in a lecture within the Gnostic Teaching that the universe was
created by seven Masonic Lodges and this undoubtedly linked
primeval Masonry with the Father, this being the reason why
I have the concept that in synthesis, Masonry is the common
denominator of all religions, and therefore it proceeds from
Gnosis. Would you like to clarify this for me?*

Answer: Esteemed gentleman, those who have studied the Masonry of Ragon or Leadbeater profoundly know very well that occult esoteric Masonry existed not only under the porticoes of the Temple of Jerusalem but also in ancient Egypt and in submerged Atlantis. Unfortunately, this honorable institution entered into the involuting, descendent circle within the Kali Yuga age or the Iron Age in which we currently find ourselves.

Nevertheless, it is clear that in the future Sixth Great Race it will have a brilliant mission to fulfill, precisely when the powerful esoteric civilizations of the past revive.

We do not deny the divine origin of this institution. We already know that the Seven Cosmocrators officiated with holy Liturgy at the dawning of the Great Day, when they fecundated the chaotic matter so that life would come forth.

From century to century, throughout the different cosmic Rounds, the "workshops" became increasingly denser and denser, until finally reaching their present state.

We recommend the Masonic Brothers to study in depth the esotericism of Solomon and the Divine Wisdom of the land of the Pharaohs.

It is necessary, it is urgent, that the Masonic Brothers not fall into Marxist-Leninist skepticism, a dialectic for fools; that they not pronounce themselves against the Divinity, because this, besides being contrary to an esoteric Order of divine origin, will inevitably lead them to the Seventh Dantean Circle, the tenebrous region of the Violent against God.

Question: Venerable Master, how does one classify the concrete case of some Gnostics who believing that they are identified with the Doctrine of Christ, are also identified with the opposite side, which is Marxist atheism?

Answer: Distinguished gentleman, it just so happens that some sincere elements who truly aspire to work for a better world never cease to exist in esoteric or occultist type currents.

It is unquestionable that poisoned by red propaganda and desiring to create the "Soviet paradise" here in the Western world, they work with enthusiasm in order to achieve the total realization of that great longing.

They are sincere but mistaken and people with magnificent intentions, yet mistaken. Remember that the path that leads to the Abyss is paved with good intentions.

If these individuals lived for a while as workers in the Soviet Union, I am sure that upon returning to this region of the Western world they would demonstrate rabidly as anticommunists...

It proves very interesting to know that there are more communists in the Western hemisphere than in the Soviet Union. What happens is that over there, behind the iron curtain, people already know Communist reality, they have lived it, and therefore they cannot be cheated by the red propaganda. On the other hand, since here we still do not have a government of a Marxist-Leninist type, the red agitators can play with incautious people in the same manner that a cat plays with the mouse before devouring it.

From a rigorously esoteric point of view, we can emphatically affirm the following: in the Submerged Worlds, in the tenebrous Regions of the Seventh Dantean Infra-dimension, Communists dress in black tunics. They are truly personages of the Left Hand, priests of Black Magic.

I will conclude by saying: the Venerable Great White Lodge has classified Marxism-Leninism as authentic and legitimate Black Magic.

Those who have seen the Secret Path that leads to final Liberation could not militate within the ranks of the left hand without committing, for this reason, the crime of Violence against God.

Question: Dear Master, although all of us know what fraud is and that we always relate it to matters of an economic type, does this crime which is purged in the Seventh Dantean Circle include all type of frauds?

Answer: Friends, there are many types of fraud and it is good to clarify all of this. Dante symbolizes fraud with a horrifying, tenebrous image. Dante depicts the monster of fraud in the following manner:

His face was the face of a saintly person, so placid was the surface of the skin, but his whole trunk was the shape of a snake. He had two paws, with hair up to his armpits; his back and breasts and both of his flanks were painted gaudily with knots and loops. Tartars or Turks never wove a cloth with more colors in background and design, nor did Arachene ever loom such webs...

Dante says that this monster had a terrible stinger at the end of its tail –this symbol expresses the crime of fraud very well–. Let us think for a moment of the various colored snares with which the fraudulent envelops his victim, the venerable face that fraudulent people take on, their poisonous snake body, their horrible claws and the sting with which they hurt their victims...

The types of fraud are so varied that one is really astonished.

There is fraud in the one who forms an esoteric circle and thereafter abandons it.

There is fraud in the one who opens a Lumisial and thereafter disturb it with his crimes, be it romancing the neighbor's wife, be it seducing with the purpose of practicing Sexual Magic, secretly committing adultery, desiring the Isis of the temple, exploiting the brothers of the sanctuary, promising what he cannot fulfill, preaching what he does not practice, doing the contrary of what he teaches, creating scandals, drinking alcohol in front of the surprised devotees, etc., etc., etc.

There is fraud in the man who promises matrimony to a woman and does not fulfill his word, in the woman who gives her word to a man and then disappoints him by falling in love with another man, in the parent who promises his son or daughter such and such a gift or such and such help and thereafter does not fulfill his promise, etc., etc., etc. All of these forms of fraud are Violence against the Father; that is why Dante allegorizes them with the frightful monster with a venerable face.

There is fraud in the individual who borrows money and does not return it; there is fraud in vendors of lottery and gambling games since the victims, convinced that they can win, lose their money and feel deceived.

Question: Venerable Master, we understand that the Seventh Dantean Circle is denser than all the previous ones, therefore we would like for you to explain to us the material constitution of that infra-dimension.

Answer: Friends, the Seventh Submerged Region, or of Saturn, is of a surprising material density since each atom in this submerged region possesses 672 atoms of the Absolute in its womb.

Obviously, these specific types of atoms are very heavy and for this reason the Seventh Submerged Region ends up being extremely gross and painful.

Given that an equal number of Laws –672– governs this submerged tenebrous zone, beneath the geological crust of our world, life there becomes unbearable, very difficult, terribly complicated and frightfully violent.

Question: Master, I would like to know if the element or elements in which the inhabitants of this Circle move is also not seen by them and if they think that they are also doing very well.

Answer: Honorable friends, I want you to know that this cavernous region of our planet is a mixture of mineral and fire.

Nevertheless, the flames there are only known by their effects, by the violence, by the rough, instinctive and brutal blows, etc.

I repeat what I already said at the beginning of this talk: what Dante symbolized with blood is exclusively the bloody color of sexual violence in the aura of the lost ones and in the infrahuman atmosphere of this zone.

Undoubtedly, an inhabitant of this Saturnine Region would never think bad about himself. They always suppose that they march on the path of righteousness and justice. Some of them know that they are Demons, but they comfort themselves with the idea that it is what all human beings are.

However, these individuals who do not ignore that they are Demons, would never admit the idea that they are wicked since they firmly believe that they are good, just and upright persons.

If someone were to scold them for their crimes, if they were to be admonished, if they were called to repent, they would feel offended, slandered, and they would react with acts of violence.

12

THE EIGHTH DANTEAN CIRCLE

THE SUBMERGED SPHERE OF URANUS

My friends, who are gathered here again tonight, on November 18, 1972, the 10th year of Aquarius, with the purpose of studying the Eighth Dantean Circle submerged beneath the terrestrial crust in the infra-dimensions of nature. As we enter into explanations, we have to start by reviewing what we have already said in other texts in relation to Black Tantrism. Obviously, there are three types of Tantrism:

1. White Tantrism.

2. Black Tantrism.

3. Gray Tantrism.

Hindustanis talk to us frankly about the Igneous Serpent of our Magical Powers, that solar electronic power that ascends through the spinal cord of the ascetics.

It is clear that the transcendental Fohat develops exclusively with White Tantrism. We have given the key in our previous books; nevertheless, we will repeat it: the connection of the lingam-yoni –phallus-uterus– without the ejaculation of the sacred sperm.

SAMAEL AUN WEOR

Black Tantrism is different: there is connection of the lingam-yoni, magical rites and seminal ejaculation. In this concrete case, the outcome is the awakening of the Igneous Serpent in its strictly negative form.

It is evident that in Black Tantrism the Sacred Fire is precipitated from the coccyx toward the Atomic Infernos of man. Then the tail of Satan, the Abominable Kundabuffer Organ, appears.

Gray Tantrism has other purposes: animal pleasure without transcendental yearnings.

We will now focus explicitly on the Abominable Kundabuffer Organ.

There are two Serpents.

1st The Serpent of White Tantrism is the Bronze Serpent which healed the Israelites in the desert by victoriously ascending through the spinal cord.

2nd The Tempting Serpent of Eden, the horrible Python, that writhed in the mud of the Earth and that the irritated Apollo wounded with his arrows.

The first, the Bronze Serpent, the Ascending Fire, has the power of awakening the chakras of the spinal column; it opens, shall we say, the Seven Churches of the *Book of Revelation* by St. John and transforms us into terribly divine Gods.

The second opens seven chakras that are in the lower abdomen, the Seven Doors of Hell, as the Muslims call them.

Much has been said about the Kundalini, the annular Serpentine Power that develops wonderfully in the body of every white tantric. However, we solemnly affirm that no one could enjoy the powers of the Luminous Serpent without having been previously devoured by it.

Now, friends and brothers of the Gnostic Movement, you will understand the reason why the Adepts from India have been qualified as Nagas –'serpents'.

The Great Hierophants of Babylon, Egypt, Greece, Chaldea, etc., etc., called themselves Serpents.

In serpentine Mexico, Quetzalcoatl, the Mexican Christ, was devoured by the Serpent, and that is why he received the title of Flying Serpent.

Wotan was a Serpent because he had been swallowed by the Serpent.

It is obvious and manifest that the in-depth marriage, the integral fusion of the Divine Mother with the Holy Spirit; that is, the Igneous Serpent of our Magical Powers with Shiva, the Third Logos, the Arch-Hierophant and Arch-Mage is only possible when we have been devoured by the Serpent. Then, comes the glorious resurrection of the Secret Master within us, here and now.

Now, I invite the whole auditorium who is listening to me and all of the Gnostic Movement in general, to an in-depth reflection on the antithesis...

It is unquestionable that the horrible serpent Python is the negative and fatal opposite, the shadow, the radical antithesis of the Serpent of Light, so to speak. Undoubtedly, truth disguises itself as darkness in the Abyss.

If in the Superior Dimensions of nature and of the cosmos we are devoured by the Bronze Serpent that healed the Israelites in the desert, then obviously, in the Eighth Dantean Circle the condemned are devoured by the horrible Tempting Serpent of Eden; they then turn into frightfully malignant, poisonous vipers.

I want you to integrally comprehend that the Serpent will always have to devour us; whether in the luminous aspect or in the tenebrous Eighth Infernal Circle.

The fatal supper of the horrible Tempting Serpent of Eden is pathetic, devouring the lost ones with the purpose of destroying them, disintegrating them, reducing them to cosmic dust, in order to liberate the Essence, in order to restore its original pristine purity. Only in this manner is the Soul able to emancipate itself from the painful "Tartarus".

It is very interesting to know that the Serpent always destroys the Ego, either through the Luminous Path, based on conscious work and voluntary sufferings, or through the Tenebrous Path, in the Eighth Circle of fatalities.

It is wonderful to know that the Ego always has to be dissolved, no matter the cost, according to our will or against our will, and that the Serpent must inevitably swallow us, victorious or failed...

That Tempting Serpent of Eden, that horrible Python, is the negative aspect of the Divine Mother. Once her labor within the Avernus is completed, she returns to her positive polarization within the luminous Region...

See then friends, how the Divine Mother loves her child...

Those that are lost, the Black Tantrists, inevitably condemn themselves to Second Death upon developing the Serpent of Fatalities.

The red turbaned Dugpas will never be able to flee from the Divine Mother Kundalini. She will devour them inevitably, no matter the cost.

In the Eighth Infernal Circle dwell unfortunately the false alchemists, the Black Tantrists, the falsifiers of metals, those who crystallized negatively, to be clearer, those who instead of crystallizing the Sexual Hydrogen Si-12 into the Superior Existential Bodies of the Being, got it to crystallize negatively to truly turn themselves into Adepts of the Tenebrous Face, who inevitably end up being devoured by the horrible Serpent of Fatalities.

I want everyone to realize that there are two types of Alchemy, two types of death for the Ego, and two types of feasts that the Serpent feeds on.

You can choose the path... Choose! Knowledge is given unto you. You have before you the dilemma of To Be or Not To Be of Philosophy.

Woe to you, candidates for Second Death! Your tortures will be frightful! Only in this way will you be able to die in the tenebrous Avernus.

In what other manner could the Essence emancipate itself? In what other manner could it be set free to re-initiate a new evolving cycle, which undoubtedly has to begin from the hard rock?

In the Eighth Infernal Circle we also find money counterfeiters, falsifiers, impostors, the incestuous, the sowers of discord, bad counselors, those who promise and do not fulfill their promise, those who create scandals and also those who cause schisms, false and deceitful people, etc., etc., etc.

This Eighth Submerged Region is the antithesis, the opposite, the negative aspect of Uranus.

This planet of our solar system is very interesting. We have been told that the North and South Pole of Uranus point alternately towards the Sun.

When the positive pole of that planet is in the direction of the sun star, then the masculine force imposes itself upon the face of the Earth.

When the negative pole of that world is in the direction of the resplendent Sun, then the feminine force commands on our afflicted world.

Each cycle or magnetic period of Uranus lasts 42 years. Thus, this is how men and women alternate their command here on the Earth, in cycles or periods of 42 years.

The complete period of planet Uranus comprises 84 years, 42 of a masculine type and 42 of a feminine type.

Let us observe well the customs of peoples during history and we will see intensive periods of masculine activity, such as piracy for example, when all of the seas of the Earth were filled with corsairs, and periods like the present one, or like the one when the Amazons established their lunar cults and governed a large part of Europe, making the world shake.

Each masculine cycle is proceeded by a feminine cycle and vice-versa. Everything depends on the polarization of Uranus and on the type of energy that comes to Earth from that planet.

It is good to know, for the good of the Great Cause, that the sexual glands are governed by Uranus.

We need to integrally comprehend that the feminine ovaries are also governed by Uranus.

This planet, as regent of the New Age of Aquarius, brings a complete revolution to our afflicted world.

It is then not surprising that in the Submerged Region of Uranus, beneath the crust of the Earth, the sexual aspects of the definitively lost are defined, and that the Tempting Serpent of Eden guzzles the fallen to begin the destructive process on a grand scale, until concluding with Second Death.

In our last book entitled *The Three Mountains*, we said that in the Submerged Mineral Kingdom of planet Uranus, the Initiate has to disintegrate the bad thief Cacus or Gestas, as it appears in the Christian Gospel.

Agatho or Dismas, the good thief, is that intimate power that, from the depth of our Being, steals the Sexual Hydrogen Ti-12 for our own Intimate Self-Realization.

Cacus, the bad thief, the horrible Gestas, is that tenebrous, sinister power that steals the creative energy for evil.

It goes without saying that the Abominable Kundabuffer Organ, the outcome of the bad use of the creative energy stolen by Cacus, develops not only within the black alchemists or tenebrous tantrists, but also within the decidedly lost, even if they possessed no magical knowledge.

Now, moving onto the antithetical sphere of Uranus, in the abysmal depths of planet Earth, by the Law of Contrasts and of Analogy of the Contraries and of Simple Correspondence, the horrifying Cacus must also be destroyed.

See then, ladies and gentlemen, these luminous and tenebrous antithetical aspects, the way they correspond and how they develop...

Question: Master, is the Tempting Serpent of Eden the same as the Sacred Serpent?

Answer: My dear frater, I find your question very interesting and I hasten to answer.

It is clear that in the Avernus truth disguises itself as darkness. It is incredible to learn that the Serpent can polarize itself in a positive or negative manner.

This means that the Tempting Serpent of Eden, even though it is the tenebrous contrast of the Serpent of Light, is undoubtedly the negative polarization of the Bronze Serpent that healed the Israelites in the desert.

It is surprising to learn that the radiating Serpent polarizes itself in this fatal manner, and this invites us to comprehend that it does so for the good of its own child, to destroy —within the Avernus— the infrahuman elements that we carry within, and to liberate us from the frightening claws of pain. This is the love of every Divine Mother.

Question: Beloved Master, since it is evident that the majority of the inhabitants of this planet do not practice White or Black Tantrism but Gray Tantrism —which is sexual intercourse with the spilling of the Ens Seminis and without any transcendental longing— I ask you if all of these masses automatically enter the Eighth Dantean Circle, as those who practice Black Tantrism.

Answer: Distinguished gentleman, your question is very intelligent and I want you to understand my answer. It is good for you to know that all Gray Tantrism inevitably becomes Black.

When someone descends into the Avernus, he awakens negatively. That fatal awakening is due to the development of the Abominable Kundabuffer Organ.

It is therefore urgent to know that any fornicator, even if they do not know Black Tantrism, is in fact tantric and he inevitably becomes a tenebrous personality with the Tempting Serpent of Eden completely developed.

Question: Master, when we talked about the Second Infra-dimensional Circle, you explained to us that fornicators dwell there, and just to clarify the concept, I would like to know the difference between the fornicators that inhabit the Circle of Mercury and those that enter the Eighth Dantean Circle.

Answer: Friends, lust is the root of the Ego, of the "I," of the Myself, of the Oneself. This invites us to comprehend that lechery, fornication, unquestionably exists in each one of the nine natural infra-dimensions beneath the geologic crust of our world.

Nonetheless, there is a difference in all of this: in the Submerged Sphere of Mercury, the frightening Coatlicue or Proserpine, the Tempting Serpent of Eden, does not yet devour her children; only in the Submerged Eighth Region does She have her frightful feast. Now we can explain to ourselves why the Florentine Dante sees millions of human beings turned into pieces, bleeding, hurting themselves with their nails and with their teeth, decapitated, etc., etc. in the Eighth Circle.

It is obvious that in such a submerged Region the process of ossification, crystallization, mineralization and destruction of all the Ego begins.

Question: Venerable Master, the narrative that you have just given us about the love of the Divine Mother is truly impressive, that whether it be in the aspect of Light or in that of Darkness, she liberates her child, the Essence, even in the most painful manner within the entrails of the Earth. Why, then, do many Black Magicians with awakened Consciousness, knowing the pain that they have to endure, persist in treading the path of Black Tantrism and Second Death?

Answer: Distinguished gentleman, it is good for everyone present here to know that some awaken for Light and others for Darkness, as I have already said in former books.

Nonetheless, there is a radical difference between those who awaken positively and those who do it in a negative manner.

Undoubtedly, the lost ones, those who have awakened in evil and for evil, even when they know that they must involute within the entrails of the world until Second Death before achieving the restoration of the original pristine purity of the psychic matter, do not regret the path that they have chosen because they have made their involution and the fatal Wheel of Samsara a religion, a mystique...

It is important to inform this audience that the Adepts of the Left Hand have temples in the Submerged Regions where they worship the negative aspect of the Serpent.

Certainly, these infrahuman beings are never unaware of the fate that is reserved for them; they even wish to hasten it so as to emancipate themselves and go out free into the light of the sun with the purpose of once again starting a new evolution that will have to reinitiate, as I have already said, beginning with the hard rock and continuing as plant and animal, until re-conquering the state of intellectual humanoid.

When one converses with Yahve, one can clearly witness that the lost ones abhor the Solar Logos and that they are totally in love with the vicious and fatal circle, the Wheel of Samsara.

Question: Venerable Master, I do not understand how it is possible that an inhabitant of this Submerged Infra-dimension of the Eight Dantean Circle, whose Essence is bottled up in the tremendous "I" of lust, can even briefly awaken the Consciousness, since for this to happen the Essence must be liberated from the Ego.

Answer: Distinguished gentleman, I will repeat what I have already said: some awaken in Light and others in Darkness. Upon reaching this point of tonight's lecture, we are going to quote a verse from Daniel the Prophet.

Let us look at the Bible, Daniel XI, XII:

"And many of them that sleep in the dust of the earth shall awake, some to everlasting life, and some to shame and everlasting contempt. And they that be wise shall shine as the brightness of the firmament; and they that turn many to righteousness as the stars for ever and ever. But thou, O Daniel, shut up the words, and seal the book, even to the time of the end; many shall run to and fro and science shall be increased."

Since we are already in the end of times and since science has scandalously increased, it is good to remove the seal from the book and to clarify the prophecy.

I repeat: the Abominable Kundabuffer Organ has the power to awaken the Consciousness of those who enter the Abyss where only crying and gnashing of teeth are heard.

We can, therefore, awaken Consciousness in a luminous and positive manner by means of the voluntary dissolution of the Ego, or awaken it in evil and for evil by means of the development of the Abominable Kundabuffer Organ. Each one can choose their path. The prophecy of Daniel has been clarified.

Question: Venerable Master, I know many spiritual mentors who very sincerely live separated from sexual practices, in other words, they are celibate. Therefore, as I understand, they are not classified within any of the three Tantras that you have spoken to us about. Will these persons perhaps not enter into this Region of the Avernus?

Answer: Woe unto you, hypocrites, Pharisees, whitened sepulchers, perverse generation of vipers, for you make clean the outside of the cup and of the platter, but within you are full of rot.

The Pharisee "I" is found active in the depth of many devotees; they boast of being saints and sages, chaste and perfect, but deep within they are frightful fornicators.

The Pharisee "I" blesses the food when sitting at the table, has pietistic attitudes, deceives himself believing to be virtuous but within the profundity of himself, hides unspeakable designs and Machiavellian objectives that he justifies with good intentions.

Within the Eighth Dantean Circle these beati are irremediably devoured by the Tempting Serpent of Eden.

Question: Master, what can you tell us about the density and the elements that integrate this infra-dimension?

Answer: Distinguished friends, the Eighth Dantean Circle is at the same time, a petrous and igneous Region; fire really tortures the lost there.

This Submerged Zone of Uranus beneath the geologic crust of planet Earth has crystallizations of unbearable materialism.

It is important to remember with complete clarity that amazes that in this mentioned zone, each atom carries in its womb 768 atoms of the Sacred Absolute Sun.

Therefore, each one of these atoms is terribly dense, and thus it is not surprising that materiality in this Region is even denser than in the seven previous Circles.

An equal number of laws –768– control all of the activities of the Eighth Infernal Circle and for this reason life is extremely complicated and difficult in this submerged zone of the Avernus. As a result, sufferings intensify terribly in the tenebrous zone of the negative aspect of Uranus below the epidermis of the Earth.

13

THE NINTH DANTEAN CIRCLE

THE SUBMERGED SPHERE OF NEPTUNE

ery dear friends, gathered here tonight we intend to study the Ninth Dantean Circle, with the purpose of going deeper into this matter.

In the course of these talks we have reached the very center of the Earth, which is of a frightful inertia, given that it is the very nucleus of our planet.

Upon reaching this part, Dante in his *Divine Comedy* unexpectedly cites the lance of Achilles. We have been told that if in the beginning that lance wounded and caused harm or bitterness, thereafter it became a true blessing.

This clearly reminds us of the lance of Longinus, with which the Roman centurion wounded the side of the Lord.

This very same lance, wielded by Parsifal, the marvelous hero of the Wagnerian drama, came to heal the side of Amfortas.

Already in our previous texts we spoke concretely about this weapon of Eros.

We said then that this spear is phallic in type, and when wisely handled it can be utilized for the disintegration of the pluralized "I."

The fact that Dante mentions the lance of Achilles precisely in the Ninth Sphere is quite obvious and this is something that should make us meditate...

It is good to remember that the Holy Lance is the very emblem of the phallus, where the beginning of all life resides, the transcendental sexual electricity with which we can disintegrate and reduce the pluralized "I" to cosmic dust.

In this talk I also want to cite the Holy Grail, that divine Cup or miraculous Chalice from which the great Kabir Jesus drank at the Last Supper.

It is clear that such a jewel is the living symbol of the uterus or divine yoni of the Eternal Feminine.

Given that we have entered into the topic of the Ninth Sphere, we could not have forgotten to mention in this talk the Chalice and the Lance of the Great Archaic Mysteries.

In the Ninth Sphere the involuting creatures definitely disintegrate. What happened to Nimrod and his Tower of Babel? What will become of the modern fanatics of that Tower? Vain will be their attempt to assault Heaven with their rockets. Cosmic travels are not allowed to intellectual animals; attempting it is a sacrilege. Such voyages are exclusively for authentic, legitimate and true Man.

After the great catastrophe that is approaching, the intellectual rascals of the Tower of Babel will enter into the Infernal Worlds to be reduced to cosmic dust in the Ninth Sphere.

What became of Ephialtes? He succeeded in moving the incarnated Gods in ancient Atlantis, nonetheless he was reduced to dust in the Ninth Dantean Circle.

And what became of Briareus, the one with one hundred arms, living allegorical representation of the Lords of the Tenebrous Face who inhabited the submerged Atlantis in times of yore...? Within the Ninth Infernal Circle, or that of Neptune, he was dissolved, becoming dust of the earth.

In this Submerged Neptunian Zone traitors are reduced to dust. Woe to Brutus, Cassius and the inner Judas of every living being!

And what became of you, Alberigo de Manfredi, Lord of Faenza? Of what use were your good intentions, and the fact of having entered the Order of the Jovial Friars? The divine and humans know very well the horrible crime that you committed. Were you not the one who slew your kindred in the midst of a banquet?

The legend of the centuries says that while pretending to reconcile with them, you assassinated them at that famous banquet, precisely at the end, at the very moment when desserts were being served. Nevertheless, you continued to live; this is how it appeared to people, however, in reality you entered the Ninth Infernal Circle at the very moment in which the crime was committed. Who then remained, inhabiting your body? Was it not perhaps a Demon?

Woe to the traitors! Woe to those who commit such crimes! They are immediately judged by the Tribunals of Objective Justice and sentenced to death. The Cosmic Executioners execute the sentence, and these wretched ones disincarnate immediately, passing to the Ninth Dantean Circle even though their physical bodies do not die, for it is known that any Demon, replacing the traitor, remains inside the physical body, so that the karmic processes of the persons or relatives who in one way or another are related to such perverse personalities are not altered.

Even though it might seem incredible, currently many living dead, whose true owners live in the Infernal Worlds, walk the streets of cities.

Question: Venerable Master, if the Essence bottled within the pluralized "I" is the one that transmigrates into the Infernal Worlds, does this replacement that you are speaking to us about perhaps mean that another Essence takes over the body of the living dead?

Answer: Friends, I repeat: any Demon can replace the ex-owner of the body. There can also be the case where the Demon who becomes the owner of the situation, master and lord of that abandoned vehicle, is one of the least harmful Demons that made up the Ego that was precipitated into the Avernus.

Thus, the judges of Heavenly Justice condemn the crimes of high treason with the penalty of death.

Question: Master, what is meant by "a crime of high treason?"

Answer: Friends, there are many sorts of treason, yet some are so serious that they are in fact paid with the penalty of death.

The act of inviting this or that person or persons to a banquet and then murdering them in that same banquet, arguing this or that motive, is such a serious crime that it cannot be paid in any other manner; in this case the traitor disincarnates immediately and his body remains in the hands of some Demons.

It is evident that in no way do people realize what has happened deep down in the personality of the traitor, but the Judges of Heavenly Justice are only interested in that the sentence be executed, and that is all.

Question: Master, I have not fully understood this matter regarding the Essence, since I do not comprehend how the Demon that replaces the ex-owner of the body of the traitor has a physical life devoid of Essence.

Answer: What does Master G. tell us about this? Master G. says that there are many people in the streets with only their personality but devoid of Essence, that is, they wander around alive, yet they are dead.

Friends, it comes to my mind that little verse that says:

Dead are not those who rest in peace within the cold tomb; dead are those whose Souls are dead yet they are still alive.

The Demon that replaces the owner of a body might no longer have any type of Essence; and with this my explanation is completely clarified. These are the cases of the soulless people cited by H.P.B. in her *Secret Doctrine*. I am not the first to mention this matter, nor the last, but I am indeed the first to clarify it totally.

Question: Venerable Master, would you like to give me an explanation in regards to what you previously said about the Cosmic Executioner?

Answer: I see in the audience an International Gnostic Missionary who has asked this question very sincerely...

The Tribunals of Objective Justice, so as to differentiate them from the subjective justice of this vain world in which we live, have Cosmic Executioners at their service.

In these moments what comes to my mind are two of them who are very famous and worked in the ancient Egypt of the Pharaohs. This type of Executioners act according to the Great Law and they are beyond good and evil; they have power over life and power over death...

I remember with complete crystal clarity something unusual that occurred to me in my present existence... After having concluded all the esoteric-initiatic processes, I was submitted to many trials, but there was one that I regrettably always failed. I am referring emphatically to the sexual issue.

At that time, many years ago, the inevitable always happened to me: I failed in the decisive moments, and I would unfortunately swallow the apples of the Garden of Hesperides...

In the physical world I observed the most absolute chastity. The disaster always happened to me outside of the body, in the Superior Worlds; I would fail in the presence of many ineffable ladies.

Over and over again I would succumb before the immodest processes of Gundrigia, Kundry, Salome, the seductive Eve of Hebrew mythology... The serious thing about this case is that, in spite of having triumphed in all of the previous esoteric-initiatic trials, these failures happened to me precisely at the end of the Mountain of Initiation.

My case was truly pitiful, and in all of those scenes of an erotic type, under the Tree of Science of Good and Evil, I was not the owner of myself. A Demon would enter my mind, take control of my senses, control my will and in this way I would fail miserably...

I would suffer the unspeakable, the wound of Amfortas bled in my side and the remorse was frightful...

Thus, finally one day, mortally wounded in the depths of my Soul, I cried out to my Divine Mother Kundalini asking for help, and I did not have to wait for long...

On a given night, my adorable Mother got me out of my physical body and took me before the Tribunals of Objective Justice.

Great was my terror when I saw myself in the presence of the Judges of the Tribunal of Karma. Many people filled the hall. There was dread on all of their faces and anguish in all of their hearts.

I advanced some steps into the hall of Truth-Justice and the Judge opened the book and read: Crimes against the Moon Goddess, adventures of Don Juan Tenorio, in the era of medieval troubadours and of errant knights and of feudal cities.

Then, with a thundering voice, he pronounced the sentence of death and in an imperative manner he commanded the Cosmic Executioner to carry it out at once.

I still remember the unspeakable terror of those moments. My legs trembled in the precise moment when the Executioner unsheathed his flaming sword and menacingly directed it towards my defenseless person.

In those seconds that seemed to me centuries of torture, all of the sacrifices for humanity, my struggles for the Gnostic Movement, the books I had written, etc., etc., etc., passed through my mind and I said to myself, "So, this is the fate that now awaits me, after having suffered so much for humanity? Is this the payment that the Gods give me? Woe! Woe! Woe!"

Suddenly, I feel that something moves and agitates itself violently inside of me as the Executioner directs the tip of his sword towards me...

Then, I see with mystical amazement, a lustful, terribly perverse Demon that takes the shape of a neighing horse as it emerges from my body through the spinal column...

The Executioner now points his sword towards the malignant beast, and it falls headlong down into the bottom of the dark precipice. Its legs and tail are turned upwards, and finally the whole body of that frightful abomination penetrates totally beneath the epidermis of the planetary globe, to lose itself within the tenebrous entrails of the Avernus...

Thus, friends of mine, this is how I was freed of that lustful "I" that I created in the Middle Ages when, as a fallen Bodhisattva I wandered on a regal mount on cobbled roads from castle to castle, through the lands of the feudal lords.

Once I was freed of that abomination of nature, I felt happy; I did not fail again in the sexual trials, I was master of myself and thus I was able to continue on the Path of the Razor's Edge.

Here then ladies and gentlemen, is the great benefit that the Cosmic Executioner bestowed upon me. Unquestionably, these types of beings are beyond good and evil and they are terribly divine.

By no means do I want to practice demagogy; that is why I do not even remotely intend to praise the infamous executioners of subjective justice, of earthly justice, of that vain justice that is bought and sold. I am referring exclusively to those sacred individuals of Objective Justice, of Heavenly Justice, and this is radically different...

Question: Master, at the beginning of your impressive narration regarding the beings that enter into the Ninth Dantean Circle, you referred to the present builders of the Tower of Babel, and you mentioned the men of science who send rockets into space. Can you clarify what these sages of modern science are guilty of?

Answer: Distinguished gentleman, with great pleasure I hasten to answer your question...

Old texts of Ancient Wisdom say that the Titans of submerged Atlantis wanted to assault Heaven and they were precipitated into the Abyss.

I want you ladies and gentlemen to fully realize that the sages of the 20th century are not the first ones to launch rockets into space, nor the only earthlings that have been able to send astronauts to the Moon.

Nimrod and his followers, the fanatics of the Tower of Babel, inhabitants of the submerged Atlantis, created better rockets propelled by nuclear energy and sent men to the Moon.

This I know for a fact; I saw it, and I give testimony of it because I lived in Atlantis. I still remember an airport of the submerged continent. Many times from a neighboring restaurant, –Caravansin or Asana-, many times I saw those spaceships take off amidst the enthusiastic shouts of the excited multitudes. What remained of all this? What became of the Titans? Now we can only find dust in the Ninth Infernal Circle...

Friends, ladies, do not forget that space is infinitely sacred, and consequently, interplanetary navigation is controlled by very severe Cosmic Laws.

The error of these modern followers of the Tower of Babel is precisely in their self-sufficiency. These learned ignoramuses, these know-it-alls, set off from the mistaken principle that they are already Men, they do not want to realize that they still have not reached this stature, they are only rational homunculi, intellective humanoids.

In order to be Men, one needs to have given oneself the luxury of creating, for one's personal use, an Astral Body, a Mental Body, and a Causal Body. Only those who have created such

Supra-sensitive Vehicles will really be able to incarnate their Real Being, which would in fact place them within the Kingdom of Men.

It is therefore absurd for rational animals to abandon the zoo –planet Earth– in order to travel through infinite space.

Therefore, it is necessary to know that these know-it-alls of the Tower of Babel will be fulminated by the terrible Ray of Cosmic Justice and will perish in the Ninth Dantean Circle.

Attired with the Eidolon –Astral Body– I have spent long hours in the entrails of the Earth, in the very center of permanent gravity, in the nucleus of our world.

This region is terribly dense since each atom of the said zone carries in its womb 864 atoms of the Sacred Absolute Sun.

An equal number of laws –864– control the wretched creatures that are in the process of complete disintegration in this zone ...

Walking about, I saw a stone and upon it was a head similar to that of a human; it moved very slowly, mechanically repeating everything that came to my mind that I say. It was someone who had already become totally mineralized and who unquestionably was decomposing and disintegrating to finally reduce himself to cosmic dust.

Continuing on my way within the entrails of the world, I suddenly felt upon my shoulders as if a diabolic entity had alighted upon me. I shook myself forcefully, and that creature fell to the ground a little further away....

Thereafter, continuing on the solitary path of the tenebrous "Tartarus" in those frightful profundities where time is terribly long and tedious, I entered into a filthy room where there was a prostitute romping in the bed of Procrustes, slowly disintegrating. That whore was losing fingers, arms, legs..., slowly, little by little, and she copulated incessantly with however many larvae would approach her...

I got out of there, out of that horrible bedroom, terribly shaken... Lastly, something unusual happens: I see a pair of witches dressed in black, slowly floating above the floor, heading towards a kitchen. There these harpies are preparing their potions, their filters, their magic spells, to cause harm to other wretched ones from the tenebrous "Tartarus"...

Time passes and I begin to feel annoyed in this crude materiality; I then long to get out of it, to ascend to the surface of the Earth, to again see the soft light of day...

My longing is not in vain. Soon I am assisted and my Real Being once more takes me out of those abysses to contemplate anew the lovely mountains, the profound seas, the light of the sun and the twinkling stars...

Friends, remember the city of Dis in the Ninth Infernal Circle. There, those who have involuted in time exhale their last breath...

Lucifer-Prometheus, the adversary, that vile worm that pierces the heart of the world, had the most beautiful face, although now he is found chained to the fatal rock of impotence...

Let us not think of a dogmatic Lucifer, but of the inner Lucifer of each one, in that reflection of the Logos that is found within the intimate depth of each person.

It is said that he weeps with six eyes, and this number invites us to do reflection. The number of the Great Whore is 666 and by adding each digit we obtain the result: 18. Continuing with new additions we would reach the following synthesis: $1 + 8 = 9$, the Ninth Sphere, the Ninth Dantean Circle.

Lucifer is therefore that revolutionary force found in the depths of our sexual system, and which when handled wisely can transform us into Gods.

To whom shall I compare those who do not know how to handle the Luciferian force? Possibly to the apprentices of electricity, or to the gullible, who not having such a profession, ignoring the danger, dare to play with high tension electrical cables; undoubtedly, they are fulminated and precipitated into the Abyss.

The negative aspect of Lucifer-Prometheus inevitably leads us to failure and this is why it is said that he is the adversary who dwells in the heart of the world. The antithesis of Lucifer or its superior aspect is the Solar Logos, the Cosmic Christ.

Lucifer is a ladder to descend into the Avernus and a ladder to ascend. Comprehension is indispensable; remember that our motto is Thelema – 'will'...

It is necessary to learn to distinguish between a fall and a descent; we need to descend into the Ninth Sphere –sexuality– in order to create the Superior Existential Bodies of the Being and to dissolve the Ego.

In the Ninth Circle is the well of the universe, the center of planetary gravity.

It is important to remember that the creative organs of the human species have their full representation in the Ninth Submerged Sphere.

No one would be able to ascend without having previously taken the trouble to descend. Each exaltation is preceded by a terrible and frightful humiliation.

To descend into the Ninth Sphere is indispensable. Some do it during life by means of their own will, spontaneously, and for their Intimate Self-Realization and others, the majority, the multitudes, do it in an unconscious manner when they descend into the Abyss of perdition.

Question: Venerable Master, I would like you to explain to us why sex is also called the Ninth Sphere. Is it perhaps related with the center of the Earth?

Answer: Friends, it is urgent to comprehend that in the Superior Dimensions of nature, submerged beneath the epidermis of the Earth, by Law of Antithesis, there is a Ninth Circle of Glory, where the Initiates of the Universal White Fraternity can see, traced in a concrete manner, the sign of the infinite, the Holy Eight, placed horizontally. Those who have studied esoteric Kabbalah know the intimate significance of this magical figure very well.

The upper part of this symbol represents the brain, the lower part allegorizes sex, and the center of this magnificent figure is the atomic point where the Nine Submerged Regions gravitate. You have there then: the brain, heart, and sex of the Planetary Genie...

The fight is terrible: brain against sex, sex against brain. When sex overcomes the brain, when it is out of control, we are then precipitated headlong into the Abyss. When the brain and sex are in balance, we self-realize ourselves intimately.

All the creatures that exist upon the face of the Earth have been created in accordance with this holy symbol of the infinite; now you can explain to yourselves why sex corresponds to the Ninth Sphere.

The child remains nine months within the maternal womb. For nine ages humanity was within the womb of Great Nature, Rhea, Cybele, etc., etc. etc. With this explanation I seriously believe that I have answered the gentleman's question.

Question: Venerable Master, I would like to know how the Essence comes out into the light of the sun once the Ego has been reduced to cosmic dust in this Ninth Circle of the center of our planet.

Answer: After having spoken about the sign of the infinite and the Superior Dimensions of nature, let us now return, then, to the matters related with the Infernal Dimensions or Infra-Dimensions of nature.

After exhaling its last breath in this region where the throne of Dis is situated, the Essence, the psychic material, what we have of the Soul, is free, without Ego, since, as we have already said, the latter is reduced to cosmic dust.

Once the Essence is emancipated, it takes on a very beautiful child-like shape, filled with radiant beauty. This is the solemn moment in which the Devas of nature examine the liberated Essence.

After having verified to satiation that it no longer possesses any subjective, infrahuman element, they awarded him a ticket —document— of freedom. What I mean to say with this is that they grant unto the Soul the bliss of Liberation...

Happy are those moments in which the Soul of the deceased penetrates through certain luminous atomic doors that allow it to immediately exit into the light of the sun.

Once freed, the creature on the epidermis of our world, reinitiates a new evolution. It then becomes a Gnome or Pygmy of the Mineral Kingdom; thereafter it will continue its evolution, ascending through the Plant and Animal levels, until some distant day, it reconquers the state of intellectual humanoid that was once lost.

14

CONTINUOUS MOVEMENT

Dear audience, distinguished gentlemen, honorable ladies; we are going to talk a little bit about Continuous Movement.

Every now and again, the rascals of the intellect concern themselves with Continuous Movement, and it is clear that public opinion is intensely stirred up.

There have always been attempts to invent some mechanism that functions perpetually, but this is not possible due to the inevitable wear and tear of materials. It is clear, that if the pieces of any machine wear out, Continuous Movement disappears.

Some people, trying to discover the Law of Continuous Movement, have ended up in an asylum.

One cannot help but laugh when contemplating so many devices that have not given any result. What ingenious mechanisms haven't the rascals of the intellect invented! Nonetheless, the problem continues without a solution.

Frankly, we have already discovered the Law of Continuous Movement in the marvelous cylinder of the Archangel Hariton.

It is said that its main part is made of amber with platinum axes, while the interior panels of the walls are made of anthracite, copper and ivory, and of a very strong cement resistant to cold, heat, and water and also to radiations of cosmic concentrations.

From our way of seeing and understanding things, it is obvious that both the exterior levers and the cogwheels must be renewed from time to time because although they are made of the strongest metal, prolonged usage wears them out.

We are speaking unquestionably about the Wheel of Samsara, which rotates eternally.

All of us, without exception, have turned many times with this Great Wheel, and if this Continuous Movement has not been interrupted, it is due exclusively to the infinite quantity of disposable elements.

Let us think for a moment on the axis of this Great Wheel, the one that is said to be of platinum; it could also be emphatically affirmed that it is of silver.

Anyone knows that silver or platinum are completely lunar in type, it is obvious that the axis of the fatal Wheel could not be of any another material.

As for amber, it is clear that the latter is found diluted in everything created; we must not forget that this substance completely unifies the Three universal Forces.

It is extraordinary that even though the Three Primary Forces of Creation each work independently and on their own, remain unified thanks to that magnificent substance called amber.

Each one of us has not only passed through the mill many times, but also through each cog of the mill.

With this said, I want to emphasize the information that we have incessantly rotate through successive eternities within the Wheel of the Archangel Hariton, that is, within the extraordinary Wheel of Samsara.

The disposable materials are the Egos, that descending with the tragic Wheel are disintegrated in the Avernus.

On the right Anubis always ascends evolving and on the left Typhon always descends involuting.

We have repeated *ad nauseam* in all of these lectures that each one of us is always assigned 108 existences. It is clear that once the cycle of successive lives is finished, if we have not attained the Intimate Self-Realization of our Being, we turn with the Wheel of the Archangel Hariton, descending within the Submerged Mineral Kingdom.

With this we want to speak very clearly and say: one evolves to a point that is perfectly defined by nature, and thereafter one involutes.

We ascend evolving on the right side of the Wheel and we descend involuting on the left side of it.

The evolving ascent, in itself, begins from the Mineral Kingdom.

Any esotericist investigator with Awakened Consciousness will be able to verify the crude reality of the evolving creatures in the Superior Mineral Kingdom, to differentiate it from the Submerged Inferior.

Many times, moving outside of the physical body with the Eidolon, I have opened certain rocks or fragments of stone to study these multiple creatures that inhabit that Superior Mineral Kingdom.

I can tell you without fear of exaggerating that those innocent creatures are beyond good and evil.

On a certain occasion, when I opened a rock fragment, I was able to see many ladies and gentlemen elegantly dressed that were at the most 5 to 10 centimeters tall. There is no doubt that these small Mineral Elementals like to dress themselves up in our humanoid garments.

Traveling by car on different roads of Mexico, I have seen with mystical astonishment certain superior Elementals of the rocks, who have warned me about dangers, or have advised me to be cautious on the roads.

This second type of Mineral Elementals is unquestionably more advanced than the first type, and it takes on shapes very similar to those of the intellectual humanoid, although they wear garments of the color of the rocks they inhabit.

A more advanced third type of Mineral Elementals are those known by the name of Gnomes or Pygmies. These types of creatures look like true dwarves with long white beards and gray hair. There is no doubt that this last type knows the Alchemy of metals in depth and cooperates in the work of nature. Obviously, these are more advanced creatures, and many texts of occultism talk about them clearly. We need only to recall for a moment *The Elementals* by Franz Hartmann, who mentions these creatures...

There is no doubt that the advanced Mineral Elementals enter the Plant Kingdom.

Each plant is the physical body of a Plant Elemental.

Each tree, each herb, as insignificant as it might be, possesses its own particular Elemental.

I do not want to say with this that the Elementals of plants, trees and flowers, etc., are inside their immobile body at all times; this would be absurd and even unfair. Plant Elementals have complete liberty to enter and leave their bodies at will; one is amazed when one encounters them in the Fourth Coordinate, in the Fourth Vertical.

Normally, the Elemental creatures of the Plant Kingdom are classified in family groups.

One is the family of the orange trees, another is that of mint, another that of pine trees, etc. etc. etc.

Each family has their own Temple in Eden, in the Fourth Dimension.

Many times, attired in the Eidolon, I have entered into these paradisiacal Temples.

To quote something about the latter, I now want to refer to the Sanctuary of the orange trees.

I found many innocent children within the Sanctuary of the mentioned plant family; they were busy listening to the teachings that their Guru-Deva was imparting to them.

That instructor, wearing an outfit like that of a bride, resembled an exquisitely spiritual feminine beauty.

I have made similar visits to other plant Temples located in the Promised Land, in that land where the rivers of pure water flow with milk and honey...

The advanced Elementals from the Plant Kingdom will enter into the diverse departments of the Animal Kingdom later on.

These creatures, distributed in multiple families or species, also have their guides and their Temples located in the Terrestrial Paradise, that is, in the Fourth Coordinate, called the Etheric World by occultists.

On a certain occasion, while in meditation, I was able to clearly verify the intelligent meaning of the language of birds.

I clearly remember this one bird perched on the crown of a tree arguing with another. The first one was calm when all of a sudden it was disturbed by the arrival of the second one. The latter perched itself menacingly on top of the tree, making many recriminations to the first one...

I was alert, listening in meditation to what was happening. I clearly remember the insults of the threatening bird:

"A few days ago, you hurt my foot and I have to punish you for that mistake..."

The threatened creature apologized, saying,

"What happened is not my fault, leave me in peace..."

Unfortunately, the aggressor bird did not want to listen to reason and pecking his victim with force, he incessantly reminded the other of his wounded foot.

On another occasion, finding myself also in profound inner meditation, I was able to hear the barking of two neighbor dogs. The first one was telling the second one everything that happened in his house, he told him:

"My master treats me very bad; here in this house they constantly hit and whip me and the food is terrible; everybody, in general, insults me and I lead a very unhappy life."

The second one would answer with his barks, saying:

"For me, it is much better; they give me good food and treat me very well."

The people who would come and go on the street would only hear the barking of two dogs, they did not understand the language of the animals; nevertheless, for me that language has always been very clear.

On a certain occasion, a neighbor dog warned me that a great failure awaited me if I took a certain trip towards the north of Mexico. The aforesaid animal shouted telling me:

"A failure, a failure, a failure!"

And I did not want to listen to him.

Around that time, upon arriving a certain town very close to the Sonora desert, I told the driver of the vehicle that we were traveling in that it was indispensable for us to find a hotel since I did not wish in any way to continue that trip that night.

Nonetheless, that good man with sleeping Consciousness did not wish to obey. I therefore warned him in the following manner:

"You will be responsible for what is going to happen, you are warned; you hear me, you are warned..."

Hours later, the car —automobile— turned over in the desert, and there were injured people; no one died. I then reminded that gentleman of the mistake he had committed for not obeying me... There is no doubt, that the man acknowledged his offence and asked for forgiveness, but it was too late, the incident had happened.

Unfortunately, people with sleeping Consciousness are this way; this is how they wander about in the world from the day they are born until they die.

What I am saying might seem a little strange to you, for in no way you notice the difference when listening to the song of a bird. You would never understand their language, and much less that of a dog.

You only hear the sounds of nature: barks, whistles, singing, etc. and nothing else.

The same can happen to these animal creatures: when they listen to human language, they only perceive the raising and the lowering of the voice, more or less high-pitched, more or less low-pitched sounds, squeaks, roars, neighs, snoring, snorting and croaking.

Nonetheless, we understand each other; we have our earthly languages, etc.

The most advanced Elemental creatures enter the Kingdom of Intellectual Humanoids; there is no doubt that these tri-brained or tri-centered bipeds are much more dangerous...

Everyone who enters the Kingdom of the Rational Homunculi is always assigned 108 existences, as we have already said *ad nauseam*; but he who fails, who does not attain Intimate Self-Realization within the cycle of existences that have been assigned to him, ceases to return or to reincorporate into humanoid organisms and plunges involuting in the entrails of the Earth, in the infra-dimensions of nature.

Through our investigations of an esoteric type, we have been able to verify, with complete crystal clarity, what the involutive processes are.

It is clear that we have to retrace our steps and go down the steps we climbed up before.

After recapitulating past humanoid experiences in the Avernus, we must repeat animalistic and vegetaloid states before total fossilization and Second Death.

I remember a very interesting case. On a certain occasion I warned a lady of the Abyss about the following:

"On the involutive path that you are on, you will have to disintegrate in the Ninth Sphere, become cosmic dust; this is what Second Death is like."

The lady responded:

"I do not ignore it; we know that, and that is precisely what we want."

The Demon that accompanied her, furious, attacked me with his infernal psychic powers, and I had to defend myself with the Flaming Sword.

Yahve has made this entire Wheel of Samsara a mystic, a religion, and his followers are faithful to him.

When one converses with Yahve, one can verify that this fallen Angel possesses a sparkling intellectuality, with which he can totally seduce anyone.

All of Yahve's lectures begin by talking against the Cosmic Christ —this given Demon is terribly perverse and mortally hates the Solar Logos.

Those who want to self-realize intimately with the purpose of avoiding the descent into the Infernal Worlds must enter the Path of the Revolution of the Consciousness. This means separating oneself from the Wheel of Samsara and parting completely from the Laws of Evolution and Involution.

Now you will clearly explain to yourselves why the Cosmic Christ, during his time on Earth, spoke to us about the strait gate and the narrow and difficult path that leads to Light...

The Ego is never immortal; it has a beginning and an end. Either we voluntarily annihilate it, or nature takes charge of disintegrating it in the Avernus.

We must choose. We face the dilemma of the To be or Not to be of Philosophy, and those who do not want to listen to us now will have to suffer the consequences later on.

The voluntary processes of the dissolution of the "I", here and now, are very interesting.

In the beginning we must eliminate the humanoid weaknesses and then continue dissolving or disintegrating all those animal or bestial aggregates that we carry within, and much later on it is indispensable to work with the double-edged axe of Ancient Mysteries, to crush and reduce to dust the vegetaloid memories of all the lust and morbidities of the past.

Lastly, we must work with the tools of the laborer to crush the fossil or mineraloid states of the different yesterdays that sleep within the profound depths of the subconscious.

With this I want to say that what nature is to do with us in the Abyss, we can do it ourselves here and now, if we truly want to avoid infernal bitterness.

Question: Beloved Master, when we self-realize intimately and separate ourselves from the Wheel of Samsara, does this mean that we are no longer in Continuous Movement?

Answer: I hear a question from the audience, and I hasten to answer it with greatest pleasure. Distinguished gentleman, it is urgent that you comprehend what Continuous Movement of the Wheel of Samsara is, in each and every one of its aspects.

Undoubtedly, Continuous Movement exists not only in the cylinder of the Archangel Hariton, but also in any cosmic cylinder.

Remember clearly sir that there are Cosmic Days and Nights. Everything flows and ebbs, comes and goes, rises and falls, increases and decreases...

There is rhythm in everything and Abstract Absolute Space is electric vibration and, as a result, Continuous Movement.

Frankly, I do not acknowledge absolute immobility; what happens is that there are multiple and infinite forms of Continuous Movement.

Question: Venerable Master, you talked to us about three types of Elementals, and I want to ask you if these exist within the Wheel of Samsara both in evolution as well as in involution or are they exclusive to evolution?

Answer: Distinguished frater, observe in detail all the phenomena of nature and you will have the answer...

Many thinks that monkeys, simians, apes, orangutans, gorillas, etc. etc., are evolutive in kind. Some even suppose that man comes from the ape, but such a concept collapses spectacularly when we observe the habits of these animalistic species. Put a simian in a laboratory and observe what happens.

Unquestionably, the various families of simians are involutions that descend from the intellectual humanoid.

The humanoid does not come from the ape; the truth about this is the other way around: simians are involuting, degenerated humanoids.

Let us move on now and observe the family of pigs. In the times of Moses, the Israelites that would eat the meat of this animal were decapitated.

It is clear that this type of Elemental is in a natural involutive process.

We can discover analogous states of involution in plants and in minerals.

Copper for example, within the interior of the planetary organism in which we live is the specific center of gravity of all involutive and evolutive forces.

If we apply the positive force of the universe to copper, we can then contemplate, with the spatial sense, multiple marvelous evolutive processes.

If we apply the universal negative force to the aforementioned metal, we will be able to perceive, by means of integral clairvoyance, infinite involutive processes that are very similar to those of the multitudes which inhabit the entrails of the Earth.

If we apply the neutral force to copper, the evolutive as well as the involuting processes remain in a static state.

The laws of Evolution and Involution constitute the mechanical axis of all nature, the silver axis of the Wheel of Samsara...

The laws of Evolution and Involution work in a coordinated and harmonious way in all of creation.

Obviously, the Elementals of the Mineral, Plant, and Animal Kingdoms evolve and involute in their own natural scales. We could never conceive the hare-brained idea that the Elementals of nature, due to failure within this or that living species, could make the Wheel turn backwards so as to return to the Abyss through the door from which they came out.

I want for all of you, ladies and gentlemen, to comprehend that in the "Tartarus" one enters through one door and exits through another.

This means among other things, that evolving Anubis will always ascend to the right, and that involuting Typhon will perpetually descend to the left. The chakra of Samsara does not rotate backward, understood?

Question: Venerable Master, there is a belief among us who understand these Laws pertaining to certain species of animals, and we would like an explanation only in the concrete case of crows, rats, and other species that are more or less repugnant.

Answer: With great pleasure, I will answer the new question from the audience. Beyond any doubt, there are repugnant creatures in nature that show signs of marked involution.

For example, ancient Egyptians abhorred rats; and it is obvious that they are in a state of marked involution. Another is the case of crows, and these, even though they feed on death due to the fact that they unfold in the Ray of Saturn, possess certain marvelous powers that indicate evolution.

I have been able to witness what the faculties of the crow are. On a certain occasion, when I was in a small town in Venezuela, in a certain house where a little boy was seriously ill, I saw with astonishment, a group of crows that had very calmly landed on the roof of that house.

Those simple people then clarified the following to me: This child will die.

When I asked the reason for such a sentence, they pointed to those black crows as a response; then I comprehended...

The case was a lost cause and the child really did die. What amazed me the most were the faculties of those Elementals; they knew that the child was going to die and settled on the roof of that mansion, awaiting the supreme moment for the feast. Undoubtedly, the macabre feast never took place because the child was given a Christian burial, however, the birds did come and the Law was fulfilled.

Question: Very beloved Master; because of the aspects that you have explained to us at length, does this mean that all those animal creatures like cats, dogs, pigs, etc., have passed through the human form at some point and are on the path towards disintegration? Is it possible that these same creatures are on their way to human form?

Answer: Distinguished brother, allow me to inform you that many Elementals of nature passed through the Infernal Worlds. I shall clarify with other words: after Second Death, every Soul becomes an Elemental of nature and begins its evolutive processes as I have already said, from the hard rock, continuing through plant and animal, until reaching the state of intellectual humanoid.

In the interim, the Elementals of the different Kingdoms evolve and involute, but they would not be able to return to the Avernus since they do not possess the Ego. Only humanoids can enter into the Avernus because they do have the Ego within their interior. With this, the question has been clarified and the answer given...

Question: Master, what relationship is there between the Essence and the Elementals?

Answer: It is good that this honorable audience that is listening to me fully understands that there is certainly no difference between the Essence and the Elementals.

It is clear that the Essence is the Elemental itself, and the Elemental is the Essence itself.

When the Ego is disintegrated in the Infernal Worlds, we become Elementals of nature.

However, when the Ego is disintegrated here and now through conscious works and voluntary sufferings, instead of becoming Elementals we become Masters, this is what is important.

Question: Master, I am curious to know, based on what you have explained to us with respect to the Elementals being beyond good and evil, and therefore innocent, if this innocence can be lost.

Answer: Distinguished gentleman, honorable audience who is listening to me, I beg you all to comprehend my words...

There are two types of innocence: that of the victors and that of the failures.

The Soul that escapes from the Avernus after Second Death to become an Elemental of nature is obviously a failure, even though it has re-conquered its innocence.

The Soul that disintegrates the Ego in a voluntary and conscious way, here and now, re-conquers its innocence in a victorious manner and becomes a Buddha.

There are Elementals that enter the Wheel of the Archangel Hariton for the first time. They have never been humans; they long to reach the state of humans.

There are Elementals that, before being elementals, lived as humanoids and involuted in the Infernal Words.

Here are the two extremes, the two aspects of Elementals:

1. Elementals that begin.

2. Elementals that repeat the elemental processes.

Question: Very beloved Master, since we have the opportunity of your wisdom I would like to know if it is easier for an Elemental to attain Self-Realization when it enters a human womb for the first time because it comes without Ego.

Answer: Honorable audience that is listening to me tonight, it is urgent to know that the Essence, the Soul that comes from the three inferior Kingdoms into a human womb, does not yet have the necessary and indispensable experience that is required to attain the Intimate Self-Realization of the Being.

Normally, every Essence that enters into a human organism for the first time makes many mistakes, forms Ego, acquires karma and suffers the unspeakable afterwards.

Only later can this Soul attain Self-realization if it so wishes.

Nonetheless, I now repeat what I have already said in past lectures: not all Souls attain Mastery. For this to happen, a certain intimate yearning is indispensable, and this is only possible when the Monad, that is, the Immortal Spark of the Spirit, truly resolves to work on its human Soul.

It is clear that not all the Monads, Spirits or Virginal Sparks are interested in Mastery; given that we have already said this in past lectures, it is not necessary to continue making clarifications on the matter.

Question: Venerable Master, in any case, I consider that by voluntarily and progressively eliminating the Ego, we are really in a process of evolution because we have always understood that evolution means ascent, which is why I sustain that those who affirm that there is permanent evolution until reaching unitotal Perfection are not mistaken. Do you have any objection to this concept?

Answer: I like the question from the audience. Obviously, the question in itself has a completely reactionary undertone; nonetheless, I hasten to answer it.

Do you perhaps think, gentlemen that the Ego can evolve? Do you suppose that dissolving it is evolution? Any educated clairvoyant is able to verify the involutive processes of the "I", of the Myself, of the Oneself.

It is amazing to verify how the Ego plunges on the involutive path, descending through the animal, plant and mineral scales when we tread the Path of the Revolution of the Consciousness.

Or do you think, friends, that with the dissolution of the Ego, the Essence reinitiates a new evolving ascent adhered to the Wheel of Samsara? Or do you believe that the Being, the Spirit, must perpetually live bottled up within the evolving processes of nature and of the cosmos?

We have never denied the Laws of Evolution and of Involution, we only clarify them.

The evolving and involutive processes correspond exactly to the Great Wheel of Samsara. Those processes could not be infinitely repeated within the World of the Spirit, because this would in fact mean perpetual slavery.

Remember friends that Jesus the Great Kabir never wanted to bottle himself up in the dogma of evolution.

That Great Hierophant only talked to us about the Path of the Revolution of the Consciousness, about the narrow, strait and difficult Path that leads us to Light, and that very few are those who find it.

Gentlemen, when are you going to understand this? In what era? When are you going resolve to enter through the strait Gate and the narrow Path? Or do you perhaps want to set Jesus the Christ straight?

Those who dissolve the Ego achieve radical transformation, and that is total revolution.

Question: Master, it seems to me a concept of total injustice and contrary to the love that identifies the Great Architect of the Universe, to admit that after having achieved the human state and having developed the intellect to the heights where we currently find ourselves —where the advances and feats of modern scientists astonish– that we must return to the state of horses, dogs and pigs. How can such a concept even superficially appear in the mind of rational and intelligent man? Frankly, I believe that this insults the eminent dignity of man, made in the image and likeness of God!

Answer: I see among the audience a gentleman who is trying to find fault with the author of the Doctrine of the Transmigration of Souls, the great Avatar Krishna, who lived a thousand years before Christ.

The Great Hindu Avatar never said that the chakra of Samsara turned backwards, that the Wheel of the Archangel Hariton processed itself the other way around, stopping its motion to turn in the opposite direction.

Ladies and gentlemen, the Wheel of the Arcanum 10 of the Tarot always follows its course, it never turns backwards.

Any car can go in reverse, but the Wheel of Samsara never reverses.

Repetition of cycles according to the Law of Recurrence is different, and this we see proven in the Days and Nights of Brahma, with their ever-incessant repetition; in the seasons that repeat each year; in the diverse cosmological Yugas that never stop repeating themselves, etc., etc., etc.

None of this is regression my friends, all of this moves in accordance with the Wheel; all of this is part of Continuous Movement.

Nevertheless, it is necessary to understand that the Law of Recurrence repeats itself in spirals, sometimes higher and sometimes lower. The spiral is the curve of life.

If we have exhausted the diverse processes of humanoid, we must obviously go up or down. Some go up, others fall into submerged involution.

Those who have dissolved the Ego ascend; those who have not dissolved it descend.

The victorious transform themselves into Buddhas, into Masters; the failures are transformed into Elementals of nature, after

Second Death announced by our Lord the Christ, by John in the *Book of Revelation*,

There are no backward movements, but rather continuity of cycles or periods of cosmic manifestation.

We have already said in past lectures that all these cycles or periods are counted, and in this, there is no backward movement.

The Wheel moves forward, it never turns back. It begins with cycle number 1 and it ends with cycle 3,000. The counting of cycles or periods of manifestation never moves inversely, therefore, mathematics clearly demonstrates that the Doctrine of the Transmigration of Souls is exact.

Ladies and gentlemen, it would be very serious if the Ego did not have a limit and if it continued developing and unfolding itself eternally. Think about what this would mean: the evil of the world would never have a limit, it would extend victoriously throughout the spaces of the infinites and it would dominate all the Seven Cosmoses. In this case, there would indeed be injustice.

Distinguished ladies and gentlemen, fortunately, the Great Architect of the Universe, cited by the gentleman who asked the question, has put a check on evil.

15

THE DISSOLUTION OF THE EGO

istinguished friends, esteemed ladies, today, on December 9th of the tenth year of Aquarius –1972– we meet here once again, in this place, with the longing to study profoundly the topic of the dissolution of the Psychological "I."

Before all else, it is indispensable for us to carefully analyze this question of the Ego.

Diverse schools of a pseudo-esoteric and pseudo-occultist type emphasize the harebrained idea of a double "I": they call the first one Superior "I"; they qualify the second one as Inferior "I."

We say that superior and inferior are two sections of the same thing.

Much has been said about the Alter Ego and it is even praised and deified and considered divine.

In the name of that which is the Truth, it is indispensable to say that the Superior and Inferior "I" are two aspects of the same

Ego, and that therefore, praising the first one and underestimating the second one is, without a doubt, something incongruous.

Focusing directly on this matter, looking at the Ego as it is in itself and without these kinds of arbitrary divisions –Superior and Inferior– it is clear that we can correctly make a differentiation between what the "I" is and what the Being is.

We could face the objection that such a differentiation is nothing more than another concept emitted by the intellect.

Those who are listening to us might even look for escape routes, asserting that one concept more or one concept less in matters of high Philosophy is something that does not have the least importance.

There are even those who can afford to listen to these affirmations and then forget them, in order to pay attention to something they do consider important.

The people of sleeping Consciousness tend to disregard these types of affirmations, due to the fact that they are already tired of so much theory. These persons tell themselves: "What does one more theory matter? What does one theory less matter?"

We must speak with complete frankness and base ourselves on facts, on direct experiences, and not on simple opinions of a subjective type.

I am going to tell you, friends of mine, what I know, what I have seen and heard, and if you want to accept my affirmations well, you do so, but if you want to reject them, it is your business... Every human being is free to accept, reject or interpret the teachings as he wishes.

In the beginning of my present reincarnation, I too, like many of you, had read several pseudo-esoteric and pseudo-occultist books.

Searching as you have done, I went through diverse schools and came to know a great many theories.

It is obvious that because of so much reading and re-reading, I also came to believe in the existence of the two "I's", the Superior and the Inferior.

Different preceptors told me that I had to dominate the Inferior "I" by means of the Superior "I," to someday be able to reach Adepthood.

I confess, frankly and without circumambages, that I was completely convinced of the existence of the so-called two "I's". Fortunately, a transcendental mystical event was to shake me intensely at the very bottom of my Soul...

It happened that one night, the date does not matter, nor the day, nor the hour, when I found myself outside of my physical body in a completely conscious and positive manner, my real Inner Being, the Intimate, came to me. Smiling, the Blessed One said to me:

"You have to die!"

These words of the Intimate left me perplexed, confused, astounded. Somewhat fearful, I interrogated my Inner Being –Atman– saying to him:

"Why do I have to die? Let me live a little bit longer! I am working for humanity...!"

I still remember the moment when the Blessed One, smiling, repeated it to me a second time:

"You have to die!"

Thereafter, the Adorable showed me within the Astral Light, what had to die within myself. Then I saw the pluralized "I" formed by a multitude of tenebrous entities, a true cluster of perverse creatures, distinct types of psychic aggregates, living Demons personifying errors.

It was in this manner, my friends, that I came to know that the "I" is not something individual, but a sum of psychic aggregates, a multiple sum of quarrelsome and vociferous "I's."

Some of these represent anger, others greed, those lust, these others envy, those others pride, then sloth, gluttony and all its infinite derivatives continue.

I actually did not see in the Ego anything worthy of being adored, any type of divinity, etc....

Upon arriving to this point of my exposition, it would not be surprising if some of the attendees were to object to my words, telling me: "It is possible that you, sir, saw your Inferior "I," sum of psychic aggregates, as oriental Buddhism asserts. Your concept would be very different if you would have perceived your Superior "I" in all of its greatness."

I know very well, friends, the diverse forms of intellectualization that you have, your evasiveness, your elusiveness, your different justifications, your reactions, your resistances, the desire of always making everything that has the flavor of Ego stand out.

It is clear that the Ego does not feel like dying and that it wants to continue in some exquisitely subtle form, if not in the most dense and gross forms.

Nobody wants to see their beloved "I" reduced to cosmic dust just for the sake of it, just because some guy said it in a lecture hall.

It is quite normal that the Ego does not wish to die and that it looks for consoling philosophies that will promise it a little corner in Heaven, a place on the altars of churches, or a beyond filled with infinite happiness.

We truly regret having to disillusion people, but we have no other choice than to speak bluntly, frankly and sincerely regarding these very serious matters.

Since we Gnostics like to talk based on concrete, clear and definitive facts, I will now have no problem in narrating another unusual event, with the purpose of demonstrating to you that the Superior "I" does not exist...

The other day, while in profound meditation, in accordance with all the rules that Jnana Yoga commands, I entered into something known as Nirvikalpa-Samadhi. I then abandoned all the Super-sensitive Bodies and penetrated into the world of the Solar Logos, converted into a Dragon of Wisdom.

In such logoic moments, beyond the body, the affections and the mind, I wanted to know something about the life of the Great Kabir Jesus; it was precisely in that very instant, when I saw myself transformed into Jesus of Nazareth performing miracles and wonders in the Holy Land.

I still remember the moment when I was to be baptized by John in the Jordan River... I saw myself inside a temple located on the shores of that river; the Precursor was wearing a beautiful tunic, and when I approached him, he steadily looked at me and exclaimed:

"Jesus, take off your garment, because I am going to baptize you!"

I went inside the Sanctuary and pouring upon my head the anointing oil and then a little bit of water, he prayed and I felt transformed.

What happened afterwards was marvelous. While seated inside a hall, I saw three divine suns: the first one was the blue of the Father, the second one was the yellow of the Son and the third one was the red of the Holy Spirit.

These are the three Logoi: Brahma, Vishnu, and Shiva. When coming out from that ecstatic state, upon returning to my physical body, my confusion was tremendous. Me –Jesus of Nazareth? Me– the Christ? Oh God and Holy Mary! A miserable sinner, a slug from the mud of the earth, who is not even worthy of untying the sandals of the Master, transformed, just like that, into Jesus of Nazareth!

Quite concerned about all of this, I resolved once again to enter into meditation and to repeat the mystical experience, changing only the motive of it: now, instead of wanting to know something about the life of Jesus, I interested myself in John and the baptism of the Nazarene.

Then came the previous mystical state; I abandoned all the Supersensitive Bodies and once more I was in the logoic state.

Once I returned to such a state, I fixed my attention with greater intensity on John the Baptist, and I then saw myself transformed into John, performing the activities of the Precursor, baptizing Jesus, etc., etc., etc.

Upon losing the ecstasy, upon returning to my physical body, I then comprehended that in the World of the Logos, in the World of Christ, there isn't any type of Superior "I" or Inferior "I."

It is urgent for all of those present to comprehend that in Christ we are all one and that the heresy of separateness is the worst of heresies.

My friends, everything in this world in which we live passes: ideas pass, persons pass, things pass. The only thing that is stable and permanent is the Being, and the reason of being of the Being is the Being himself. Distinguish then, between what the "I" is and what the Being is.

Question: Master, what substance are the psychic aggregates that constitute the Myself made of?

Answer: Ladies and gentlemen, it is indispensable for you to comprehend what the mind and its functions are.

The intellectual animal mistakenly called man still does not possess an individual mind, he has not created it, he has not formed it.

Strictly speaking, the Mental Body can only be created by means of sexual transmutations. I want all of those present to understand that in the sacred sperm there exists the Sexual Hydrogen Si-12.

Undoubtedly, the esotericist who does not spill the Cup of Hermes —who does not ejaculate the semen— actually gives origin to the marvelous transmutations of the libido within his organism, the result is the creation of the individual Mental Body.

The Manas, the mental substance, strictly speaking, is found in the interior of any individual, but it lacks individuality; it possesses diverse forms, it is constituted in the form of aggregates which have never been foreign to esoteric Buddhism.

I beg this kind audience that is listening to me to patiently follow the course of my dissertation...

All of those multiple, quarrelsome, and vociferous "I's", which together form the Myself, the Oneself, are made up of more or less condensed mental substance.

Now you can explain to yourselves the reasons why every person constantly changes opinions.

Let us say we are, for example, real estate salespersons. A client approaches; we talk to him, we convince him of the necessity of buying a beautiful house; the person becomes enthusiastic and emphatically affirms that the deal is sealed and that nothing can make him desist from his wish. Unfortunately, after a few hours, everything changes: the client's opinion is no longer the same; another mental "I" now controls the brain, and the enthusiastic "I" that, a few hours earlier, was passionate about the purchase of the property is displaced by a new "I" that has nothing to do with the deal nor with the given word. Then the castle of cards falls to the ground and the poor real estate agent feels deceived...

The "I" that swears eternal love to a woman, is displaced tomorrow by another that has nothing to do with the oath and then the person goes away, leaving the woman disappointed...

The "I" that swears loyalty to the Gnostic Movement is displaced tomorrow by another "I" that has nothing to do with the oath and the person withdraws from Gnosis, leaving all the brothers of the sanctuary confused and astounded...

See for yourselves, dear friends of mine, what the infinite forms of the mind are; in what way they control the capital centers of the brain, and how they play with the Human Machine.

Question: Master, in this planet in which we live, the "I's" make life bearable, since it is easy to comprehend that if we dissolve them and recede from everything that is our desires, our life would be terribly sad and boring, is that not so?

Answer: Distinguished ladies and gentlemen, authentic happiness lies radically in the revalorization of the Being.

It is unquestionable that each time the Being goes through intimate revalorization he experiences authentic happiness.

Unfortunately, people of today confuse pleasure with happiness and bestially enjoy fornication, adultery, alcohol, drugs, money, gambling, etc., etc., etc.

The limit of pleasure is pain and every type of animal pleasure changes into bitterness.

Obviously, the elimination of the Ego revalorizes the Being, producing happiness as a result. Unfortunately, the Consciousness imprisoned within the Ego does not understand, does not comprehend the need for intimate revalorization, and prefers beastly enjoyments because it firmly believes that the latter is happiness.

Dissolve the pluralized "I" and experience the happiness of the revalorization of the Being.

Question: Master, based on everything that you have presented, we feel the evident and unpostponable need to form a Mental Body, in order not to have so many minds.

Answer: I have heard a question from a gentleman and I hasten to answer it.

Certainly, the intellectual animal, mistakenly called man does not possess an individual mind, as we have already said in this lecture. Instead of one mind he has many minds and this is different. What I am affirming can upset pseudo-esotericists and pseudo-occultists quite a bit, who are completely convinced by the theories that they have read, which affirm that the rational homunculus possesses a Mental Body.

Allow us the liberty to dissent from such affirmations. If the intellectual animal had an individual mind, if he truly did not possess those diverse mental aggregates that characterize him, he would have continuity of purpose; everyone would keep their word, no one would affirm today to deny tomorrow. The presumed real estate buyer would return the following day with cash in hand after having given his word, and Earth would be a paradise.

Creating the Mental Body and dissolving the pluralized "I" is urgent when one wants the authentic revalorization of the Intimate Being. Only those sacred revalorizations can grant us true happiness.

Question: Venerable Master is it possible that a person who gives money to the church, who reads the Bible, who goes to confession, who does charitable works in institutions, who spreads the Gospel, who only has his own wife and other virtues, can also have "I's?"

Answer: Distinguished ladies and gentlemen, allow me to inform you that the "I" disguises itself as a saint, as a martyr, as an apostle, as a good husband, as a good wife, as a mystic, as a penitent, as an anchorite, as a splendid charity worker, etc.

Between the cadence of verse crime also hides, among the perfumes of the temple crime hides, under the shadow of the cross adultery and fornication are committed, and the worst abject criminals take on pietistic poses, sublime figures, martyr-like expressions, etc.

It is good to know that many virtuous people possess very strong psychic aggregates. Remember that there is a great deal of virtue within the wicked, and a great deal of evil within the virtuous.

In the Abyss, in the nine Dantean Circles, there are many mystics, anchorites, penitents who believe that they are doing very well. Do not be surprised then, that in the Avernus there are also exemplary priests and devotees who follow them.

Question: Master, what becomes of the spiritual value inherent in the good intentions of a sincere person who lives mistakenly?

Answer: Very good friends of mine, I find the question from the audience very interesting and I am pleased to answer.

Remember that the path that leads to the Abyss is paved with good intentions; many are called and few are chosen.

The wicked of all times have had good intentions. Hitler, filled with magnificent intentions, trampled upon many peoples and because of him millions of persons died in gas chambers or in concentration camps or in front of firing squads or in filthy underground prison cells.

Undoubtedly, this monster wanted triumph for great Germany, and he spared no effort whatsoever in this regard.

Nero burned Rome for the sake of his art, with mystical intentions of making the lyre resound universally and he threw the Christians into the Roman circuses so that the lions would devour them with the desire of liberating his people from what he considered an epidemic or a calamity: Christianity.

The executioner that fulfills an unjust command, full of magnificent intentions, murders his fellowman.

Millions of heads fell under the guillotine during the French Revolution and the headsmen worked with magnificent intentions because they wanted the triumph of the people.

Robespierre, filled with magnificent intentions, led many innocent people to the scaffold.

We must not forget what the Holy Inquisition was. Then the inquisitors, with magnificent intentions, condemned many wretches to the stake, to the torture rack, to agony.

I want you then, ladies and gentlemen, to comprehend that what is important are good deeds and not good intentions that could be more or less mistaken.

The Lords of Karma in the Tribunals of Objective Justice, judge the souls on their deeds, on clear, definitive and concrete actions, and not on good intentions.

The results are always what count. It is useless to have good intentions if the actions are disastrous.

Question: Master, what is the procedure to follow to liberate ourselves from the psychological defects that so torment our mind?

Answer: Honorable audience, it is urgent, undeferrable and unpostponable to annihilate the Ego, to reduce it to ashes in a voluntary and conscious manner, if we truly want to avoid the descent into the Infernal Worlds.

I want you to know that in relations with people, when interacting with our relatives or with our fellow workers, etc., etc., the hidden defects spontaneously emerge, and if we are in a state of alert perception, alert novelty, then we see them just as they are in themselves.

A discovered defect must be judiciously submitted to analysis, to in-depth meditation, with the purpose of comprehending it in a unitotal, integral manner...

It is not enough to comprehend a defect; one has to go even deeper. It is indispensable to self-explore ourselves, to find the intimate roots of the defect that we have comprehended, until attaining its deep meaning.

Any spark of Consciousness can immediately illuminate us, and in millionths of a second truly capture the deep meaning of the comprehended defect.

Elimination is different. Someone could have comprehended some psychological error and may have penetrated its deep meaning, and nonetheless continue with it in the different levels of the mind. It is not possible to be free from such and such an error without elimination.

The latter is vital, cardinal and definitive when one wants to die from instant to instant, from moment to moment.

Nonetheless, it is not with the mind that we can extirpate errors. By means of our understanding we can label our diverse psychological defects, give them different names, juggle them from one level to another in the subconscious, hide them from ourselves, judge them, excuse them, etc., etc., but it is not possible to fundamentally alter them nor to extirpate them.

What is needed is a power superior to the mind; we need to appeal to a transcendental power, if we really want to eliminate errors and die in ourselves here and now.

Fortunately, such a superior power is found latent in all human creatures. I want to refer to the Kundalini, the Igneous Serpent of our Magical Powers.

During full chemical copulation, we can beg our particular Divine Mother to eliminate the psychological error that we have not only comprehended but we have also felt its profound significance.

You can be sure that our particular Cosmic Mother, wielding the spear of Eros, will mortally wound the psychic aggregate that personifies the error that we need to eliminate.

It is precisely with this Holy Staff, a marvelous emblem for creative energy, the weapon with which Devi Kundalini will eliminate from us, here and now, the defect that we want to annihilate.

Naturally, the elimination of these aggregates is done in a progressive manner, since many of them process in the 49 levels of the subconscious.

This means that any psychological defect is represented by thousands of psychic aggregates that are begotten and developed in the 49 subconscious levels of the mind.

Someone might not be a fornicator in the intellectual zone, and nonetheless be one in the more profound zones of the subconscious.

Many mystics who were extremely chaste in the merely intellective level, and even in 20 or 30 subconscious levels, failed in more profound levels when they were subjected to esoteric tests.

Someone might not be a thief in the merely rational level and even within 48 subconscious levels, and nonetheless be a thief in level 49. So, the defects are multifaceted, and very holy individuals can be frightfully perverse in the deepest levels of the subconscious.

By means of esoteric tests the Initiates self-discover themselves. Failures in the tests point to, indicate, the diverse psychological states in which we find ourselves.

Question: Venerable Master, can you tell us how we who are single can do this work?

Answer: Distinguished ladies and gentlemen, the spear of Eros, the Holy Staff, can always be handled by Devi-Kundalini, our particular Cosmic Divine Mother.

Nevertheless, there is a difference between married and single people. When the Staff is handled during the sexual trance, it has a marvelous electrical power that is more superior.

When the spear is not utilized during the erotic trance, it possesses a marvelous power that is inferior.

Single men and single women can also progress, even though their work will be a little slower; however, when they get married, their work will become stronger, more powerful in the complete sense of the word.

Single men and single women can progress to a certain point that is profoundly defined by nature; beyond this limit, it is not possible to progress without Sexual Magic.

16

THE DEVIL

Friends of mine gathered tonight, December 18, 1972, in the tenth year of Aquarius; we enter into the second part of our dissertations.

Much has been said about the Devil, quite a lot has been written on the topic, but few have actually explained it.

The origin of this myth must be sought in the initiatic crypts of the past and in archaic caverns.

Let us reflect for a moment upon what the Sun is. Unquestionably, the king star illuminates us and gives us life, however, it contrasts with darkness.

Any midday, however resplendent it may be, has its shadows, be it under the leafy trees of the solitary road, within the grottos of the mountains, or simply below any mobile or immobile body.

Each one of us projects our shadow, here, there and everywhere.

Light and shadow, in harmonious antithesis, outline a complete duality whose extraordinary synthesis is wisdom.

Let us now go a little bit further. Let us go deeper into the profoundness, into the unknown of our Being.

We know that beyond the body, the affections and the mind, there is the inner divine Logoi ... Unquestionably, that which is ineffable, that which is Real, projects its own reflection, its particular shadow, within ourselves here and now.

Undoubtedly, the intimate Sun of each one of us also has its shadow, and it fulfills a specific mission within the very depths of our own Consciousness.

Obviously, such a shadow, that Logoic reflection, is the psychological trainer, Lucifer, the tempter...

In the psychological gymnasium of human existence, a trainer is always required whose purpose is the development of powers, faculties, extraordinary virtues, etc., etc., etc.

How could virtues spring forth in us, if temptation did not exist?

Only through struggle, through contrast, through temptation and rigorous esoteric discipline can the flowers of virtue spring forth from within us.

Therefore, the Devil is not that tenebrous personage created by the dogmatism of some dead sects, and against whom the Marquis of Merville was to cast all of his anathemas. Nor is the Devil that fabulous entity that deserved to be forgiven, as written by Giovanni Papini in his famous book entitled *The Devil*, a work which resulted in the excommunication of this compassionate writer. We all know very well that Giovanni Papini was the spoiled child of the Vatican; nonetheless in the time of Pius XII he was disqualified...

Ladies and gentlemen: Satan, Lucifer, the Devil, is much more than all of this; it is the reflection of our own intimate Being in ourselves and within our Consciousness, here and now.

Examining old mythologies from ancient times, we come to clearly render evidence that this satanic myth was divulged in all of the corners of the world by the priests of the heliolithic or heliocentric religion, which was definitely universal before.

Let us remember that there were eras in the past when Temples to the Sun and to the Dragon were built everywhere, in all places of the planet Earth. Then, Dragonian Cults existed, and the sacerdotes of that universal religion called themselves Children of the Dragon, or simply qualified themselves as Dragons.

The symbol of the Dragon was taken from those gigantic flying reptiles that existed in the era of Atlantis and Lemuria. It is interesting that such a symbol has been used to allegorize every shadow of the Sun, every reflection of the king star, including the particular intimate Lucifer of every human being.

In the Egypt of the Pharaohs, the Midday Sun, the Sacred Absolute Sun, was always symbolized by Osiris, while his shadow, his reflection, his Lucifer, is allegorized by Typhon.

In the Greek Mysteries, the Spiritual Sun, the Star of Christmas, the Demiurge Creator, was always represented by Apollo, while his shadow, his Lucifer, his Satan, his divine reflection, was definitely allegorized by Python.

In the *Book of Revelation* by St. John, the resplendent Christ Sun is always symbolized by Michael, the warrior divinity, while his cosmic shadow is personified by the Red Dragon.

In the Middle Ages, the Logos was allegorized with the personality of St. George, while his shadow is symbolized by the Dragon.

Let us observe what are Bel and Dragon, the Sun and its shadow, day and night.

The Devil, then, is not that personage that some dead sects have seated on a throne of ignominy in order to frighten the weak. With good reason Goethe placed in the mouth of his God that phrase with which the divinity addressed Mephistopheles:

"Of all of your species, genius rebels to my Law, the least harmful and prejudicial is you."

Much has been said about the satanic myth, and some suppose that it reached the Western world from the land of Egypt.

We do not deny in any manner that many Solar Gods with their corresponding Dragons originating in Hindustan arrived to the land of the Pharaohs; nor do we deny that the allegory of Osiris and Typhon was to be portrayed in old Europe; nevertheless, we go even further. We have the right to think of the Hyperboreans and their Solar Cults, together with their Dragons and Infernos.

Pre-Vedic India was not the only one exclusively to send its Solar Gods and their cults to Egypt. Beyond all doubt, submerged Atlantis also left in the country of Sais and on the banks of the Nile, archaic cults to the Sun and its Dragons.

To defeat the Dragon, to kill the Dragon, is urgent when one wants to be swallowed by the Serpent, when one wishes to be transformed into a Serpent.

This means coming out triumphant in all of the temptations placed by the Dragon, to come out victorious, to eliminate the Ego, to disintegrate all the psychic aggregates that constitute it, to reduce to cosmic dust all the memories of desire, etc., etc.

Indubitably, after having been devoured by the Serpent we are transformed into Serpents. Thereafter, the Eagle, the Third Logos, the Arch-Hierophant and Arch-magus, our Real Being, the Secret Master, swallows the Serpent. Then we are converted into Feathered Serpents, into the Mexican Quetzalcoatl, into the Mahatma and the Work is done.

Upon arriving to these transcendental heights of the Being, to these intimate revalorizations, the reflection of the Logos, his particular shadow within ourselves, the Devil, returns to the Logos, commixes with Him, fuses with Him, because deep inside He is He...

Question: Master, if I have to forget even the memories of desire, what stimulus will I utilize in order to work in the Lit Forge of Vulcan?

Answer: I will gladly answer this question coming from the audience...

The Sacred Scriptures emphatically affirm that first is the animal and then the Spiritual.

Indubitably, when the work in the Forge of the Cyclops begins, desire —*"istu"* in Sanskrit— is needed, because the profound revalorizations of the Being have not yet been fulfilled.

It would be impossible to demand Maithuna, Transcendental Sexology, Sex-Yoga or Kundalini-Yoga, with the radical exclusion of desire from beginners. However, later on with the dissolution of the Psychological "I," it is unquestionable that the factor desire becomes unnecessary. The reason: once every subconscious animal agent is eliminated, desire cannot radically exist.

Upon arriving to these transcendental heights of the Being, we can work in the Ninth Sphere exclusively with the force of Eros, with the power of the Sexual Hydrogen Si-12, with the transcendental electricity of the zoosperms.

Therefore, my friends, in the final analysis, desire is not indispensable for the work in the Lit Forge of Vulcan.

Question: Beloved Master, given that Satan is the reflection of God, consequently Satan is love, then wouldn't it be incongruent to state that the Ego is Satanic?

Answer: Distinguished gentleman, friends, ladies, remember that there are two types of darkness: the first we shall call darkness of silence and of the august secret of the sages; the second we shall qualify as darkness of ignorance and error.

Obviously, the first is super-darkness. Indubitably, the second is infra-darkness.

This means that darkness bipolarizes, and that the negative is only the unfoldment of the positive.

By means of simple inductive logic, I invite you to comprehend that Prometheus-Lucifer, chained to the solid rock, sacrificing himself for us, subjected to all the tortures, even if he is the needle of the scales, the giver of Light, the measure and the weight, the guardian of the Seven Mansions that does not allow anyone to enter but those who have been anointed by Wisdom and who hold in their right hand the lamp of Hermes, inevitably unfolds into the fatal aspect of the egotistic multiplicity, into those sinister psychic aggregates that constitute our "I," and which have been properly studied by Tantric Buddhist Esotericism.

Gentlemen, with this explanation I gather that you have understood my words.

Question: Master, if the practice of Maithuna-Yoga exists since time immemorial, why then are complicated erotic stimuli offered to the public eye as bas-reliefs on the very temples in Vedantic India? It seems to me that such stimuli make the practice of Maithuna even more difficult.

Answer: With great pleasure I will give precise response to the question that a distinguished esotericist gentleman has formulated with complete clarity...

Certainly, in the Hindu *Kama-Kalpa* there is a tantric photograph of a sacred sculpture that exists in a very ancient temple. I want to emphatically refer now to that work of Sexual Magic...

If we carefully observe the photograph of the cited Hindustani book, we will see a woman in Siddhasana: her head is down, and legs upwards, with the particularity that these are not in the lotus figure, but opened from right to left, even though her knees are bent, leaving the lower part of the legs horizontal; the head is supported upon the hands and forearms, as this sacred asana is known in the world of Yoga.

What is most interesting is the following: a magician, practically sitting between her legs with the phallus forcibly introduced within her uterus, is practicing the Maithuna.

Undoubtedly, this tantric woman could not remain in that position, with the head downwards, if two other women were not helping her to the right and to the left.

One can clearly see a pair of young women helping to hold the body of the female yogini. These female assistants, semi-nude, feel terrible lust, and this can be clearly seen in their eyes.

The mage enjoys himself while caressing the breasts of one and of the other, while keeping his phallus connected to the feminine yoni.

Indubitably, this complicated and difficult tantric practice, among four persons, is unnecessary and totally rejected by the Universal White Brotherhood.

It is not superfluous to remind the audience that these complicated sexual practices carried out by more than two persons certainly correspond to Black Tantrism, and this can be evidenced when we study the sinister teachings of the Dag-Dugpa clan, in the Church of the Red Cap Sacerdotes, in the region of the Himalayas in Eastern Tibet.

It is obvious that the Adepts of the Yellow Church, White Tantrists, or True Urdhvareta Yogis, only practice the Sahaja Maithuna in accordance with the mandates of the Gnostic Church —sexual union of husband and wife in legitimately constituted homes.

Therefore, the sexual act or Maithuna between more than two persons, as it has been portrayed by the *Kama Kalpa*, is unquestionably Black Magic.

Obviously, Left Tantrism is different from White Tantrism, and this illustration from the *Kama Kalpa* is manifestly sinister and tenebrous; it could never be accepted by the White Tantric Initiation of the Yellow Buddhist Church.

There is no doubt that the multiple asanas of the Black Tantrics, instead of awakening the Kundalini or sacred Prana to make it ascend through the spinal cord, stimulate and develop the Abominable Kundabuffer Organ, then the aspirant transforms himself into a tenebrous personality, into a Black Mage of the worst kind.

We are not unfamiliar with the *Kama Sutra* and the *Kama Kalpa*. Unfortunately, the *former* has been adulterated in a shameful way in order for it to be widely known in the Western world, and regarding the latter, it has been tainted with black tantras or sadhanas of the dugpas.

Let my affirmations be corroborated, may they be clearly verified through previous study of Buddhist canons and occult secret books in subterranean crypts of Central Asia.

Given that I am an Adept and that I am in direct contact with the Masters of the White Lodge, such as K.H., Morya, Hilarion, etc., it is clear that I can make these clarifications in a completely conscious and precise manner.

Question: Master, how could we differentiate when Lucifer is acting in us and when the Ego is acting in us?

Answer: I will answer this question with great pleasure... We have already spoken clearly of the Luciferian Super-Darkness and of the Infra-Darkness of ignorance and error.

Lucifer, the tempter, the great trainer in the psychological gymnasium of existence, works by tempting us, and these internal impressions tend to polarize negatively or fatally by means of egotistical activity.

Indubitably, it is only by means of serene self-reflection and profound inner meditation that we can make a clear differentiation between direct Luciferian intimate impressions and bestial egotistical impressions.

Normally, people with sleeping Consciousness are not duly prepared to make such a differentiation of impressions. This requires a lot of psychological training.

Question: Master, the Devil is always allegorized with the trident. Does this symbol have some special significance?

Answer: This question from the audience reminds me of the trident of the mind that is used by the Brahmins of India and Pakistan. However, we go even further: we reach the Three Primary Forces of the universe, allegorized by the trident. It is clear that by defeating the Dragon we can crystallize these Three Forces within ourselves, and then we transform, in fact, into true Solar Gods.

Is not the Dragon the reflection of the Sun? Comprehend then what the trident represents.

Question: Beloved Master, when we are working with Lucifer in the Ninth Sphere in order to eliminate the Ego, are we doing so with the positive as well as negative forces of Lucifer?

Answer: Distinguished gentleman, ladies, Lucifer is obviously the ladder to descend and the ladder to ascend, and the power to work and dissolve the Ego in the laboratory of sexual Alchemy.

Unquestionably, it is only by means of the luciferian Fire that we can reduce to ashes the negative crystallizations of our psyche, the infrahuman elements, the psychic aggregates, the wretched deviations of the luciferian force. This is how, friends, the transcendent Fohat, the sexual electricity, the marvelous power of Christ-Lucifer, redeems, works, disintegrates what is useless, in order to liberate the Essence, the Consciousness, the Buddhata.

17

THE DRAGON OF DARKNESS

My friends, gathered here tonight after the Christmas of 1972, we are going to talk a little bit about the Dragon of Darkness.

Remember that these Teachings will constitute the Christmas Message of 1973-1974.

Indubitably, today, this matter of the Devil stirs public opinion quite a lot, and therefore it is necessary to clarify, to indicate, to point out with precision, the crude satanic realism.

Frankly, I do not believe in that Devil of dogmatic religions, and I think that you also would not accept that fetish of the profane clergy.

It is obvious that in Atlantis, before the second transalpalnian catastrophe, a flying reptile of a rather Neptunian type and full of scales existed in the land of Mu.

The Chaldeans always wanted to symbolize the darkness of the night, the reflection of the Logos in the universe and within each one of us, with the famous Atlantean amphibian.

H.P. B. conceptualizes such a creature is Makara, the tenth sign of the Zodiac; however, we go a little bit further on this point, because I am firmly convinced that that mysterious creature specifically, is of a completely Neptunian type.

In any case, the Scaly One, the flying reptile of the Chaldeans, was later taken by the Jews and, I repeat, by the Christians... The most regrettable thing in this matter is that this allegory or symbol has been converted into that frightening and horrifying figure of the orthodox Devil.

It is now good to remember the Gnostic community of the Naassenes, worshippers of the Serpent. The Adepts of that Order symbolized the Dragon or reflection of the Logos by the brilliant constellation of seven stars. I am referring emphatically, clearly and precisely to the constellation of the Dragon.

Some suppose that John, the seer of the *Book of Revelation* is the author of that allegory. Such a supposition is, in fact, mistaken because the Dragon belongs to Neptune, to Atlantean Magic...

The seven stars of the constellation of the Dragon stand out in the hand of the Alpha and Omega, that Verb of the *Book of Revelation* that appeared to John.

It is, then, the Dragon, Prometheus-Lucifer, Satan or the Devil, in its superior aspect is the Logos itself, the "born by itself", the Hindu Aja. In its inferior aspect, it is the esoteric, authentic and legitimate Dragon or Devil, different from that of dogmatic orthodoxy. Every Hierophant, every true Self-Realized one is a Dragon of Wisdom.

Therefore, my friends, I want you to comprehend what that dogmatic fetish or fantastic orthodox Devil is, and what the reflection of the Logos truly is, the shadow of God within each one of us, the real Devil, or Lucifer, or sacred Prometheus.

I feel that deep down inside of you, in your own subconscious, there is some resistance, due to the education you received and the mistaken ideas that you all have had about the Devil until now.

I am not at all surprised by this prejudice that conditions your intellect. You were taught to believe in a terrible Devil, seated on a throne of ignominy, with a steel fork in his right hand, dominating the entire world. And now it is clear that upon hearing my words, upon telling you that the Devil of the dogmatic sects is a mere fantasy, that he does not exist and that what truly exists is the Devil of the good Law, the shadow of the Spiritual Sun inside each one of us, the shadow of the night by opposition to the day, the shadow of the trees on the side of the road, etc., it is obvious that it moves you and even surprises you...

But without leaving behind that apprehension proper of a false belief that was instilled in you from the first years of childhood, how could the shadow of the Eternal Living God be bad? Please, reflect on this a little...

In the British Museum, there is a representation of the Scaly One, which is certainly very interesting. In the mentioned museum, there is also a very ancient, archaic painting, where the Tree of Science of Good and Evil appears, the apple tree of Eden...

Interestingly, close to this tree, we can see Adam and Eve in the painting, the man and the woman, trying to get the apples with the purpose of devouring them. Behind the trunk of that tree is the Dragon-Serpent, and up above in the clouds, some beings appear, cursing the tree, living representation of all exoteric or profane clergy, who do not know about the Sexual Mysteries.

There is no doubt then that the two human beings, man-woman, are before the Tree of Science of Good and Evil.

The Serpent-Dragon is the initiator, and one must know how to profoundly understand this.

I am going to explain this frankly to you, I am going to say what all of this is, so that you understand and march with firmness on the strait and difficult Path that leads the Initiate to Final Liberation.

Unquestionably, the Serpent is the sexual fire that must ascend through the spinal canal degree by degree up to the brain.

Naturally, this igneous element possesses extraordinary powers, thus when it ascends through the dorsal spine, it transforms us radically.

Regarding the Dragon, he is indubitably the most extraordinary psychological trainer that each one of us carries within.

The divine Daemon, cited many times by Socrates, the very shadow of our individual Spirit, leads us into temptations with the purpose of training, educating us; only in this manner is it possible for the precious gems of virtues to spring forth in our psyche. Now, I ask myself and I ask you: where is the evilness of Lucifer? The results speak for themselves: if there is no temptation, there are no virtues; the stronger the temptations, the greater the virtues will be. The important thing is to not fall into temptation, and for this, we must pray to the Father saying: Do not let me fall into temptation...

Seeing then these two aspects that hide behind the Tree of Science of Good and Evil, we reach the logical conclusion that the Dragon and the Serpent, or the Serpent-Dragon, to speak in synthesis, is without a doubt the great practical initiator.

We have given the key many times and we will not get tired of repeating it to satiety: the connection of the phallus and the uterus without ejaculating the semen. Only in this way is the Sacred Fire of sex put into motion, which by rising itself through the spinal column, degree by degree, from vertebra to vertebra, finally comes to transform us radically.

That the Dragon tempts us during the work? It is his duty... He must make us strong; he must educate us in the sexual gymnasium; he must convert us into athletes of Sexual Magic.

Much later, the Igneous Serpent of our Magical Powers must swallow us, and then we will, in fact, be transformed into Serpents...

However, before that extraordinary event, before that banquet of the Serpentine Fire, we must defeat the Dragon, that is, we must triumph over temptation...

In the end, the Scaly One, Lucifer, the shadow of the Eternal One, the intimate reflection of our true divine Being, will return to Him, will fuse with Him, will shine within Him...

Upon reaching this level, we will be able exclaim with the ancient Initiates: "I am a Dragon, I am He, He, He...!"

Question: Master, does the divine Daemon tempt us only in the work with sex or also in the work of the dissolution of the Ego?

Answer: Distinguished lady, it is urgent for you to understand that the root of the Ego is found in sexual abuse, in lust, in fornication, in adultery... If we take away the roots of a tree, it is clear that the latter will die. Something similar occurs to the Ego.

Unfortunately, Lucifer must educate us in sex. There, we must submit ourselves to a rigorous training through the most severe temptations. It is clear that if there, in sex, we come out victorious, the disintegration of the Ego is inevitably precipitated.

I do not want to say with this that we must not work on all the psychological defects with the purpose of reducing them to ashes; I am only putting a certain emphasis on the sexual aspect, given that the original sin is found in fornication.

Question: Venerable Master, I have heard that in one of the Gospels the Great Kabir Jesus said: you are sons of Satan, but not sons of God. *Can you explain this to us?*

Answer: Distinguished gentleman, I hear your question and with the greatest pleasure I hasten to answer...

Obviously, all of us are sons of the Dragon, of Satan, of the Devil, of Darkness.

If someone wants to become a Son of God, he must defeat the Dragon, the tempter, the Scaly One. Then we will have transformed into Sons of God and into Dragons of Wisdom.

Nevertheless, the Great Kabir Jesus never cursed his shadow. In none of the Four Gospels has it been said that Jesus extended his right hand to curse his own shadow.

When Jesus, the Great Gnostic Sacerdote, was tempted by Satan, he only exclaimed: *"Satan, Satan, it is written: 'You shall not tempt the Lord, thy God, and you will obey only Him...'"* It is thus clarified that Satan, Lucifer-Prometheus, must obey God. His duty is to tempt the Initiate; it would be absurd for the shadow of the Eternal One to tempt the Eternal One, or in other words, for the Devil to tempt God.

It is clearly seen in the words of the Great Kabir Jesus, that Lucifer is the minister of the Highest, the guardian of the Seven Mansions, the servant of Divinity.

Those, who anathematize the shadow of the eternal living God, are obviously anathematizing the same God because God and his shadow are one, understood?

Question: Master, could it be that the Devil of dogmatic orthodoxy with his horns, tail, and trident, exists in reality as a representation of the psychic aggregates that constitute the Ego?

Answer: Distinguished gentleman, I have already said in past lectures that we must make a clear differentiation between what is the divine Daemon and what is the Ego. Undoubtedly, the Ego in itself, with all its psychic aggregates, is perverted Astral Light, malignant mind; it has nothing to do with Lucifer. It is rather his antithesis, his fatal opposite.

Question: Master, I understand that the divine Daemon and the Ego are totally different, but since it is formed by the Red Devils of Seth, I believe that the Devil with the trident that we all know could well represent the Ego. Don't you think so?

Answer: Distinguished gentleman, the basis of your question is mistaken; it is founded on an error, on a prejudice. I don't know why, ladies and gentlemen, there has been a desire to convert a flying reptile of ancient Atlantis into a malignant fetish.

Therefore, I do not think that it is correct that such an error serve as the basis for a question; I do not agree that a poor, innocent amphibian has to forcibly represent the perversity of the Ego.

I agree that such a reptile symbolizes the shadow of the Eternal, but that it allegorizes our psychological defects frankly seems incongruent to me.

We could very well allegorize the Ego in any other form; let us recall the classical Three Furies, or the Medusa, etc. We can symbolize the Ego and its psychic aggregates with these classical figures.

Question: Master, the Catholic religion, for example, does not put the Dragon as the Devil, but represents him as a man with horns, tail, hooves, and trident. What can you tell me about this?

Answer: Here in the audience, I see a lady that has asked a very interesting question, and it is clear that I will answer it with complete clarity.

Ladies and gentlemen, this Devil of the Catholic religion is nothing more than a deviation from the same pictorial Dragon of the Chaldeans, inspired by a poor flying reptile from the Atlantean continent.

I invite you to comprehend that this innocent animal was later painted in the form of a Dragon, and finally, in the most recent figure as that fetish with hooves, horns, and black wings that terrifies the ignorants so much. It is necessary to cast aside ignorance, to inquire, to investigate, to study...

Question: Venerable Master, when we talk about the Tree of Science of Good and Evil, what does evil really mean and what does good mean?

Answer: This question that comes from the audience seems very interesting to me, and I am pleased to answer ...

Friends, I want you to know that "good", in the most objective sense of the word, is all that we do consciously and in accordance with the Great Law; "evil" is all that causes us remorse after it is done.

Question: Master, there are many people who although they do evil, do not feel any remorse. Can you tell us why?

Answer: Distinguished lady, your question deserves to be examined carefully. First of all, what is remorse?

If the transcendental aspects of our intimate Being confront themselves with our own Logoi or with the Sacred Absolute Sun, then we can verify the psychological errors of the inferior parts of our psyche for ourselves and this causes remorse in us.

Normally, the mentioned process, what I have just said, takes places in all normal beings; although these in the physical world ignore it radically, anyway they feel remorse after a bad action.

The fate of the decidedly perverse is very different. The latter, given that they have already distanced themselves too far from the Sacred Absolute Sun due to their evil deeds, it is clear that deep down inside them such processes no longer take place, and consequently remorse becomes impossible.

Question: Master, you have explained to us that the Dragon of Darkness is in synthesis the great trainer in the gymnasium of life that we must defeat in order to create virtues. But when defeating the Dragon, what we are doing is decapitating the Ego, and since the work with the Igneous Serpent of our Magical Powers –who is undoubtedly our Divine Mother– is of primary importance in this process, I cannot avoid relating the Dragon of Darkness with our Divine Mother, in other words, with Devi-Kundalini. Is this incongruent?

Answer: I hear the question and I am going to answer with greatest pleasure.

Ladies and gentlemen, in this moment I am going to bring up once again the Chaldean painting of the British Museum: behind the Tree of Science of Good and Evil the Dragon-Serpent appears, that is, the great effective and practical initiator.

Obviously, the Dragon only represents the Serpent, and this is unquestionable.

It is said that we must defeat the Dragon or kill the Dragon; symbolical affirmation of the triumph over temptation.

As we are trained and educated, as the precious gems of virtues progressively glow within the depths of our Soul, the Ego begins dissolving, and this is indisputable, irrefutable.

In any case, we must defeat the Dragon to be devoured by the Serpent. Blissful is the one who transforms into a Serpent.

Question: Master, could the inner Dragon drastically perform a miracle? For example, do something spectacular with the purpose of correcting someone.

Answer: My friends, a story comes to mind in these moments, quite interesting by the way, from a Gnostic brother in Costa Rica.

The narrator tells us that in a town of his country an unusual and unsuspected event occurred.

It involved a lady prostitute. She would get incessantly drunk on all types of alcoholic beverages and in the midst of her drinking spree, she would exclaim, "I can possess ten or fifteen men a day and every man who crosses my path, I possess and if the Devil crossed my path, I would possess him, too...!"

On a certain occasion a sailor arrived at her door, he had a handsome appearance. That woman did not have any inconvenience in romping with him in the bed of Procrustes...

After the fornication, that woman sitting at the door of the brothel looked into the street... Suddenly, the young lad called her from inside, saying:

"You do not know me. Turn around and look at me so that you can get to know me."

The wretched woman, obeying the instructions of the lover, got up to go back into the abominable bedroom, and upon looking at the one who had been her instrument of pleasure, saw something horrifying, terrible and tenebrous.

The Scaly One, disguised in the manner that the orthodoxy of the Roman Catholicism gave him, stared at her fixedly, while a strong smell of sulfur filled the place...

The prostitute was not able to resist and she fell unconscious to the floor, emitting at the same time some shrill screams ... When the neighbours heard the screams, they came to help her, but the smell of sulfur made them run away terrified.

Later on, the wretched woman after having narrated at the hospital what had happened, died on the third day; the Devil took her away.

The narrator tells us that the smell of sulfur persisted for some time in the brothel, and for that reason, people avoided passing by the street where that house was located.

By judiciously analyzing this story, we discover practically an operation of moral asepsis; a method of urgency taken by the woman's own inner Lucifer.

There is no doubt that her intimate God commanded his shadow, his Lucifer, his particular inner Dragon, to materialize in that shape before the wretched woman, to become visible and tangible before her, and then to even copulate with her....

Obviously, her divine inner Sun could not have carried out that copulation, that apparition, but his particular shadow, since it is polarized negatively with regards to the positive light, could clearly and manifestly carry out all of this concretely.

The outcome will be marvellous later on. The wretched woman died filled with terror, and when she returns to reincorporate, when she is reborn in this world, when she takes on a new body, it will be very difficult for her to return to prostitution; that terror, that psychic "shock" has remained in the Consciousness.

So, most likely in her future existence she will decide to walk on the Right Path, on the path of chastity.

This is how the Dragon can work and operate drastically at a given moment.

18

SUBTERRANEAN CRYPTS

Today I see with joy a very select group of gnostic visitors, who came to Mexico after having attended the International Gnostic Congress in the Republic of El Salvador...

We are going to continue with our lectures and I hope that all of you will get the utmost benefits from them.

After this preamble, let us enter the topic that concerns us today.

In ancient Chaldea and in Egypt there were marvellous catacombs, subterranean crypts where the Mysteries were cultivated.

It is good to remember the crypts from Thebes and Memphis – unquestionably, the former ones were even more renowned.

From the occidental side of the Nile there were, in those times, large profound passages that reached the Libyan Desert. In those crypts the secrets related to the *Kuklos Anankes*, the inevitable cycle, the circle of necessity, were cultivated.

In these moments as we are talking about this, the Temple of Serpents in San Juan, Teotihuacan comes to mind.

The esoteric investigator can see there the rattlesnake in detail, chiselled on the rock and the most amazing thing of all this is that beside the sacred Viper of the Aztec Mysteries, the Conch, carved on the living rock also stands out.

Various Conchs shine beautifully on each side of the divine Serpent.

There is no doubt that in the subterranean crypts of Chaldea, Thebes and Memphis the Wisdom of the Serpent was truly cultivated.

The transcendental study of the inevitable cycle or circle of necessity, which processes itself in a spiraloid or conch form during Cosmic Manifestation, is also very well-established.

So, observe dear Gnostic brothers who accompany me tonight, the intimate relationship that always exists between the Serpent and the Conch. Reflect for a moment on the profound significance that both the Serpent and the Conch intrinsically possess.

Obviously, the Serpent is the transcendental sexual power, the marvellous power that brings us to existence, the force that originates all life.

Any authentic esotericist knows very well that the sexual Serpentine Power of the entire universe has power over the tattvas and therefore over the Elementals of nature.

The universal Serpentine Power originates infinite creations; Devi-Kundalini creates the Mental, the Astral, the Etheric and the Physical Body.

Now then, Maha-Kundalini, or in other words, the Cosmic Mother, Mother Nature, has created the entire universe, has taken the shape of the world.

Obviously, she has also realized all her processes based on the spiraloide line, so vividly allegorized by the Conch.

Any internal progress, any inner development, is based on the spiral of life.

Therefore, speaking in a personal way, we can say that each one of us is a bad conch within the bosom of the Father.

Every soul is given or assigned 108 existence for its Self-Realization, and these are processed in spirals, sometimes higher, sometimes lower; therein is the Conch.

But, let us go a bit deeper, dear brothers who are attending our lecture tonight. We are going to study the *Kuklos Anankes*, the inevitable cycle or circle of necessity.

The concrete fact that this profound subject-matter was studied solely in these subterranean crypts is very interesting.

Undoubtedly, this is the same Doctrine of the Transmigration of Souls that the Avatar Krishna taught later on in Hindustan.

However, it is noteworthy that the Egyptian *Kuklos Anankes* was even more specific...

We have already said a lot, we have already affirmed in these lectures, what the descent into the Infernal Worlds is; we have put certain emphasis by saying that once the cycle of 108 lives assigned to each Soul is completed, if we have not self-realized, we enter the Infernal Worlds.

Obviously in those Submerged Regions, we involute frightfully until reaching the Ninth Circle, situated in the heart of the world. There the lost ones are disintegrated, they are reduced to cosmic dust.

After Second Death —and this is something that we have already said in all our previous lectures–, the failed Soul or Souls resurge, come out under the light of the sun again to restart the journey, starting a new evolution, which inevitably must start from the lowest step, which is the Mineral Kingdom.

The interesting thing about the Egyptian *Kuklos Anankes* is precisely the specifications, the diverse analysis and synthesis.

It is clear that we must take into account the Ray in which each Essence that springs forth from the Abyss develops, and consequently its line of individual development.

Varied are the plant families, varied are the animal species, different are the mineral elements, etc. etc. etc.

The Rectors of Nature cannot make all the Essences that have sprung forth from the Abyss pass through the same mineral element, be it iron, copper, or silver, etc., or through a determined plant family, or through a determined animal species.

The Gurus-Devas must wisely distribute life, because some Essences can live in the iron, others in the copper, others in silver, etc.; not all could pass through the same mineral element.

The plant Elemental Families are very well organized in the Etheric World and not all the Elementals could be pine trees or peppermint plants; each plant Family is different: there are Lunar, Mercurial, Venusian, Solar, Martian, Jupiterian, Saturnine plants, etc. etc. etc.

Each one of the Essences, according to their Ray of Creation, will have to relate with this or that Plant Department, and solving all of this, knowing how to distribute them, is something that corresponds to the Rectors of Nature...

The animal species are very varied, and it would be absurd to reincorporate determined Essences in animal organisms that do not correspond to their Ray of Creation. Certain Essences can evolve in the Kingdom of Birds, others within the quadrupeds, others amongst the fish of the immense sea...

The Rectors of Life must know how to wisely handle these currents of elementals in order to avoid confusions, anarchies, unnecessary destructions.

Finally, the entrance of the currents of life into the Kingdom of Rational Humanoids is very delicate; a lot of wisdom is required to avoid catastrophes.

See then, what this Doctrine of the Transmigration of Souls is, studied in depth by the Egyptians.

Votan also talks to us about a snake hole, which he had the joy of having penetrated.

The relationship between this snake or serpent hole mentioned by Votan here in Mexico, and the crypts of Egypt and Chaldea is well-known.

This serpent or snake hole is nothing more than a subterranean cave, a crypt of Mysteries, where this Great Initiate entered triumphantly...

Votan says that he was able to enter in that serpent hole, inside the interior of Earth, and reach the roots of Heaven because he himself was a Snake, a Serpent.

The Druids from the Britannic Celtic region in Europe also called themselves Serpents.

It is not superfluous to remember the Egyptian Karnak and the Breton Carnac, both are living symbols of the Serpent's mount.

There is no doubt that you, my visiting friends, already know very well what the Serpent is, you already have this information; therefore, it doesn't seem to me that this news is new.

The Hindustanis clearly speak about the Serpent; it has to do with a marvellous sexual electric power, the Sacred Fire that is found hidden in each one of us.

It is undoubtable that this Igneous Power or Serpentine Power really looks like a snake; this is how clairvoyants see it.

From the occult anatomical point of view, I can affirm to you emphatically that it looks like a Serpent of Fire coiled three and a half times within the magnetic centre of the coccyx, the fundamental base of the spinal column.

Sometimes I fear that you have not understood me, but I know that you have read my books and therefore the teaching we are giving tonight should by no means surprise you...

First, we must awaken the Fire and make it ascend through the spinal column up to the brain; only in this way can we transform ourselves radically.

Then —and this is what is most tremendous— we must be swallowed by the Serpent; only in this way can we convert ourselves into Serpents. This is the teaching of Votan; this is the Doctrine of the Mayas and of the Aztecs.

We could never have fruition of the Powers of the Snake without first being swallowed by Her, and this is something that many pseudo-esoteric and pseudo-occult writers unfortunately do not know.

However, I want you to understand that it is not possible to be devoured by the Snake without previously having defeated the Dragon.

I also cite the Dragon in my previous book entitled *The Three Mountains*, but then I was making reference to an abominable monster that every human being carries within, along with the Three Traitors, and which we must inevitably disintegrate in the Lunar Infernos.

Now I am speaking about a different Dragon. I am referring to the reflection of the Logos in each one of us, here and now, the authentic Devil, the Sacred Dragon of the Dracontias, which is not at all wicked or perverse, as ignorant people suppose.

That Red Dragon, that shadow of the Solar Logos within us, that psychological trainer that each one carries within their interior, leads us into the alleys of temptation with the purpose of training us on the path of virtue.

We have already said, and I will not get tired of repeating it to satiety, that without temptation there is no virtue; the stronger the temptations, the greater the virtues if we succeed in coming out victorious. Temptation is fire; triumph over temptation is light. Therefore, let us not look with disdain at Typhon Baphomet, the Devil, because every person carries him within, and he is the shadow of the intimate God.

Remember, brothers, that each Devil is all contrast; the Devil is the shadow of the Sun, the shadow of every tree under the light of the king star, the night, etc., etc., etc.

Looking at this from another angle, considering this matter from another aspect, we could say that as Devil, he is the flip side of any coin. For the tenebrous, for the people who live in the Abyss, for the Demons, the Devil are Angels, Gods, Light, Kindness, Beauty, etc., etc.

If people who live in Light are terrified when they see Demons, it is obvious that Demons are also terrified when they see people who live in Light, when they see Angels, Archangels...

I am speaking about something that I know of for a fact, something that I have been able to live, to experience for myself in a direct way.

Many times, while entering in the Infernal Worlds, I have seen the tenebrous horrified, I have heard them exclaim: "A Demon has gotten in! Let us defend ourselves!" They have certainly felt horror in my presence. I am a White Demon to them, and they are Black Demons to me; therefore, the Devil is a matter of contrasts, of oppositions, etc., etc., etc.

Among the Dracontias, the Dragon was revered, in other words, the shadow of the Logos, the shadow of the Spiritual Sun, its reflection in the universe and within ourselves.

Do not forget that behind this Sun that illuminates us is the Phoenician Elon, or the Jewish Elion, the Central Sun of this universe where we live, move, and have our Being.

It is normal for this Sacred Absolute Sun to have its contrasts and oppositions. In any case, its shadow in us and within us is Lucifer, the great psychological trainer that we have for our own good.

But please, I beg the brothers here that are listening to me to comprehend what I am saying, do not be afraid...

The resistances that are in some of you who are listening to me at this moment are due to the prejudices, the fear, the mistaken information of some dogmatic priests.

All of us as children have received a certain education, and so, negative and prejudicial, erroneous and absurd ideas were inculcated in us.

We were told that Lucifer was a terrible devil that commanded the entire Earth, who took us into an orthodox Inferno to torture us in pots or pans with fire, etc. etc. etc.

I want you, my friends, to know once and for all that the Devil of orthodox religions does not exist; the true Devil is carried by each one in his interior.

In the Middle Ages the Gnostic community of the Satanians existed. That of the Iscariots also existed. The Adepts of those communities were burnt alive at the stake during the Inquisition.

It is a pity that the community of the Satanians cannot now be restored due to the concrete fact that the documentation was destroyed.

The concrete fact that Judas Iscariot, until this date, is really considered as a traitorous disciple also causes certain pain.

If we judiciously analyze what Satan, the Devil, Lucifer is, if we comprehend that he is only the reflection of God within us, the shadow of the intimate Sun within each one, located within the depths of our Soul for our own good, in fact and in its own right, we will be doing justice to that Gnostic community.

Ladies and gentlemen, the orthodox, dogmatic Satan of the clerical sects does not exist. The authentic Lucifer is in each person, and only in this way must it be understood.

Judas Iscariot is another very interesting case. In reality, this Apostle never betrayed Jesus the Christ; he only played a role, and this role was taught to him by his Master Jesus.

The Cosmic Drama, the life, passion, and death of our Lord the Christ, was represented since ancient times by all the Great Avatars.

The Great Lord of Atlantis, before the second transapalnian catastrophe, represented in the flesh the same drama of Jesus of Nazareth. On a certain occasion, a Catholic missionary that arrived in China found the same Cosmic Drama amongst the people of the yellow race: "I believed that we, Christians, were the only ones who knew about this drama!", the missionary exclaimed. Confused, he left the priesthood.

That drama was brought to Earth by the Elohim. Any man that seeks the Intimate Self-Realization of the Being will have to live it, and become the central character of the cosmic scene.

Hence, each one of the twelve Apostles of Jesus of Nazareth had to play their part in the scene. Judas did not want to execute the part chosen for him; he asked for Peter's part, but Jesus had already firmly established the part that each disciple had to symbolize.

The part that Judas played had to be learned by heart, and it was taught to him by his Master.

Judas Iscariot, therefore, never betrayed the Master. The Gospel of Judas is the dissolution of the Ego; without Judas the Cosmic Drama is not possible. This Apostle is, therefore, the most exalted Adept, the most elevated amongst all the Apostles of the Christ Jesus.

Indubitably, each one of the twelve had his own Gospel. We cannot negate Patar, Peter. He is the Hierophant of sex, he who holds the Keys to the Kingdom in his right hand, the great initiator. And what shall we say about Mark, who was to guard the mysteries of the Gnostic Unction with so much love? And what of Philip, that great Enlightened being whose Gospel teaches us how to project in the Astral Body and to travel with the Physical Body in the Jinn state? And what of John, with the Doctrine of the Verb? And what of Paul with the Philosophy of the Gnostics? It would be too long to narrate here everything that is related to the twelve and the Cosmic Drama.

The moment has come to eliminate from our minds ignorance and old religious prejudices! The instant has come to study Christic Esotericism in depth!

Question: Master, with regard to the Demons that supposedly frighten or torment people on the roads, is that true?

Answer: With great pleasure I will answer the question that comes from the audience. When we deny the Devil of dogmatic orthodox, we are not denying the authentic Devil that exists inside of each person; we are also not denying the tenebrous Demons of the Avernus that torment people.

However, we must make a clear differentiation between what the shadow of the Logos is within us –Lucifer– and what the Demons or psychological aggregates are, or Fallen Angels, etc. etc. etc.

Demons exist everywhere, inside and outside of us: Demons are our psychic aggregates; Demons are the psychic aggregates of our fellowmen; Demons are Bael, Moloch, Belial and many millions, billions or trillions more; they exist inevitably and we must fight against them.

Question: Beloved Master, what is the effective manner to defend ourselves from the devils that attack us?

Answer: Friends, there are many ancient conjurations with which it is possible to defend ourselves from the attacks of the tenebrous. Let us remember the Conjuration of the Seven from Solomon the Sage, the Conjuration of the Four, the Pentagram, etc. etc. etc.

In a very special manner, it is good to know that the Pentagram with the superior angle pointing upwards and the two inferior angles pointing downwards, makes the tenebrous flee.

Question: Master, I would like for your excellency to tell me if the Fifth Angel, who comes in war to give the intimate Wisdom of the Being, can liberate and give the great Teaching on Judas Iscariot to humanity.

Answer: Friends who are listening to me tonight, respectable Gnostic lady who has asked this question, in the Middle Ages certain reactionary elements, understanding that Samael, my Real Inner Being, the Fifth of the Seven, teaches revolutionary Occult Wisdom, gave the name of Samael to the shadow of the Logos; that is, they tried to make me fit into their terribly narrow molds.

It is now up to me to unveil, to indicate the Path with clarity, to perform a dissection on many words and concepts, in order to see what truth they hold.

I am not the only Initiate who knows the Mysteries of the Cosmic Drama; neither am I the only one who has the honor of knowing the part of Judas, since we already know that the Gnostic community of the Iscariots existed, who specialized precisely in the Gospel of the Great Master Judas, faithful disciple of our Lord the Christ.

The learned ignoramus, the rascals of the intellect, the followers of many dead sects, struck out against us for the very fact of having disclosed these matters.

However, we fulfil our duty, and with the greatest of pleasures we cast light on darkness, regardless of the cost.

I repeat justice has not been done to Judas, in spite of the fact that he was the most exalted of all the twelve.

What happens is that humanity dislikes horribly eliminating the Ego, and since the Doctrine of Iscariot is precisely against the "I", against the Myself, then the most natural thing is that even the erudite themselves of the diverse pseudo-esoteric and pseudo-occultists schools mortally hate him.

In any case, the Four Gospels cannot be interpreted literally, they are written in code: they have been precisely elaborated by Initiates and for Initiates.

Question: Venerable Master, then, if Judas Iscariot was the most exalted of the disciples of the Great Kabir Jesus, who was the traitor?

Answer: I will answer this question that comes from the audience... Friends and Gnostic brothers who are listening to me: the true traitor of the Christ is inside each one of you.

This means that not only did you betray the Christ but moreover, you betray him daily, from instant to instant, from moment to moment...

The Masonic Brothers know very well who the Three Traitors of Hiram Abiff are: Judas is the Demon of Desire, who betrays the intimate Christ from second to second; Pilate is the Demon of the Mind, who is always giving excuses, justifying himself, washing his hands, declaring himself innocent, etc., etc.; Caiaphas is the Demon of Ill Will —each person carries him deep within— he who does not know how to do the Will of the Father, he who always does what he wants, whatever he feels like doing, who does not give a hoot about the Commandments of the Blessed One.

These Three Traitors murdered Hiram Abiff, the Secret Master.

Jesus, the Great Kabir, before crystallizing within himself the Three Primary Forces of the universe, had to eliminate the intimate Judas, as each one of you must do.

Having understood all this, comprehending that Iscariot only fulfilled a duty obeying his Master and playing a part he had learnt by heart, we must now do justice to this Adept before the solemn verdict of public awareness.

Question: Master, from the beginning of Christianity, the Sacred Bible, known as the book of divine Truth does not mention the Apostles as you denominate them, nor does it teach that Lucifer is the shadow of God. Why should we give more credit to your words than those that are read in the Holy Gospels?

Answer: With greatest of pleasure I am going to answer the question that comes from the audience...

Distinguished gentleman, the Four Gospels were written 400 years after Christ, not by the Apostles, but by the disciples of the Apostles, and as I have already said, they are written in code. They are, indeed, four Treatises of Alchemy and Kabbalah.

Judiciously analyzing the words of the Great Kabir Jesus, we see within them the Chaldean and Egyptian parable; Pythagorean mathematics, and Buddhist moral. Unquestionably, the Great Kabir Jesus travelled through India, Chaldea, Persia, Greece, Egypt etc., etc.

Only those of us who have studied Gnosticism, only those of us who have delved into Cainite, Satanian, Iscariot, Naasenian, Essenian, Pedaticenian Esotericism, etc., etc., etc., know indeed what the Mysteries of Lucifer are, and the part that Judas played, and the part that each one of the Apostles of the Master Jesus had to play in the Cosmic Drama.

It isn't precisely the Bible that is going to explain the part of each one of the twelve.

You must begin, distinguished gentleman, by knowing in depth the esotericism of the twelve Zodiacal Signs, and then let yourself be guided by the study of comparative religions and Gnostic Scriptures.

You will be able to intuit a lot by studying the *Pistis Sophia*. It is a pity that we only find this book in English; however, I hope that one day it will be translated into Spanish.

In any case, we should not study the Bible literally, since it is written in a symbolic manner and only the Initiates can understand it.

I am not the only one who knows all of these Mysteries, but I am the first to unveil them, to make them public for the good of humanity.

Question: Master, please do me the favor of explaining to us why Peter denied the Christ three times.

Answer: I will most gladly answer this question. It is said that Peter denied the Christ three times, and it is good to know its significance. Obviously, this is completely symbolic. Through this we are meant to understand that the Initiate falls into temptation again and again, whether in the physical world or in the Internal Worlds, and he weeps and suffers the unspeakable, but if he perseveres, if he is firm, if he finally eliminates the Ego and reduces it to cosmic dust, he then converts into a Master and reaches Intimate Self-Realization.

19

WAR IN THE HEAVENS

My friends, ladies and gentlemen who are listening to me, tonight we are going to study the topic related to War in the Heavens.

Much has been said about the great rebellion of the Angels against the Eternal; it has been affirmed that Michael with his hosts of Light had to fight against the Dragon and his henchmen.

All of this, my friends, is totally symbolic; we must know how to understand it so as to not fall into error.

In previous lectures we gave lengthy explanations about the Devil, the Dragon, and now we will enter deeper into all of this matter.

Between parentheses, I want to tell everyone present here that I have a bet with the Devil, and this might surprise you a little bit...

On a certain occasion, the date or time does not matter, both of us seated at a table face to face, I heard from the lips of my own intimate Lucifer the following affirmations:

"I will defeat you in chastity, and I will prove it to you; you cannot overcome me ..."

"Do you want to make a bet?"

"Yes," Satan answered, "I am willing to seal the bet. How much shall we bet?"

"For this much and it is done."

Thus, I left that personage, who is nothing more than the reflection of my own intimate Logos, in truth I treated him a little bad...

In the name of truth, I want to tell you my friends that so far I am winning the bet, as the Devil has not overcome me; by no means has he succeeded in making me fall into temptation, even though I have had to fight tremendous battles against him.

The war is tremendous; I am defeating the Draon and I can say I have vanquished him.

This is the same thing that Michael did against Lucifer, the same fight every Initiate has to do against his Dragon.

Just as Michael won against all the rebellious Angels, likewise, each one of us must defeat and disintegrate all the devil "I's" or psychic aggregates that personify our errors.

Looking at this matter of War in the Heavens from another angle, we find that this allegory also represents the fight that occurred between the primitive Adepts of the Aryan Race and the Sorcerers from Atlantis, the Demons from the ocean, etc. etc. etc.

It is unquestionable that after the submersion of that ancient continent, the Black Mages from that ancient land swallowed by the waters continued to incessantly attack the Adepts of the new Race to which we all belong.

The allegory then, of the War in the Heavens has different meanings: it can symbolize religious, astronomical and geological events, and moreover, it possesses a very profound cosmological meaning.

In the sacred land of the Vedas much is said about the battles of Indra against Vritra. Obviously, the resplendent God Indra is called by the sages Vritra-Han for being the slayer of the Dragon, in the same way as Michael is the vanquisher of the same.

It is clear that every Initiate that slays or defeats the Dragon is swallowed by the Serpent, and in fact, converts into a Serpent, like Votan.

Nevertheless, sexual temptations are usually dreadful; rare are those who do not fall into temptation.

Satan, the Dragon, Lucifer, or whatever we want to call him, makes tremendous super-efforts to make the Initiate fall into temptation, and it is clear that almost all fail; that is why it is very difficult to obtain self-realized people. The weakness of people is found precisely there, in sex, and no matter how strong they may feel, in the long run they succumb.

This issue of War in Heaven is therefore something terrible, almost impossible to describe with words –sexual temptations are not a piece of cake–...

Is it perhaps easy to defeat the Dragon? The most serious thing in all of this is that people have the Ego alive; the Red Demons of Seth have not died, and the Consciousness of each one, bottled up in its sinister aggregates, functions truly within its own conditioning, and it even justifies itself washing its hands as Pilates or puts off the error saying: "Today I cannot but later on, with time, I will triumph", etc. etc. etc.

In this way, the "Michaels" who defeat the Dragon are very rare; one must search for them with the lamp of Diogenes; these people are too weak, fragile, ignorant and absurd.

Much has also been said about the fallen Angels in the old texts of classical antiquity, but this is neither understood by the learned ignoramuses nor by the rascals of the intellect.

Any Guru-Deva who falls into animal generation in fact converts into a fallen Angel, and even into a Demon.

It is unquestionable that when an Adept commits the crime of spilling the Glass of Hermes, all the inhumane elements he had previously disintegrated resurrect in him and for this reason becomes, in fact, another Demon.

We have now arrived at the root of a much-discussed topic, abundantly studied and rarely comprehended.

What happens is that, in order to comprehend this matter, it is necessary to have lived it; suppositions or vain rationalisms are useless here.

Since I lived all of this in a very remote archaic past, when multitudes of Lemurian Bodhisattvas committed the error of falling into animal degeneration, this is why I can give testimony of all of this and crudely explain it as it is and without suppositions or utopias of any kind.

I do not care if people believe me or not; I am stating what I have lived and that is all; for the rest, everyone does with their life as they please; I affirm what I know, what I have been able to see, hear, touch, and feel...

This topic of the fallen Angels is represented in Hindustan with the religious battles of Iranians against Brahmans, Gods against Demons, Gods against Asuras, as it appears in the war of *Mahabharata*, etc. etc.

This issue of the battles against the Dragon, we can also see in the Scandinavian *Edda*, where the Aesirs appear fighting against the ice giants, Aesir-Thor against Jötunn.

Therefore, my friends, I want you to comprehend the necessity to fight against the Dragon; I want you to understand that you must defeat him in pitched battles if you truly aspire to convert yourselves into Serpents of Wisdom and into terribly divine Gods.

Please, I beg you, overcome the ignorance that you are in; I beseech you to study these books and to live them, it truly hurts me to see all of you converted into weak and miserable shadows.

Question: Master, would you like to explain to me if when a person who is working in the Lit Forge of Vulcan falls, the "I" or "I's" she succeeded in disintegrating, resurge again in her?

Answer: Distinguished Gnostic sister, it is unquestionable that with any sexual fall, some infrahuman subjective element does in fact and in its own right resurrect. That is why our Lord the Christ said: The disciple must not allow himself to fall, because the disciple who allows himself to fall must fight a lot in order to recover what was lost.

Question: Master, you talk to us about the War in the Heavens, and we know from the teachings that the battles against the Secret Enemy must be carried out in the Avernus, in other words, descending into the Infernos. Could you please clarify this for me?

Answer: Friends, the allegorical meaning of all religious writers is unquestionable, whether they are Christians, Buddhists, Mohammedan, etc., etc. This matter of "heavens," refers to states of Consciousness; indubitably, our different conscious states are altered during the fight. The battle against the Secret Enemy can take us to definitive Liberation or to radical failure.

Certainly, it would be incongruent to suppose, even for a moment, passionate temptations within divine, ineffable regions; therefore, we must translate here the word "heavens" as states of Consciousness or as functions of the Essence, etc. etc. etc.

Question: Master, when you mentioned that you made a bet with your own intimate Lucifer, can we understand that your own Soul is at stake in this?

Answer: Friends, Gnostic brothers, there are valorizations and devaluations of the Being. There are also cosmic capitals equivalent to virtues.

What is at stake in this bet is based on a determined cosmic capital; this is valued in a manner similar to how the currency of the world is valued, and as a result, I would remain deprived of a certain amount of virtues and devalued or intimately devaluated. I think that with what I have expressed here, the brothers in this auditorium have understood me.

Question: Master, we have been told that when working in the Lit Forge of Vulcan the Ego can be disintegrated. What can you tell us in this regard?

Answer: Distinguished lady, we have already talked very extensively in previous lectures about the modus operandi for the dissolution of the Myself, of the Oneself.

We have also given extensive explanations on the same topic in our book entitled *The Mystery of the Golden Blossom.* We said then that it was necessary to work with the lance of Eros during the chemical coitus or metaphysical copulation.

I believe that this audience no longer ignores our Gnostic esoteric procedures; the most important consists precisely in knowing how to pray during the Sahaja Maithuna.

In those moments, one must plead the particular Divine Mother Kundalini —because each person has their own— so that She eliminates the error we need to eradicate or extirpate from within our own psyche.

It is indisputable that the transcendental sexual electricity can reduce any psychological defect to ashes.

Undoubtedly, our Divine Mother Kundalini, handling the Holy Lance with dexterity can turn any psychic aggregate, any intimate defect into dust.

In past lectures we also mentioned the necessity of first having comprehended the defect that we want to extirpate from our nature; it is clear that only through the technique of Meditation can we comprehend any error in an integral manner.

Comprehension and elimination are basic for the dissolution of the Myself, of the Oneself.

Question: Master, would you like to explain to us if the Kund-abuffer Organ is developed by spilling the Glass of Hermes?

Answer: Distinguished ladies and gentlemen, it is urgent to comprehend that when the Glass of Hermes is spilled in a continuous and habitual way, the Abominable Kundabuffer Organ is also developed, the famous Satanic tail of the tenebrous, the sinister, negative Fohat, which in the long run leads us down the descending, infra-human path towards the Abyss and Second Death.

Question: Master, would you like you tell us if by working in the Lit Forge of Vulcan, without spilling the Glass of Hermes, but without disintegrating the pluralized "I", in the long run the Kundabuffer Organ also develops?

Answer: Friends, distinguished lady who asks the question, it is very necessary to comprehend the necessity of an upright conduct when one is working in the Forge of the Cyclops.

He who does not die within himself, he who does not dissolve the Ego, develops the Abominable Kundabuffer Organ in the long run, even if he is working in the Lit Forge of Vulcan —Sex-Yoga—.

We already said in prior chapters that the Abominable Organ of all fatalities develops in adulterers, in those who betray the Guru, in the sincerely mistaken who are accustomed to justify their crimes, in the wrathful and perverse, etc., even if they are working with White Tantrism, even if they do not spill the Glass of Hermes.

Only by dying within ourselves and truly working in the Ninth Sphere, and by sacrificing ourselves for our fellowmen, is how we can develop the Igneous Serpent of our Magical Powers in our intimate nature.

Much later, we must totally defeat the Dragon, if we truly long to be devoured by the Serpent to transform ourselves into Serpents.

Question: Master, should we understand that the war the Archangel Michael fought against the Dragon and the rebellious Angels was done with the lance of Longinus?

Answer: Friends of mine, the lance of Longinus is the same lance of all magical pacts, the same with which Saint George wounded his Dragon.

There is no doubt that this Holy Lance, this staff of Achilles, is the marvellous emblem of sexual energy with which we can radically incinerate, burn, destroy, the diverse parts of the Myself, the Ego, the Psychological "I".

Question: Venerable Master, what do the rebellious Angels allegorize?

Answer: Friends, it is said that Michael fought against the Dragon and his rebellious Angels, as we must do against our intimate Lucifer and the psychic aggregates; all of this is related to internal, secret, terrible and very painful battles.

Each one of us must transform then, into a Michael, incessantly fighting against the Dragon and his fatal hosts.

20

THE LAW OF ETERNAL RETURN

My friends gathered in this house this evening, today we are going to study the Law of the Eternal Return of all things.

At the hour of death, the Angel of Death always comes to the deathbed. There are legions of them, and they all work in accordance with the Great Law.

Three things go to the graveyard or cemetery: First: the physical corpse. Second: the Vital Body —it escapes from the Physical Body with the last exhalation–. This vehicle floats above the sepulcher and slowly decomposes as the Physical Body disintegrates. Third: the ex-personality, which unquestionably can escape from the tomb sometimes and wander around the cemetery or travel to some places that are familiar to it.

There is no doubt that the ex-personality dissolves slowly over time; there is no tomorrow for the personality of the dead; it is transitory in itself...

That which continues, that which does not go to the sepulcher is the Ego, the Myself, the Oneself.

Death itself is a subtraction of fractions; once the mathematical operation is done only the values remain.

Obviously, the sums of values attract and repel each other in accordance with the Law of Universal Magnetization, they float in the atmosphere of the world.

Eternity opens its jaws to swallow the Ego and thereafter it expels it, it casts it out, it sends it back into time.

We have been told that in the precise moment of death, at the very moment when the deceased exhales his last breath, he projects an electro-psychic design of his personality; that design continues within the Supersensitive Regions of nature and later on saturates the fecundated egg. This is how when we return, when we reincorporate within a new physical body; we come to possess very similar personal characteristics to those of the previous life.

That which continues after death is not then something very beautiful. That which is not destroyed with the physical body is nothing more than a bunch of Devils, of psychic aggregates, of defects.

The only decent thing that exists in the depth of all of those cavernous entities that constitute the Ego is the Essence, the psyche, that which we have of Soul.

Upon returning into a new physical vehicle, the Law of Karma enters into action, since there is neither effect without cause, nor cause without effect.

The Angels of Life are in charge of connecting the Silver Cord to the fertilizing zoosperm. Unquestionably, many millions of zoosperms escape in the instant of copulation, yet only one of them is endowed with sufficient power so as to penetrate into the ovum in order to realize the conception.

This force of a very special type is not a product of chance or hazard; what occurs is that it is propelled from within, in its intimate energetism by the Angel of Life that in those instants realizes the connection of the returning Essence.

Biologists know very well that the masculine and feminine gametes each carry 24 chromosomes that when added together give the total sum of 48, which constitute the germinal cell.

These 48 chromosomes remind us of the 48 Laws that govern the physical body.

The essence then comes to be connected to the germinal cell by means of the Silver Cord. Given that this cell divides into 2, and the 2 into 4, and the 4 into 8, and so forth successively for the process of fetal gestation, it is clear that sexual energy becomes in fact the basic agent of that cellular multiplication. This signifies that by no means could the phenomenon of mitosis take place without the presence of creative energy.

The deceased, the one who is preparing to take a new physical body does not penetrate the fetus; he only comes to reincorporate at the moment in which the baby is born, at the precise moment when it draws its first breath.

It is very interesting that with the last exhalation of the dying person, dis-incarnation occurs, and that with the first inhalation we return into a new organism...

It is completely absurd to affirm that one chooses in a voluntary manner the place where one shall be reborn. Reality is very different. It is precisely the Lords of the Law, the Agents of Karma who select for us the exact place, home, family, nation, etc., where we must reincorporate, return.

If the Ego could choose the location, place or family, etc., for its new reincorporation, then the ambitious, the arrogant, the misers, the greedy... would seek palaces, the houses of millionaires, rich mansions, beds of roses and feathers and the world would be all riches and sumptuousness. There would be no poor people; there would be no pain or bitterness. No one would pay karma, we could all commit the worst crimes without being caught by Celestial Justice, etc., etc., etc.

The crude reality of facts is that the Ego does not have the right to choose the place or family where it must be born. Each one of us has to pay what we owe; it is written that whosoever sows thunder shall reap the whirlwind; the Law is the Law and the Law is fulfilled.

It is therefore very unfortunate that so many famous writers of contemporary spirituality emphatically affirm that each one has the right to choose the place where they should be reborn.

What lies beyond the sepulcher is something that only awakened men can know, those who have already dissolved their Ego, people who are truly conscious of themselves.

There are many theories in the world, of a spiritualized type or of a materialized type and the reasoning of intellectual humanoids allows for anything: it can create spiritualized theories as well as materialized ones.

By means of the most severe logical processes, rational homunculi can elaborate within their cerebral encephalon a materialistic theory as well as a spiritualistic theory, and in one as well as the other, in the thesis as well as in the antithesis, the basis of its logic is really admirable.

Unquestionably, as a faculty for investigation, reasoning with all its logical processes has a beginning and an end. It is too narrow and limited, since as we have already said, lends itself for everything, it is useful for everything, for the thesis as well as for the antithesis.

Thus, clearly the processes of logical cerebration are not in themselves convincing because of the concrete fact that with them any spiritualized or materialized thesis can be elaborated, both demonstrating the same logical vigor, seeming very plausible indeed to any reasoning humanoid.

Therefore, it is not possible for reasoning to truly know anything of what is in the next world, of what is beyond, of what continues after death...

Emmanuel Kant, the great German philosopher already demonstrated in his great work entitled *Critique of Pure Reason* that reasoning itself cannot know anything about the Truth, about what is real, about God, etc., etc., etc.

We are not then throwing ideas out a priori, what I am saying with so much emphasis can be documented with the cited book by the mentioned philosopher.

We obviously have to discard reasoning as an element of suitable cognition for the discovery of what is Real...

Now that the reasoning processes have been archived in this question of practical metaphysics, we will from this very moment establish a solid base for the verification of that which is beyond time, of that which continues and which cannot be destroyed with the death of the physical body...

I am asseverating something that I know, something that I have experienced in the absence of reasoning. It is not superfluous to remind this honorable audience that I remember all of my previous lives.

In ancient times, before the submersion of the Atlantean continent, people had developed that faculty of the Being known by the name of Instinctive Perception of Cosmic Truths.

After the submersion of that ancient continent, that precious faculty entered into the descending involutive cycle and was completely lost.

It is possible to regenerate that faculty by means of the dissolution of the Ego. Once that goal is attained, we will be able to verify the Law of Eternal Return of all things for ourselves, in a self-conscious manner.

Indubitably, that mentioned faculty of the Being allows us to experience what is Real, that which continues, that which is beyond death, beyond the physical body, etc., etc., etc.

Since I possess that developed faculty, I can affirm with complete authority what I know, what I have lived, what is beyond, etc., etc.

Speaking sincerely and straight from the heart, I can tell you the following: the dead normally live in Limbo, in the antechamber of Hell, in the Region of the Dead –the Inferior Astral– a region that is fully represented by all those grottoes and subterranean caverns of the world, that united or intimately linked together make up a whole in their conjunction...

The state in which the deceased find themselves is lamentable: they resemble somnambulists, their Consciousness is completely asleep, they wander around everywhere and firmly believe that they are alive; they are unaware of their death.

After disincarnating, the storekeepers continue in their stores, the drunkards in the taverns, the prostitutes in the brothels, etc., etc.

It would be impossible for people like this, for these types of unconscious somnambulists, to afford the luxury of choosing the place where they must be reborn.

What is most natural is that they are born without knowing when or how, and that they die completely unconscious.

Many are the shadows within the deceased; every disincarnated is a bunch of unconscious shadows, a bunch of larvae that live in the past, who are unaware of the present, who are bottled up within all of their dogmas, within the rancid things of yesterday, within the events of times of yore, within affections, within family sentimentalisms, within egotistical interests, within animal passions, within vices, etc., etc., etc.

Upon being born again, the Essence expresses itself during the first three or four years of childhood, and then the child is beautiful, sublime, innocent and happy.

Unfortunately, the Ego starts to express itself little by little as we approach the age of seven, and it fully manifests itself when the new personality has been totally created.

It is indispensable to comprehend that the new personality is created precisely during the first seven years of childhood, and that it strengthens itself with time and experiences.

The personality is energetic, it is not physical as many people assume, and after death it slowly decomposes in the cemetery until reaching radical disintegration.

Before the new personality is totally formed, the Essence can afford the luxury of manifesting with all its beauty, and it even renders small children, very psychic indeed, sensitive, pure clairvoyants, etc., etc.

How happy we all would be if we did not have the Ego, if only the Essence expressed itself in us! Then, indisputably, there would be no pain, Earth would be a Paradise, an Eden, something ineffable, sublime.

The return of the Ego into this world is truly revolting, horrifying and abominable. The Ego in itself irradiates sinister and tenebrous vibratory waves which are in the least pleasant.

I say that every person, as long as they have not dissolved the Ego, is more or less black, even if they boast of sanctity and virtue.

The incessant return of all things is a Law of life, and we can verify this from instant to instant, from moment to moment.

The Earth returns to its point of departure each year, then we celebrate the new year. All heavenly bodies return to their original point of departure; the atoms within the molecule return to their initial point; the days return, the nights return, the four seasons return: spring, summer, fall and winter; the cycles, Kalpas, Yugas, and Maha-Manvantaras return, etc.

Hence, the Law of Eternal Return is something indisputable, irrefutable and unarguable.

Question: Master, you have told us that there is no tomorrow for the personality of the dead, and that the Etheric Body disintegrates little by little. I would like to know if the personality takes longer than the Physical Body to disintegrate.

Answer: I find the question that comes from the audience interesting, and I hasten to answer it with the greatest pleasure...

Unquestionably, the ex-personality lasts longer than the eliminated vital base.

I want to affirm with this that the Vital Body decomposes as the Physical disintegrates in the sepulcher.

The personality is different. Since it becomes invigorated through time with the different experiences of life, it obviously lasts longer; it has a firmer energetic note; it usually resists for many years.

It is in no way an exaggeration to affirm that the discarded personality can survive for entire centuries. It is intriguing to contemplate various discarded personalities conversing with each other.

What I am now speaking about might appear strange to some of you. I have been able to count up to ten discarded personalities corresponding to the same owner; in other words, ten returns of one and the same Ego.

I have seen them exchange subjective opinions, gathered together due to psychic affinity.

However, I want to clarify this a little bit more to avoid confusion. I have said that one is not born with the personality, that one has to develop it, and that this is possible during the first seven years of childhood. I have also affirmed that in the moment of death that personality goes to the cemetery and that sometimes it wanders around within it or hides within its grave.

Now, think for a moment of an Ego that escapes from the physical body after each return. It is clear that it leaves behind the personality.

If we reunite, for example, ten lives of the same Ego, we will have ten different personalities, and they can get together due to affinity, in order to converse in the cemetery and exchange subjective opinions.

Indubitably, those ex-personalities weaken little by little; they are extraordinarily extinguished until they finally disintegrate radically.

Nevertheless, the memories of those personalities continue in the Causal World within the Akashic Records of nature.

In these instants, while talking with you here tonight, comes to my mind an ancient existence that I had as a military during the period of the Renaissance in old Europe.

Once, while working as a Causal Man in the World of Natural Causes, it occurred to me to take out from the secret Archives in that region the memory of that ex-personality.

The result was certainly extraordinary: I then saw that military dressed with the uniform of the epoch in which he lived.

Drawing his sword, he attacked me violently; it was not difficult for me to conjure him in order to place him once again within the Archives.

This means that in the World of Natural Causes every memory is alive, it has a reality, and this is something that can surprise many esotericist students and occultist...

Question: Master, you tell us that the personality is not born with the Ego. What can you tell us about the birth of the Vital Body?

Answer: Friends, I want you to comprehend that the Vital Body, the basic foundation of organic life, has been designed by the Agents of Life in accordance with the Law of Cause and Effect.

Those who in their past existence accumulated very serious debts can be born with a defective Vital Body, which —as is very natural— will serve as a foundation for a likewise defective body.

Liars can be born with a deformed Vital Body, resulting in a monstrous or feeble physical vehicle.

Addicts can be born with manifestly degenerated Vital Bodies, which will serve as a foundation for Physical Bodies which are also degenerated.

For example: The passionate abuser of sex can, in the long run, be born with an improperly polarized Vital Body; this will originate a homosexual vehicle or a lesbian feminine form.

Indubitably, homosexuals and lesbians are the result of sexual abuse in former existences.

An alcoholic can be born with a defective, anomalous vital brain, which could serve as a foundation for a likewise defective brain.

An assassin, a murderer, who incessantly repeats such a horrendous crime, can in the long run be born disabled, crippled, paralytic, blind from birth, deformed, horrifying, repulsive, idiotic, or definitively insane. It is good to know that assassination is the worst degree of human corruption; by no means can an assassin return with a healthy vehicle.

It would, well, be very lengthy to talk more at this moment about this point related with the question that I was asked.

Question: Master, aren't those who are born with physical defects, hereditary defects?

Answer: Distinguished lady, your question is very important and it deserves to be examined in detail.

Hereditary defects are obviously placed at the service of the Law of Karma; they constitute the marvelous mechanism by means of which karma is processed.

Evidently, heredity is found within the sexual genes; we find it there, and through them the Law works with the entire cellular mechanism.

It is good to comprehend that the genes control the totality of the human organism; they are found within the chromosomes, within the germinal cell; they are the foundation of the physical form.

When the genes are found in disorder, when their legitimate natural formation does not exist, they indisputably originate a defective body, and this is something that has already been demonstrated.

Question: Master, the disincarnated Egos that are profoundly asleep in the Region of the Dead and believe that they are still alive, how can they represent the scenes of their life if they lack a Mental Body?

Answer: The question that this gentleman is asking is mistaken at the core; this means that it is mistakenly constructed. The pluralized Ego is mind; we have already spoken clearly, we have already said that the intellectual animal mistakenly called man does not have a mind, but minds.

Indubitably, the different psychic aggregates that constitute the Ego are nothing more than different mental forms, pluralization of the understanding, etc.

When this ensemble of minds, or quarrelsome and vociferous "I's" return, what often happens is that not all of them succeed in reincorporating. From a total sum of psychic aggregates, some of them enter submerged involution in the Mineral Kingdom, or reincorporate in animal organisms, or adhere to specific places, etc., etc., etc.

After death, each one of these aggregates lives within their own occurrences and desires, always in the past, never in the present. Do not forget, my friends, that the "I" is memory, that the "I" is time, that the "I" is a book of many volumes.

Question: Master, based on what you have just said, that we are a Legion of "I's", must I conclude then that we do not have reality either, since we are also mental forms? Am I right?

Answer: Distinguished friend, ladies and gentlemen, you must understand that intellectual animal mistakenly called man is not yet an accomplished Being; this means that one is a mathematical point in space, which accedes to serve as a vehicle to determined sums of values.

Each individual is a poor, thinking animal, condemned to the sentence of living, a machine controlled by multiple infra-human and bestial psychic aggregates.

The only worthy element within each of us is the Essence, the psychic material, the prima materia to create Soul, and it is unfortunately bottled up within all these inhumane psychic aggregates.

Being a Man is something very different. In order to be one, one needs to disintegrate the Ego and to create the Superior Existential Bodies of the Being. I believe that now you have understood me.

Question: Master, are you then saying that we are in fact mental forms without objective reality?

Answer: Friends, please understand me! When I talk about psychic aggregates I am referring to mental forms; it is clear that such aggregates are indeed crystallizations of the mind and I think that you understand this; I do not find it necessary to continue explaining it; it has already been said.

Question: Master, are you telling us that all these very distinguished exponents of the magical power of the mind, who emphasize the great importance of having a positive mind, are then mistaken?

Answer: Friends, in these times of Kali Yuga, the Iron Age, people have dedicated themselves to mentalism; and here, there and everywhere one finds in bookstores thousands of books speaking marvels about the donkey of the mind. What is interesting about all of this is that Jesus, the great Kabir, rode on the donkey –the mind– in order to enter into the heavenly Jerusalem on Palm Sunday. This is how the Gospels explain it, this is how they narrate it, but people crucify Jesus the Christ and adore the donkey. This is how humanity is my dear brothers; this is what this epoch of darkness that we live in is like.

What do the mentalists want to develop, the mental force, the force of the donkey? It would be better for the comprehensive ones to ride on that animal and tame it with the whip of the will; thus, things would change and we would become good Christians, right?

What do the mentalists want to develop? The force of the mental Ego? It would be better if they disintegrate it, if they reduce it to cosmic dust; thus, the Spirit would shine within each one of them.

Unfortunately, people these days no longer want anything to do with the Spirit; now, kneeling down, they kiss the hooves of the donkey, the ass, and instead of purifying themselves, they become miserably vile.

If people knew that they do not have a Mental Body, and that the only thing that they possess is a sum of psychic aggregates, disgusting mental crystallizations, and if, instead of fortifying and strengthening these bestial "I's", they would disintegrate them, then they would indeed work for their own good and for their own happiness.

However, by developing the strength of the beast, the sinister power of the Mental Ego, the only thing that they achieve is to become more tenebrous, left and abysmal each day.

I tell my friends, I tell the brothers of the Gnostic Movement, to reduce their mental Ego to ashes, to fight relentlessly to free themselves from the mind; this is how they will attain beatitude.

Question: Master, don't you think that an Essence without Ego would result in an extremely boring life on this planet that is so beautiful?

Answer: Friends, the Ego finds existence boring when it does not have what it wants. However, when is the Ego ever satisfied?

The Ego is desire, and desire in the long run turns into frustration, fatigue, boredom, and then life becomes boring. So, with what right does the Ego dare to speak out against boredom, when he himself ultimately becomes tedium, bitterness, disillusion, disenchantment, frustration, and boredom?

If the Ego does not know what plenitude is, then how could it launch concepts about it?

Unquestionably, once the Ego is dead, reduced to ashes, the only thing that is left in us is the Essence, Beauty, and from the latter emerges happiness, love, plenitude...

What happens is that the lovers of desire, those who want passionate satisfactions, superficial people, think incorrectly; they suppose that without the Ego life would be terribly boring.

If these people did not have Ego they would think in a different manner, they would be happy and they would then exclaim: life of the Ego is frightfully boring! Friends, do you perhaps think that it is very delightful to incessantly return to this valley of bitterness to cry and suffer continuously?

It is necessary to eliminate the Ego in order to liberate ourselves from the Wheel of Samsara.

21

THE LAW OF REINCARNATION

riends of mine gathered here, we are now going to study the Law of Reincarnation... I hope that all of you will get the utmost benefit from these talks.

It is urgent that we all together try to comprehend in an integral manner what this great Law is.

Certainly, the word Reincarnation is very demanding; let us recall the ten reincarnations of Vishnu, the Cosmic Christ.

Krishna, the Great Hindu Avatar, born some thousand years before Christ, never said that all of the intellectual animals that populate the face of the Earth would reincarnate. He emphatically affirmed that only the Buddhas, the great Gods, the Devas, the Divine Kings, etc., etc., reincarnate.

Entering into the study of the Law of Reincarnation in a more detailed manner, we can say with total clarity that reincarnation is not possible for those who do not possess sacred individuality.

Unquestionably, only sacred individuals reincarnate, this is why human reincarnations were always celebrated with great religious festivities in secret Tibet.

In the name of truth, I want to affirm clearly and without circumambages the crude reality that reincarnation or reincorporation of Souls is only possible when one possesses the Golden Embryo, the Golden Flower.

By analyzing this matter at great length, we come to understand that such an Embryo must be deliberately created, through conscious works and voluntary sufferings.

Within the merely retrospective field we discover the origin of all those infra-human elements in which is bottled up the psychic material or primal matter, with which it is possible to elaborate the Golden Flower, the Golden Embryo.

We already know, because we have explained it here in other lectures, that in a remote past, humanity developed in its organism the Abominable Kundabuffer Organ, the satanic tail.

When humanity lost that organ, the bad consequences of the aforementioned organ remained within the five Cylinders of the organic machine —mind, emotion, movement, instinct and sex–.

Indubitably, these dreadful consequences came to constitute a sort of subjective and inhuman second nature that all rational animals carry within.

It is unquestionable that the Essence, the prima materia with which we must elaborate the Golden Embryo, remained bottled up within that double nature.

Dissolving those subjective and infra-human aggregates is vital when there is a serious attempt to elaborate the Golden Flower.

In former times, when the dreadful consequences of the Abominable Kundabuffer Organ had not been specifically developed, it was possible to appeal to the intimate factor that originates the impulses of faith, hope and love in order to motivate the force or forces that could disintegrate incipient, subjective elements.

Unfortunately, that basic factor of the aforementioned impulses underwent various degenerative processes, due to the exorbitant development of the bad consequences of the Abominable Kundabuffer Organ.

It is certainly painful that the factor that originates the intimate impulses related to faith, hope and love have degenerated radically.

It is for this reason that we have to now appeal to the only factor that has not been lost yet.

I want to emphatically refer to the Essence, the psychic material that is certainly the foundation, the basis of our entire psychic organization.

Liberating that Essence is urgent, undeferrable, undelayable, if we seriously want to elaborate the Golden Flower, the Golden Embryo,

Regrettably, this primal matter, this psychic material, does not participate in the routine activities of our mis-named waking state.

It is a pity that this factor upon which all of our psychic processes are established is bottled up within the subconscious zones.

Getting that factor to come out from its merely subjective state in order to manifest itself in a self-conscious and objective manner in the activities of our daily life is vital, urgent, necessary.

It is the Ego then with all its psychic aggregates, that double anti-human nature, that infra-human appendage within which the Consciousness is bottled up.

If we want to possess sacred individuality, then we must resort to the scalpel of self-criticism in order to perform a dissection of all those false values that constitute the Myself.

Much has been said about creative comprehension; it is indispensable to know all the psychic defects that we possess in an integral, unitotal manner.

Comprehending intellectually is not all; it is indisputable and irrefutable that any psychological defect is processed within the 49 subconscious, infra-conscious, and even unconscious levels.

Comprehension in this or that level is not enough; we urgently need to understand our defects in depth; it is indispensable to perforate them, if we really want to exterminate ourselves, to annihilate ourselves.

However, even though creative comprehension is urgent and unpostponable, it is not everything.

We, Gnostics, go much further: we want to grasp, to apprehend the deep significance of what we have integrally comprehended. It is not possible to originate those intimate impulses that will cause radical changes within our psyche if we have not succeeded in grasping the deep significance of this or that psychological defect.

Obviously, we come to be duly prepared for this or that inner change when we have comprehended this or that error of our psyche. Elimination comes afterwards and then we appeal to forces of a superior type.

Someone for example, could have comprehended the defect of anger and could have even given himself the luxury of grasping its deep significance, yet nonetheless continue with it.

Eliminating is different, because the mind can provoke diverse modes of action: it can label the defects, move them from one department of understanding to another, but it cannot fundamentally alter them.

We need to appeal to a power superior to the mind if we want to extirpate defects. Fortunately, such a power exists. I want to now refer to the Serpentine Fire, to that Sacred Fire that normally develops in the body of the ascetic.

If in the past this Igneous Power was able to divide the divine hermaphrodites into opposite sexes, it is clear that it can also extirpate from our psyche the inhuman elements that as appendages constitute a dual, sinister, terribly perverse and evil nature within us.

We have already said in our work entitled *The Mystery of the Golden Blossom* that the Seminal Pearl is formed with the first percentages of liberated Essence.

We already affirmed in that book that, as the different subjective elements of man are reduced to cosmic dust, the Seminal Pearl develops and becomes the Golden Embryo, the Golden Flower; therein lies the Mystery of the Golden Blossom.

I have explained the modus operandi too often, both in these talks as well as in my previous books.

At that time I said that we must learn to direct that Serpentine Fire or Ray of the Kundalini against these or those inhumane aggregates, in order to pulverize them, with the purpose of liberating the Essence...

I explained that it is precisely in the Lit Forge of Vulcan we had the opportunity to work with the lance of Achilles.

Only with the Holy Lance, marvelous emblem of the transcendental sexual electricity, can we disintegrate defects of a psychological type.

Whoever possesses the Golden Embryo, whoever has elaborated it through deliberate works and conscious mortifications, has the right to reincarnate.

It is evident that the Golden Flower confers sacred individuality upon us, it is indubitable that the Golden Embryo comes to establish in us complete equilibrium between the spiritual and the material.

Those who still do not possess this Embryo return, come back, reincorporate into new organisms, but they do not reincarnate. Distinguish then, between Reincarnation and Return. Rare are those who reincarnate, millions are those who return.

Question: Master, can you tell us when the Kundabuffer Organ developed in humanity and for what purpose?

Answer: I will very gladly answer the question that our secretary sister has asked...

During the epoch of the continent Mu or Lemuria, located —as we have already said in past talks— in the Pacific Ocean, it was necessary to develop that organ with the purpose of stabilizing the geological crust of the Earth.

Given that the Human Machine automatically transforms cosmic energies in order to retransmit them to the outer layers of the planetary organism that we live in, any change that occurs in these machines originates determined results in the interior of our planet Earth...

It was then, in that period, about 18 million years or more ago, that the Cosmocrators gave complete freedom to the inner Lucifer of each and every one, so that the tail of the simians would develop, that Abominable Kundabuffer Organ, in each human organism.

Indubitably, this course of action of the Cosmocrators altered the energetic transformation within the human interior; giving magnificent results for the geological crust of the Earth —since it was stabilized-, but sinister ones for humanity.

Much later in the course of time, the Gods eliminated this pernicious appendage from the organism but they were not able to eliminate its consequences, since these, as we have already said, became a second nature, inhumane and perverse, within each one of us.

Question: Master, are the Cosmocrators then to blame for the inhumane consequences that humanity carries in their organisms today?

Answer: I find this question interesting. The Gods who intervened therein made some calculation errors and for that reason they are to blame. I want you to know that the Gods also make mistakes.

It is clear that in a future Cosmic Day, those ineffable individuals will have to pay their corresponding Cosmic Karma.

Question: Master, since the Essence is the only element that constitutes our psychic organization which, as you said, fortunately has not been lost –does this mean that there could be a danger of the Essence being lost?

Answer: With great pleasure I will answer the gentleman's question. With all due respect, I allow myself to tell the audience who is listening to me that the question is not very well constructed. I have not said that the Essence is our psychic organization; I have only wanted to affirm that it is the basic factor of our entire psychic organization, and this is a little different.

Clearly, it is not possible for the Essence to be lost, this is why I affirm that it is the only factor that fortunately has not been lost.

Even if the Essence bottled up within the Ego were to involute in time in the Infernal Worlds, it is evident that it would never be lost, because once the Ego is dissolved, it would remain free and ready, as we have said so many times, to enter into new evolving processes.

Question: Venerable Master, you emphasize not only comprehension but also discovering the deep significance of our psychological defects. I understand that the objective of comprehension is to identify those defects and that the objective of the deep significance is to discover the damage that the defect might cause us as an obstacle for our Self-Realization. Am I right?

Answer: It is worthwhile to answer the question from the audience. Comprehension is not identification; someone could identify a psychological defect without having comprehended it; let us distinguish then, between comprehension and identification.

This matter of comprehension is very elastic. The degrees of comprehension vary. It could be that today we comprehend this or that matter in a certain way and in a certain manner, in a relative and circumstantial manner and tomorrow we will comprehend it better.

Apprehension of the deep significance of such and such defect is only possible by means of all the parts of our whole Being.

If some parts of our Being have captured the deep significance, yet other parts of our own Being have not yet captured it, then integral and deep significance has not yet been unitotally apprehended either.

We must not develop preconceptions in regards to the deep significance of an error, in regards to its specific flavor; we can only directly experience the deep significance of this or that error in the precise moment, in the appropriate instant. This is why we could by no means develop preconceived ideas in regards to what the deep significance of our psychological errors could be.

Question: Thank you Master, for this explanation, which reveals to us that comprehension is really a function of the mind, and that the deep significance is a function of the Consciousness. Is this correct?

Answer: Friends, the mind with all its functionalisms is feminine, receptive; it would be absurd to try to make it positive; it would be foolish to elaborate ideas, preconceptions, theories.

Therefore, given that the mind is a merely passive instrument by nature, it could not by itself occupy the place of comprehension.

Distinguish between what comprehension is and what the instrument that we use in order to manifest ourselves in the world is.

Obviously, comprehension belongs more accurately to the Essence, to the intimate functions of the Consciousness and that is all.

The deep significance of this or that psychological error differs from Comprehension by the very fact that it belongs to the diverse perceptions or direct experiences lived by the diverse parts of the unitotal Being.

Question: Master, can a man who reincarnates choose the place and family where he comes back with awakened Consciousness?

Answer: I will answer this new question with great pleasure... Allow me to inform all of you present here, that whoever possesses the Golden Embryo, in actual fact, also has awakened Consciousness.

In this case, it is given to him to voluntarily choose the zodiacal sign in which he wishes to reincorporate, reincarnate, re-embody; however, it is not possible for him to alter his karma.

He could select diverse types of birth, family, nation, city, etc., etc., yet, always in accordance with his karmic debts.

This means that he could resolve to pay this or that debt in accordance with his free choice, yet by no means could he avoid those debts; he would only have the right to choose between which debt to pay first, and that is all.

Question: Master, does a fallen Bodhisattva lose his Golden Embryo?

Answer: This question is certainly quite original; and for this reason it is a good idea that we answer it concretely...

It is necessary to comprehend that the Golden Embryo is imperishable, immortal, eternal.

Therefore, a fallen Bodhisattva can annihilate himself in the Ninth Sphere, go through the destruction process of the Superior Existential Bodies of the Being, yet he would never lose his Golden Embryo. After the radical destruction or definitive annihilation of the Ego, it would re-emerge, resurface on the face of the Earth, under the light of the sun, to reinitiate or begin a new evolution.

Question: Master, does the Consciousness of a fallen Bodhisattva fall asleep?

Answer: Distinguished friends, it is clear that when a Bodhisattva falls, the harmful consequences of the Abominable Kundarbuffer Organ resurrect within him, and then the Golden Embryo, the Consciousness, indisputably remains bottled up within those infra-human factors. The result, in this case, is that the Consciousness loses a good percentage of its habitual lucidity, although it does not radically fall asleep.

Question: Master, does the man who has acquired sacred individuality totally lack desires?

Answer: Friends, when someone has dissolved the Ego, when he has de-egotized himself, he has indisputably individualized himself, yet, desire is something more profound.

Any one of those present here can radically eliminate the Ego, and for such reason acquire sacred individuality, and nonetheless continue with desire.

This truly appears paradoxical, contradictory and even absurd, yet we must analyze this a little bit.

Friends, time claims many things. Once the awful consequences of the Abominable Kundabuffer Organ are annihilated, the Teleooginoora Tapes remain. The latter can be completely conserved within the Supersensitive Worlds during the entire terrestrial period if one has not bothered to disintegrate them, to annihilate them, to reduce them to cosmic dust.

Obviously, those tapes, like living films, certainly correspond to all the scenes of desire, to all of the lustful acts of this and all of our former lives, and if they are not radically disintegrated, then one hundred percent Objective Consciousness cannot be achieved either, because a part of our Consciousness is bottled up within them.

Clearly, the disintegration of those Tapes is a superior type of work that can only be performed with the two-edged axe, which in ancient times appeared at the center of all sacred labyrinths, a symbol that very few have comprehended; and which some pseudo-esoteric and pseudo-occultist works have written about in a more or less mistaken manner.

In any case, transcendental sexual electricity must also reduce the Teleooginoora Tapes to dust.

So my dear friends, you are realizing how difficult it is to be able to give full lucidity and objectivity to the Consciousness.

It is lamentable that the Essence is so bottled up within the many varied subjective and infra-human elements.

Unfortunately, many people believe that this matter of awakening the Consciousness is something easy, and constantly write to me, complaining because they still cannot project with their Astral Body, protesting because after some months they still do not have powers, demanding that they immediately acquire the capacity of being totally lucid out of their physical body, etc., etc., etc.

Usually, those who begin our studies are seeking powers, and when they do not become omnipotent individuals immediately, they then look for the subjective path of Spiritism, or they affiliate themselves to different schools of subjective psychic kinds with the purpose of instantaneously acquiring the coveted psychic faculties...

Complete objectivity implies the radical destruction of everything inhuman element that we carry within, the annihilation of subconscious atoms, the absolute death of the dual infra-human nature, the radical pulverization of all the memories of desire.

Therefore, dear friends, anyone can have attained sacred individuality, and nonetheless, still not be completely free from the process of desire.

To destroy the Teleooginoora Tapes and some other principles that I will mention later, means to extirpate even the minutest desires from our psyche.

Question: Master, is it worthwhile to exercise the right of reincarnating when it has been acquired?

Answer: Distinguished ladies and gentlemen who are listening to me, every illusion is allowed to the reincarnating Souls; however, it is preferable to exclaim with Jesus: "My Father, if it is possible, taketh this cup away from me, but let not my will, but thine, be done."

SAMAEL AUN WEOR

In these moments that I am speaking to you, here, in the study of my own house, which is also yours, something very interesting comes to mind. It so happens that on a certain night I was telepathically called by a group of Masters from the Venerable Great White Lodge.

I left my physical body and all the parts of my inner Being integrated and attired with the Existential Bodies of the Being had to attend the call.

Floating in space, I landed softly upon the flat roof of a great building. The Adepts of the Occult Fraternity received me with jubilant exclamations saying:

"The Archangel Samael has arrived!"

Then, after the usual hugs and greetings, I was interrogated in the following manner:

"You, as the Avatar of the New Aquarian age, must answer for the benefit or detriment of delivering cosmic ships to terrestrial humanity; great responsibility lies in your answer."

Kneeling down on my knees, I then saw with my spatial sense the use that the earthlings could make of such ships in the future.

The Eye of Dhagma allowed me to see inside of those ships, in a medium-term future; merchants, prostitutes, dictators, etc., traveling to other planets of the solar system, taking discord to other corners of the universe, etc., etc., etc.

Feeling in those moments the responsibility that weighed upon my shoulders, I addressed my Father who is in secret, saying,

"My Father, if it is possible, taketh this cup from me, but let not my will, but thine, be done."

Those words vibrated in the Nine Heavens from sphere to sphere, from world to world. Years passed by and everything was resolved. My Father who is in secret gave the appropriate answer: selection of human personnel, deliver these ships to certain, very select groups of humanity. It is important to say to our friends that certain isolated human groups already possess this kind of space vehicles.

In an inaccessible region of the Himalayas, where the Communist invaders will never be able to reach, there is a community of Lamas who received a certain quantity of those cosmic ships, with which they travel to other worlds of space.

These Lamas that had the good fortune of receiving such precious gifts are sacred individuals, people with the Golden Embryo developed, Beings who reincarnate.

Therefore, my friends, we must always do the will of the Father, never ours.

Those who reincarnate can choose, in accordance with the Law of Karma, the conditions of life that they want, without escaping, of course, from Karmic Law. Yet, it is preferable that our Father who is in secret chooses what is most appropriate for us.

Question: Master, we were told that the Gods also make mistakes. Who then is the one who does not make mistakes?

Answer: Friends, I find this question to be truly important and we are going to give the appropriate answer. I request the attention of the entire audience...

Only the Father who is in secret does not make mistakes. He is ineffable, omniscient, and omnipotent.

This is why I insist on the necessity of doing the will of the Father, both in the Heavens as on Earth.

When we forget our Father who is in secret, we commit errors. It is better to consult and leave everything in the hands of the Father.

Question: Master, what is the difference between the Golden Embryo and the Consciousness?

Answer: Friends, there is no difference whatsoever between the Golden Embryo and the Consciousness, because it is the same

organized Essence, the same objectivized Consciousness, radically liberated from every subconscious process.

Question: Master, Master H.P.B. says that the only way of not suffering in this world is to cease reincarnating. What you can tell us in this regard?

Answer: I want you gentlemen to know that absolute happiness is only obtained when one has God within.

One could live in Nirvana, the world of happiness, yet if one does not have God within, one would not be happy. One could cease reincarnating, yet if one does not have God within, one would not be happy either.

Even if one lived in a filthy dungeon, among the most terrible misfortunes, or if one were to be in the Infernal Worlds, having God within, one would be infinitely happy.

It is worthwhile to remind you, friends, that over there in the Infernal Worlds, live some Masters of Compassion who are working for —helping, assisting— those who are decisively lost but since they have God within, they are happy.

THE LAW OF RECURRENCE

Friends of mine, today's talk will deal with the Law of Recurrence.

When the Ego returns, when it reincorporates, everything occurs again as it happened, plus the good or bad consequences. Indubitably, various forms of the Great Law of Recurrence exist; in this lecture we will propose to study those varied forms...

Diverse scenes of our previous lives are repeated, whether in more elevated spirals or in lower spirals.

The spiral is the curve of life and it is always symbolized by the conch. We are wicked conchs within the bosom of the Father.

Obviously, we develop, evolve and involute on the spiral line of existence.

Another form of recurrence can be evidenced in the history of the Earth and its Races...

The first sub-race of our present Aryan Race developed on the central plateau of Asia and had a powerful esoteric civilization.

The second sub-race flourished in the south of Asia, in the Pre-Vedic epoch; then the wisdom of the Rishis from Hindustan was known, and the splendors of the ancient Chinese Empire, etc., etc.

The third sub-race developed marvelously in Egypt, Persia, Chaldea, etc.

The fourth sub-race shone with the civilizations of Greece and Rome.

The fifth was perfectly manifested with Germany, England and other countries.

The sixth resulted from the mixture of the Spaniards with the indigenous races from Indo-America.

The seventh is perfectly manifested by the result of all those different mixtures of races, such as we can today evince in the territory of the United States.

Clearly, the seven branches of the Aryan trunk already fully exist and this is completely demonstrated.

The studies that we have carried out in the Causal World have allowed us to correctly verify the astounding concrete facts for our present humanity.

Since each of the great Races that have existed in the world has always ended with a great cataclysm, we can logically deduce that this one, our Aryan Race, will have to end very soon, also with another tremendous cataclysm.

We are talking about the Law of Recurrence in a superior manner, and we will continue concretizing for better comprehension.

After the Great Catastrophe that is approaching, the Earth will again be inhabited by a select people.

When arriving at this part of our talk, I must emphatically tell you that the future Race that will have to populate the face of the Earth is now being intentionally created by the Brethren of the Occult Fraternity. The modus operandi of this new creation is very special.

I want you to know that cosmic travelers from other worlds visit us constantly; and that they are already taking select seed from humanoids.

A certain time ago, some newspapers from Brazil published a very interesting report: a certain Brazilian peasant while working feverishly plowing the field was suddenly surprised by some extraterrestrials who led him into the interior of a cosmic ship that had landed nearby in the jungle.

Extraordinary scientists, brethren from space, examined him carefully; and they even extracted a little bit of blood from him with the purpose of analyzing it. Afterwards, they put the peasant in a special bedroom of the ship. That perplexed peasant, astonished, confused, lying on a bed, waiting for whatever was going to happen next...

Then, something unexpected happens: a strange woman with golden hair and yellow skin similar to that of Chinese people, lacking eyebrows, laid down next to that peasant and sexually seduced him; once the act was consummated, the peasant was taken out of the ship, and it flew away into infinite space.

Many other similar cases have occurred in different places of the world.

Moreover, there has been constant discussion about mysterious disappearances of aerial or maritime crews that have been lost forever and without any explanation...

All of this invites us to do reflection; all of this makes us comprehend that the Elder Brothers of humanity are taking the seed in order to cross it with peoples from other worlds.

This is how the Holy Gods are already creating the future Great Race, the Sixth Root Race which will come to populate the Earth after the impending great catastrophe.

It will be a new type of people, a mixture of earthlings with extraterrestrials, it will be a resplendent humanity.

Therein lies distinguished brothers, the personnel with whom the future Jerusalem will come to be formed, of which the *Book of Revelation* by St. John speaks.

It is unquestionable that the glorious esoteric civilizations of ancient times will then resurrect.

During the first sub-race of the future Great Root Race the powerful cultures of the first Aryan sub-race will emerge from within the chaos, through the Law of Recurrence, yet in a superior type of spiral.

During the future second sub-race the civilization that flourished in millenary India —before the Vedas— and in ancient China will resurrect.

During the third sub-race there will be a new Egypt, new pyramids, a new Nile, and the Egyptian civilization will resurrect. Then, the ancient pharaohs will reincarnate and thousands of souls from that glorious culture will return from the Amenti with the purpose of reviving the Hieratic Mysteries of the sunny country of Kem.

Likewise, the mysteries of Chaldea, Assyria, Babylon, Persia, etc., will again shine in that age yet on a superior spiral within the great spiral line of life.

During the fourth sub-race of that Earth of tomorrow the Mysteries of Greece and Rome will resurrect, with the advantage of the superior spiral of existence.

During the fifth sub-race a certain dangerous mechanicalness will appear again; the civilization of Englishmen, Germans, etc., will resurrect, with the advantages of being more spiritual, because of the concrete fact of being placed on a superior spiral.

During the penultimate sub-race of that Great Root Race of tomorrow, something similar to the Latin world will be seen, but with a more elevated, more dignified, more spiritual aspect.

The final sub-race of that future Root Race, although very technological, will not have the gross materialism of this Black Age of Kali Yuga. So, friends of mine, this is how the Law of Recurrence works, moving through the spiral of existence.

Now, let us think about the Law of Recurrence of the worlds, in the starry spaces, in the unalterable infinite.

Everything that happened in the ancient Moon, in that satellite that illuminates the face of the Earth during the nocturnal hours, is right now repeating on our planet Earth.

In other words, I will affirm the following: all the history of the Earth and of its Races from the dawning of life is a repetition of the history of the Selenites who once inhabited that satellite, when it was still alive and had abundant life.

Ladies and gentlemen, see how the Law of Recurrence works in all the corners of infinite space.

Now, let us move on to study the modus operandi of this Great Law in the intellectual animal mistakenly called man.

When we reincorporate, when we return, when we come back, we repeat in detail all the events of our former and past existences.

A rigorous repetition exists for some individuals, concrete cases of Egos that return through many centuries within the bosom of the same family, city and nation.

These are those who, because of incessantly repeating the same things, can predict with absolute clarity what awaits them in the future. These are those who can say, for example: "I will get married at the age of 30, my wife will have such a skin color, and such a height, the number of children, my father will die at such an age, my mother at such an age, my business will prosper or fail, etc., etc." And it is clear that all of this will later happen with surprising exactitude.

These are persons who know their role by the force of having repeated it so many times, thus they do not ignore it, and that is all!

Within this category also enter the child prodigies who astound the people of their era so much; usually, it has to do with Egos that already know their profession by heart, and when they return they marvelously repeat it from the first years of their childhood.

The Law of Recurrence is astonishing. Normal, everyday people always repeat their same dramas. Comedians repeat their same clowneries over and over again in each of their successive lives. The depraved continuously reincorporate in order to incessantly repeat the same tragedies.

All of these events proper to repeated existences are always accompanied by good or bad consequences, in accordance with the Law of Cause and Effect.

The assassin will again find himself in the same horrifying scene of assassination, but he will be assassinated. The thief will again encounter the same opportunity to steal, but he will be thrown in jail. The bandit will feel the same desire of running, of using his legs for crimes, but he will not have legs, he will be born disabled or he will lose them in some tragedy. The person blind from birth will long to see the things of life that possibly led him to cruelty, etc., but he will not be able to see. A woman will love the same husband from her previous life, the one whom she possibly abandoned on the sick bed to run off with some other individual but now the drama will be repeated inversely and the man she loves will leave her for another woman, leaving her abandoned. The highway bandit will again feel the desire of running, of fleeing, he will clamor perhaps in a state of mental delirium, attired in a new body —possibly of a feminine nature— he will have strange deliriums, he will not be able to escape from himself, he will go crazy, he will be mentally ill, etc., etc. Thus, friends, this is how the Law of Recurrence incessantly works...

Question: Master, is a country that has been affected for a long time by violence due to the Law of Recurrence?

Answer: Obviously, the violence of the masses in that country is the repetition of similar violence that occurred in a chaotic past.

Think of the civil wars that took place in periods prior to the violence that occurred; wars between political parties of the right and left repeating themselves in the present as a result of the past. Therein is the Law of Recurrence.

Question: Master, if a person has been upright, if he has behaved as a good citizen in the fulfillment of his duties, how would the Law of Recurrence operate within him in his next return?

Answer: Friends, friends, do not tell me that such a fellow has been a paragon of virtues, a spring of sanctity. As magnificent a citizen as he might have been, he had his very human errors, his scenes, his dramas, etc., and it is clear that there will be a repetition of all of this in his new existence, plus the consequences; this is how the Law of Recurrence operates.

Question: Venerable Master, there is certain confusion regarding how the Law of Karma and the Law of Recurrence relate to one another, because I have the concept that with the termination of Karma, the Law of Recurrence terminates. Would you like to clarify this point for me?

Answer: Friends, in no way can there be confusion between the Laws of Recurrence and Karma, since they are both the same thing with a different name. Indubitably, karma works on firm foundations; it is just the effect of a cause that we ourselves planted. Therefore, the event in itself has to be repeated, plus its good or bad consequences.

Question: Master, people who apparently did not do anything evil to anyone suffer due to financial hardships. Does this have to do with the Law of Recurrence?

Answer: Distinguished friends, ladies and gentlemen, the Father who is in secret, can be close to us or far from us. When the son is doing badly, the Father goes away; then he falls into disgrace; he suffers because of lack of money, he undergoes terrible necessities, he cannot explain to himself the cause of his misery.

Clearly, such people believe that they have not done harmed to anyone; if they could remember their past lives, they could evince for themselves the concrete fact that they have treaded on wrong paths, possibly they gave in to alcohol, to lust, to adultery, etc.

The Father who is in secret, our own divine Spirit, can give to us or take away from us. He knows what we deserve very well and if we presently do not have money, it is because He does not want to give it to us; he punishes us for our own good.

Blessed is the man who God punishes. The Father who loves his child always punishes him for his own good.

In the particular case of this question, the victim of the sufferings will repeat the scenes from the past, plus the consequences: poverty, pain, etc., etc.

Question: Master, does the Law of Recurrence end with the 108 lives?

Answer: Friends, once the cycle of human existences assigned to every Soul concludes, the Law of Recurrence also concludes in the infernal Abysses; with humanoid scenes and animalistic, plantoid and mineraloid states repeating themselves.

Before reaching the humanoid state, we go through the Mineral, Plant and Animal Kingdoms; but upon entering the Abyss –once the human cycle of existences is exhausted– the animalistic, plantoid and mineraloid states repeat themselves again. This is how the Law of Recurrence works.

Question: Master, does the person who succeeds in liberating himself from the Wheel of Samsara no longer repeat the Law of Recurrence?

Answer: I will very gladly reply to the lady who has asked the question... I want you ladies and gentlemen to know that the Law of Recurrence, in its superior aspect, corresponds to the Law of Katancia –Superior Karma–.

The Holy Gods have to repeat cosmic scenes from ancient Maha-Manvantaras in each new Great Day that dawns, plus the consequences.

Remember that the Gods also make mistakes. Those sacred individuals, who in the present Earth period gave the Abominable Kundabuffer Organ to humanity, will pay for their mistakes by repeating similar dramas in the future Maha-Manvantara.

Our present Earth, along with the humanity that populates it, is the result of Cosmic Karma; and it is incessantly repeating the historic periods of the ancient Moon, along with the cosmic results.

Any Great Initiate will be able to verify for himself the concrete, clear, and definitive fact that the ancient inhabitants of Selene were indeed cruel and merciless.

The results are before our eyes, in the black pages of the black history of our afflicted earthly planet.

Question: Master, who are those who are free from the Law of Recurrence?

Answer: Look at the Law of Recurrence in its superior and inferior aspects of the Great Life. We can solemnly affirm that only those who are capable of crystallizing the Three Primary Forces of the universe within their intimate nature are freed from the Law of Recurrence.

The Sacred Absolute Sun wants to crystallize these Three Primary Forces within each one of us. Let us collaborate with Him and his holy designs, and we will remain free from the Law of Recurrence forever.

23

THE SPIRAL OF EXISTENCE

My friends, today we are going to talk extensively about the spiral line of life.

Much has been said about the Doctrine of the Transmigration of Souls, presented by Lord Krishna in the Sacred Land of the Vedas, about a thousand years before Jesus Christ.

In past talks we have already presented all of these processes of the Wheel of Samsara.

We have said with complete clarity, we have repeated it over and over again, that every Soul is assigned 108 lives for its Intimate Self-Realisation.

Unquestionably, those who fail during their cycle of manifestation, those who do not attain Self-Realization within their number of assigned existences, obviously descend into the Submerged Mineral Kingdom, the Hindustani "Avitchi", the Greek "Tartarus", the Roman "Avernus".

It is obvious and evident that involution within the bowels of the planet in which we live is terribly painful.

To recapitulate animalistic, plantoid and mineraloid states, in a truly degenerating manner, is by no means very pleasant.

We also affirmed in our previous lectures that, after Second Death, the Essence, what we have of Soul, re-ascends in an evolutionary manner from the Mineral Kingdom to the intellectual animal, mistakenly called man, by passing through the Plant and Animal stages.

Nevertheless, there is something in this Law of Transmigration of Souls that we have not said; we have mentioned this other Law of Eternal Return, we have mentioned this other Law known as Recurrence, but we must clarify that these two mentioned laws develop and unfold upon the spiral line of life.

This means that every cycle of manifestation is processed in ever higher spirals or curves within the great spiral line of the universe.

Since this also tends to be a little bit abstract, I see the need to clarify it better, so that all of you can profoundly comprehend the Teaching.

When the Essence escapes after Second Death, as it resurges under the light of the sun, obviously transformed into a Gnome, it will have to reinitiate a new evolving process, but within a superior octave. This means that this Mineral Elemental creature will undoubtedly find itself within the Mineral Kingdom with a state of Consciousness superior to that one it had when it initiated a similar evolution in the previous cycle of manifestation.

Upon continuing with these explanations, you must not forget that any cycle of manifestation includes evolutions in the Mineral, Plant, Animal and Human Kingdoms –in this latter 108 existences are always assigned to us.

If we examine a conch, we will see curve upon curve, something similar to a spiral type of staircase; it is evident that each one of these cycles of manifestation develops in successively higher curves.

Now you will understand why there is such a great variety of Mineral, Plant and Animal Elementals, and diverse degrees of intelligence among humanoids.

Unquestionably, there is a very great difference between the Mineral Elementals that start out as such for the first time, and those that have already repeated the same process many times.

We can say the same thing about Plant and Animal Elementals, or about humanoids.

Since there are always 3,000 cycles of manifestation, the last one of these is really found at a very high octave.

Those Essences that during the 3,000 turns of the Wheel did not attain Mastery are absorbed by their Virginal Spark in order to definitely submerge themselves within the bosom of the Universal Spirit of Life...

It is obvious, clear and evident that during the cycles of cosmic manifestation, we must pass through all the practical experiences of life.

Indubitably, any Essence that has passed through the 3,000 cycles of manifestation has also experienced the horrors of the Abyss 3,000 times, and consequently it has improved and acquired Self-consciousness.

Thus, those Essences are in fact fully entitled to divine happiness. Unfortunately, they will not enjoy Mastery; they did not acquire it and because of this do not have it.

We already said in previous lectures that not all the divine Monads or Virginal Sparks are interested in Mastery.

Clearly, it is not the Virginal Sparks or divine Monads who suffer, but the Essence, the emanation of the mentioned Sparks, what we have of Soul in each of us.

The pain undergone by every Essence is certainly well-rewarded, because in exchange for so much suffering, Self-consciousness and happiness without limits are acquired.

Mastery is different. No one could attain Adepthood without the Three Factors of the Revolution of Consciousness, clearly expressed by our Lord the Christ: "Whoever is willing to come after me let him deny himself, take up his cross, and follow me."

To deny oneself means dissolution of the "I". To take the Cross, to place it on our shoulders, means to work with Sex-Yoga, with the Maithuna, with Sexual Magic. To follow the Christ, is equivalent to sacrificing oneself for humanity, to give one's life so that others may live.

The Virginal Sparks that did not attain Mastery during their 3,000 cycles of manifestation see the Masters, the Gods, in a manner similar to how ants see humanoids.

Aztec traditions say that in the dawn of life, the Gods gathered in Teotihuacan with the purpose of creating the Sun. They affirm that they lit a great bonfire and thereafter they invited the Conch God to hurl himself into that bonfire, yet after attempting it three times, he felt great terror.

The sacred songs solemnly affirm that the Purulent God, filled with great courage, hurled himself into the fire.

When the Conch God saw this, he imitated his example. Then, the entire assembly of Gods waited silently to see what was going to happen.

The legends say that from within the living fire sprouted to form the Purulent God again, transformed into the Sun that illuminates us today.

Minutes later, the Conch God resurged transformed into the Moon that illuminates us at night.

Dear friends, this means that if we want to transform ourselves into Gods, into Masters, we must imitate the Purulent, incinerate the Ego, the "I", by means of Sexual Fire. Only through Fire will the Purulent, the Myself, the Oneself, die.

Only through Fire can we transform ourselves into tremendously Divine Solar Gods.

Unfortunately, not all Virginal Sparks are interested in Mastery; the majority, the millions of creatures that live on the face of the Earth, prefer the path of the Conch, the lunar path.

Question: Venerable Master, at the beginning of this important dissertation, you tell us that when the Essence descends to the Infernal Worlds, animaloid, plantoid, and mineraloid states are recapitulated. Would you be so kind as to explain the word "recapitulate"?

Answer: With great pleasure I will answer this gentleman's question. I want you, friends of mine, to comprehend very well what the animaloid, plantoid, and mineraloid abysmal recapitulation is.

To descend while involuting within the entrails of the buried earth is radically different from the evolving, ascent upon the surface of the Earth.

The animaloid recapitulation in the Abyss is of a degenerative, involuting, descending and painful type.

The plantoid recapitulation within the entrails of the Earth is frightening; those who undergo such processes appear more like shadows that creep here, there, and everywhere in inexplicable suffering.

The involutive mineral recapitulative descent within the entrails of the world in which we live is more bitter that death itself; creatures fossilize, mineralize and slowly disintegrate amidst torments impossible to describe with words.

After Second Death, the Essence escapes, resurges into the light of the sun, to recapitulate similar processes in an evolutive, ascending, innocent and happy manner.

There you have it my friends, the difference between involutive and evolving recapitulations.

In any case, all of these infinite involutive and evolving processes are exclusively of a lunar type and they clearly unfold within the universal Conch.

Question: Master, you explained that in each cycle of existences, the Elementals in the evolving process awaken Consciousness because they are being processed in more elevated octaves. Is this awakening of the Consciousness perhaps the result of the sufferings during involution or is it the result of the ascending process?

Answer: Distinguished friend, it is good for you to understand that the Consciousness suffers in the evolving processes as well as in the involuting processes and that therefore, based on so many efforts and sacrifices, it awakens progressively.

Millions of humanoids have their Consciousness profoundly asleep, yet when they enter into the Abyss after the 108 existences of any cycle of manifestation, they inevitably awaken in evil and for evil.

What is interesting in this case is that they awaken anyway, even if it is only to justify their errors in the Infernal Worlds.

Any Illuminated clairvoyant will be able to verify for himself the fact that the innocent Elementals are awake in the positive, evolving sense.

We see, then, two kinds of awakened Consciousness:

1. That of the innocent creatures of nature.

2. That of the involuting humanoids of the Abyss.

There is a third type of awakened people. I am referring to the Masters, to the Gods, but we are not dealing with them at this precise moment.

Unquestionably, within the Wheel of Samsara, rotating along with it, there are innocent, awakened Consciousnesses and also involuting abysmal creatures awakened in evil and for evil...

Question: Master, when you mention this matter about more elevated octaves within higher spirals, it disconcerts me, because I am used to thinking of octaves in relation to musical notes, which are related with the transmutation of the Serpentine Fire. Would you like to clarify this for me?

Answer: Indubitably, the octaves of the Conch process musically with the notes Do, Re, Mi, Fa, Sol, La, Si, in a gradual manner.

If we carefully observe a spiral staircase, we will see a succession of curves that are increasingly higher, in such a manner that they are preceded by lower ones.

This formation, this distribution of curves in the shape of any spiral, is enough for us to comprehend that between octave and octave there are also musical pauses. Each one of these pauses corresponds to an abysmal descent.

The 3,000 turns of the Wheel resound incessantly as a unique whole within the rhythms of Mahavan and of Chotavan that sustain the universe firmly on its way...

Question: Master, the Essence being good, why does it come to suffer in this world?

Answer: Friends of mine, the Essence in itself is beyond good and evil; it is absolutely innocent, pure, and unblemished.

When the Essence ends up bottled up within the Ego it suffers, but when it is dissolved, the Essence ceases to suffer.

The Essences of the planet Earth certainly remained bottled up within the Myself due to a mistake of the Gods. We already said in past lectures that certain sacred individuals gave humanity the Abominable Kundabuffer Organ with the purpose of stabilizing the geological crust of our world.

When that organ disappeared, the consequences remained within each person and the latter crystallized, becoming the Ego, a kind of second nature within which the Essence remained lamentably bottled up.

If that second nature did not exist, the Essence would be free and happy; unfortunately, it exists as a result of the Abominable Kundabuffer Organ.

Question: Master, it is said that we are children of God and that God is perfect. Why then does he send his children to suffer?

Answer: With great pleasure I will answer this question from the audience... Ladies and gentlemen, the time has come for us to know that all of us are children of the Devil... I beg you please to not be frightened.

We already know that the Mister Satan or Lucifer-Prometheus is exclusively the shadow of our own internal Divinity, projected within ourselves for our own good.

It is evident that Lucifer is the great trainer that we carry within; thus, the sexual impulse is ultimately Luciferian.

Therefore, the Devil is not –as we have already explained in past lectures– that fantastic character that some dogmatic sects present to us, but the personal instructor of each one.

It is then the luciferian force that leads humanoids to triumph or to failure, to generation or to regeneration.

From this standpoint we can affirm that we are children of the Devil and this has been said by our Lord the Christ: "Children of the devil you are" –the great Master said-, "because if you were children of God, you would do the works of God." It is necessary for us to become children of God, and this is only possible with the Three Factors of the Revolution of the Consciousness, as we have mentioned in this lecture.

A child of God is each one who reaches resurrection; reflect then on these words and do not boast of being saints or virtuous, because all of you are children of the Devil.

Friends, God never sends us to suffer; we ourselves have created the sufferings with our own mistakes and through successive births.

Question: Master, if we are Children of the Devil, who has more power over us, the Devil or God?

Answer: I will answer this question with great pleasure. We have said that the Dragon is the shadow of the intimate God of each one of us. It is evident that each one of us is a child of that shadow, of that Dragon; consequently –in the present state in which we find ourselves– the Dragon controls us absolutely. Therefore, from this relative and circumstantial point of view in which we find ourselves, the Devil has more power over us than God himself –this does not mean that the Devil is more powerful than God.

When the Immortal Spark resurrects within us, when we transform ourselves into children of God, then everything will be different; in those days we will have overcome the Dragon.

Question: Master, what can you tell me about the Angels, Bodhisattvas and fallen Masters? How do they relate to the spiral of life?

Answer: Distinguished friends, a supreme moment exists for all the millions of Essences that populate the face of the Earth.

I want to emphatically refer to that instant when we resolve for the first time to enter the Solar Path, which is indeed very different from the Lunar Path.

For all the millions or trillions of Virginal Sparks the precise moment, the critical time arrives when they have to define themselves for the Solar Path or for the Lunar Conch. When someone deliberately chooses the Path of the Razor's Edge, the die is cast; after that moment there is no turning back.

Those who attain Mastery and who thereafter want to go back in order to enter the Lunar Path, will have to undergo frightening eternities within the Infernal Worlds, until obtaining, after many billions or trillions of years, the annihilation of the Superior Existential Bodies of the Being and the destruction of the animal Ego.

This means that the greater the degree of Consciousness, the greater the degree of responsibility, and anyone who adds wisdom, adds pain.

Unquestionably, the fallen Bodhisattvas, the black Angels, the tenebrous Archangels, that is to say, the angelic or divine creatures submerged within the Abyss for the crime of wanting to take the Lunar Path after having fully defined themselves for the Solar, will have to suffer millions of times more intensely than common, ordinary people.

Once the disintegration of Vehicles and Ego has been obtained, they will in any case restart the evolving journey from the mineral, but with a Golden Embryo and consequently with greater Consciousness than the other Elementals of nature, until reaching the humanoid state.

Once this objective has been attained, given that they possess the Golden Embryo, these beings will have to return to the Solar Path in order to create their Superior Existential Bodies anew, and reconquer the Angelic or Archangelic state, etc., that they once rejected.

Another is the fate of the Virginal Sparks that never chose the Solar Path; they, transformed into simple Elementals of nature, will submerge with their Essence into the Universal Ocean of Life free in its movement.

These are Beings who preferred elemental life, who did not aspire Mastery, who always enjoyed being within the bosom of Great Nature, and who now, as sparks of Divinity, return to it forever.

24

NEGOTIATIONS

Friends of mine gathered here tonight, we are going to very seriously study this matter of negotiations.

Allow me the liberty to tell you that I am not talking about profane business; I want to emphatically refer to the negotiations of karma.

First of all, it is necessary that people understand what the Sanskrit word "karma" means.

It is not superfluous to affirm that the word in itself means the Law of Action and Consequence. Obviously, there is neither cause without effect, nor effect without cause. Any action in our life, whether good or bad, has its consequences.

Today, I have been reflecting on the misfortune of our world: how happy these intellectual humanoids would be if they had never had that which is called the Ego, the "I", Myself, Oneself.

It is indubitable that the Ego commits innumerable mistakes whose result is pain.

If these rational humanoids were devoid of Ego, they would simply be very beautiful, innocent, pure, and infinitely happy natural Elementals.

Imagine for a moment, dear friends, an Earth like this, populated by millions of innocent humanoids, devoid of Ego and governed by Divine Kings, Gods, Hierophants, Devas, etc., etc., etc. Obviously, a world like this would certainly be a paradise, a planet of the blessed individuals.

Nobody can be obligated to become a Man by force. All those millions of humanoids, even though they are not Men in the most complete sense of the word, could have been infinitely happy if a second, malignant and terribly perverse nature had not emerged within their interior.

Unfortunately, as we have already profusely said in these lectures, due to a mistake committed by certain sacred individuals, something abnormal appeared within each individual: certain inhuman elements, in which the Consciousness became bottled up.

It is clear that such inhuman elements emerged as a result of the bad consequences of the Abominable Kundabuffer Organ. This is how, dear friends, this planetary humanity failed; becoming frightfully evil.

It would have been better if those sacred individuals had not given these wretched tri-brained or tri-centered bipeds that abominable organ of all infamies.

Let us think for a moment about the multitude of humanoids that populate the face of the Earth. They suffer the unspeakable, victims of their own errors. Without the Ego they would not have those errors, nor would they suffer their consequences.

We already stated in past lectures that not all Virginal Sparks, that not all humanoids, are interested in Mastery; nonetheless, this is not an obstacle for authentic happiness.

Within infinite space there are many blissful abodes for Elemental Humanoids who have no interest in Mastery.

Unquestionably, the 3,000 cycles or periods of time assigned to any Essence, to any Monad for their cosmic manifestation, unfold not only here in our world the Earth, but also in other worlds of starry space.

Due to all of this you will be able to see, my dear friends, that for the Souls there are many mansions of happiness, and that Mastery is by no means indispensable in order to have the right to the authentic bliss of pure Spirit. The only thing that is required in order to have the right to true happiness is before all to not have Ego.

Indeed, when the psychic aggregates –the inhuman elements that make us so horrible and wicked– do not exist within us, there is no karma to pay and the result is happiness.

Not all of the blissful creatures that live in all of the worlds of infinite space have reached Mastery. Nonetheless, they are in tune with cosmic order because they do not have Ego.

When one lives according to upright thinking, upright feeling and upright acting, the consequences are usually blissful.

Unfortunately, the correct way of thinking, the correct way of feeling, the correct way of acting, etc., become impossible when a second inhumane nature acts in us, and within us and through us, here and now.

Confusions must be avoided regarding what we have just said. It is obvious that among the many, few aspire to Adepthood, to the Intimate Self-Realization of the Being. Unquestionably, these Souls transform into true Kings of the Universe and into terribly divine Gods.

The multitudes, after their 3,000 cycles of manifestation, return into the Universal Spirit of Life as simple, blissful Elementals.

What is unpleasant is that these millions of Humanoid Elementals have created within themselves a second infra-human nature, and this in itself has made them not only wicked, but moreover, and what is worse, wretched.

If it were not for the Myself, nobody would be irate, nobody would covet the goods of their neighbor, nobody would be lustful, envious, proud, lazy, gluttonous, etc., etc., etc.

I regret very much to have to say that Archangel Sakaki and his high commission of sacred individuals —who in archaic times gave the Abominable Kundabuffer Organ to humanity— will face unspeakable bitterness, horrifying karma, in the future Great Cosmic Day, since there is no doubt that due to their mistake, this humanity lost its happiness and became monstrous... May the Holy Gods forgive me for such an affirmation, but facts are facts and we have to surrender before facts, whatever the cost.

Fortunately, my dear friends, Justice and Mercy are the two principal columns of the Universal White Fraternity...

Justice without Mercy is tyranny; Mercy without Justice is tolerance, complacency with crime.

In this world of misfortune in which we find ourselves, it is necessary to learn how to manage our own businesses, in order to maneuver the ship of existence through the diverse stops of life.

Karma is negotiable, and this is something that may come as a great surprise to the followers of diverse orthodox schools.

Indeed, some pseudo-esotericists and pseudo-occultists have become too pessimistic regarding the Law of Action and Consequence; they mistakenly suppose that it unfolds in a mechanical, automatic and cruel manner.

Scholars believe that it is not possible to alter that Law; I very sincerely regret to have to dissent from that way of thinking.

If the Law of Action and Consequence, if the Nemesis of existence was not negotiable, then where would Divine Mercy be? Frankly, I cannot accept cruelty within Divinity. The Real, that which is all perfection, that which has diverse names such as Tao, Aum, Inri, Sein, Allah, Brahma, God, or better said Gods, etc., etc., etc., could by no means be something without mercy, cruel, tyrannical, etc. Due to all of this I emphatically repeat that karma is negotiable.

When an inferior law is transcended by a superior law, the superior law washes away the inferior law.

Do good deeds so as to pay your debts.

The Lion of the Law is fought with the Scales.

Whosoever has capital with which to pay, pays and does well in his negotiation; the one who does not have any capital will pay with pain.

If we place the good deeds on one plate of the Cosmic Scales and the bad deeds on the other one, it is evident that our karma will depend on the weight on the Scales. If the plate of bad deeds weighs more, the result will be bitterness. However, it is possible to increase the weight of the good deeds on the plate of the Scale, and in this manner, we will cancel karma without the need to suffer. All that we need is to do good deeds in order to increase the weight of the plate of good deeds.

Now you will comprehend, good friends of mine, how marvelous it is to do good; there is no doubt that upright thinking, upright feeling and upright acting are the best way to negotiate.

We must never protest against karma; what is important is to know how to negotiate it.

Unfortunately, the only thing that occurs to people when they find themselves in great bitterness is to wash their hands like Pilate, to say that they did nothing bad, that they are not guilty, that they are righteous souls, etc., etc., etc.

I tell those who are in misery to examine their conduct, to judge themselves, to sit down at least for an instant on the bench of the accused, that after a brief analysis of themselves, they should modify their behavior. If those who find themselves unemployed would become chaste, infinitely charitable, peaceful, one hundred percent helpful, it is obvious that they would radically alter the cause of their misfortunes; as a consequence, the effect is modified.

It is not possible to alter an effect if the cause that produced it has not been radically modified first, since as we have already said, there is no effect without cause nor cause without effect.

There is no doubt that misery has its causes in drunkenness, in disgusting lust, in violence, in adulteries, in squandering and in avarice, etc., etc.

It is not possible for someone to live in misery when the Father who is in secret is present here and now. I want to illustrate this with a story...

On a certain occasion, my Real Inner Being, my immortal Monad, took me out of the physical body in order to give me instructions about a certain disciple. Once concluded, I did not hesitate to address the Intimate Lord with the following words.

"I am tired of having a body, and what I would like is to disincarnate."

In those moments the Lord of Perfections, my inner God, answered with a solemn voice:

"Why are you complaining? I have given you food, clothing and shelter and you still complain? Do you remember the final days of your past existence? You wandered in the streets of Mexico barefoot, with the suit torn, old, sick and in the most frightful misery. And how did you die? In a filthy shack. At that time, I was absent."

In those moments, the face of my Lord shone; the infinite Heaven was reflected in his blue eyes; his white robe of glory reached his feet; everything in Him was perfection.

"Lord," I told him, "I have come to kiss your hand and receive your blessing."

The Adorable One blessed me and I kissed his right hand.

After returning to my physical body I entered into meditation. Indeed, my dear brethren, when the child errs, the Father goes away, thus the child falls into disgrace.

I think that you are now beginning to better comprehend, my dear friends, what misery is, why it happens, how it happens...

The Father who is in secret has enough power to give onto us, as well as to take away from us. Blissful is the man who God reproves.

Karma is a medicine that is applied to us for our own good.

Regrettably, people –instead of bowing down reverently before the living eternal God– protest, blaspheme, justify themselves, foolishly make excuses for themselves and wash their hands like Pilate. With such protests, karma is not modified; on the contrary, it becomes harder and more severe.

We demand fidelity from our spouse when we ourselves have been adulterers in this life or in former lives.

We ask for love when we have been merciless and cruel.

We demand comprehension when we have never been able to comprehend anyone, when we have never learned how to see the point of view of our neighbor.

We long for immense bliss when we have always been the cause for much unhappiness. We would have liked to be born in a very beautiful home with lots of comforts, yet in past lives we were not able to provide a home and beauty for our children.

We protest against insulters when we have always insulted everyone who surrounds us.

We want our children to obey us when we have never been able to obey our parents.

Slander bothers us terribly even though we have always been slanderers and have filled the world with pain.

Gossip upsets us, we do not want anyone to talk about us, and nonetheless, we were always involved in gossip and backbiting, talking bad about our neighbor, mortifying the lives of others, that is to say, we always demand what we have not given.

We were evil in all of our former lives and we deserve the worst, but we suppose that the best should be offered to us.

The sick —instead of worrying so much about themselves— should work for others, do works of charity, try to heal others, console the afflicted, take the doctor to those who cannot afford to pay him, give away medicines, etc., and in this manner, they would cancel their karma and they would heal totally.

Those who suffer in their homes should multiply their humility, patience and serenity; not reply with bad words, not tyrannize their fellow man, not upset those who surround us, know how to forgive the defects of their fellow man with infinitely multiplied patience; this is how they would cancel their karma and they would become better.

Regrettably, my dear friends, the Ego that each one carries within does exactly the opposite of what we are saying here; for that reason, I consider it urgent, unpostponable, imperative to reduce the Myself to cosmic dust.

Question: Venerable Master, do you consider your mission accomplished if you achieve that the intellectual humanoids transform themselves into innocent elementals?

Answer: I will answer this question with great pleasure... Many Prophets, Great Avatars and Masters fought in ancient times against the bad consequences of the Abominable Kundarbuffer Organ. This is a popular type of mission, whose purpose is to make humanity return to total innocence.

Those Saints, in ancient times, also had their esoteric circle for those of the Direct Path, for those who in all ages aspired to attain Mastery.

Behold, friends, therefore the two circles: the exoteric or public, and the esoteric or secret. It is not superfluous to remind you that the great confessional religions precisely fulfill these two needs. Any confessional religion serves the multitudes as well as the Initiates. I believe that now you have completely understood the meaning of my mission on the face of this afflicted world in which we live.

Question: Master, can any type of suffering that one is under-going be attributed to the absence of the Father?

Answer: Friends, there are voluntary and involuntary suffer-ings. The first are processed within those who follow the Direct Path, the Solar Path; the second is the outcome of our own karma. It is obvious that when the child errs the Father is absent and the consequence is pain.

Question: In regards to Nemesis or karma, is it possible that any suffering can be negotiable before the Lords of Karma?

Answer: Esteemed friends, I want you to comprehend that when this or that karma has been totally developed and unfolded, it inevitably has to reach its end.

This means that it is only possible to radically modify karma when repentance is total and when every possibility of repeating the error that produced it has radically disappeared.

When Karmaduro reaches its end, it is always catastrophic. Not all karma is negotiable.

Likewise, it is good to know that when we have radically elim-inated the Ego, the possibility of delinquency is annihilated, and as a consequence karma can be forgiven.

25

DIRECT EXPERIENCE

Distinguished friends, today, March 19, 1973, the eleventh year of Aquarius, we gather in order to conclude these lectures which unquestionably will have to be published as a book for the sake of the Great Cause.

In conclusion, I want to place emphasis on the necessity of directly experience everything that we have explained.

The experience of what is Real is cardinal and definitive for Creative Comprehension.

The time has come to understand, with complete clarity, that we indeed possess a definitive psychological factor, by means of which it is possible to verify what we have said in all of these gatherings.

With great solemnity I want to refer to the very foundation of our psychic organization, to that element which has not yet been lost: the Essence.

It is indubitable that in it, in the Consciousness, are found the Buddha, the Doctrine, the Religion, and the Wisdom.

In synthesis, we can affirm that in the Essence, in the Consciousness are deposited the indispensable data for regeneration, Inner Self-Realization and for the complete experience of everything that we have stated in these lectures.

This means that if in that primary element –primordial foundation of all our psychic organization– are found the basic principles of regeneration, then obviously the first thing that we need to do is to destroy, to annihilate that second nature of an infernal type, within which the Essence is imprisoned.

It is clear and evident that upon un-bottling the Essence, when it is liberated, it radically awakens.

The advantages that the mentioned event can provide us with, as you can see, are multiple.

The first among those advantages is magnificent in itself, since it has the capacity of fundamentally guiding us by wisely directing our steps along the Path of the Razor's Edge, which should lead us to final Liberation.

The second of those advantages is it guides us along the path of those varied direct experiences until we have reached the total verification of each and every one of the affirmations that we have made in these lectures.

Integral illumination, luminous experience and practical confirmation, are the modus operandi of the un-bottled, awakened, self-conscious Essence.

Complete annihilation of all undesirable elements that constitute the Myself, the Oneself is beyond all doubt urgent, unpostponable.

We need to learn how to voluntarily direct all the functionalisms of our psyche. It is not good that we continue being enslaved; we must become masters and lords of ourselves.

As the undesirable elements are being eliminated, the Consciousness awakens. Nonetheless, we need to become serious because up to now we have not been serious people.

Each one of us is presently nothing more than a log upon the boisterous waves of the sea of existence. I repeat: we need to become serious; this affirmation implies tremendous self-vigilance from instant to instant, from moment to moment.

Remember what we have already said in previous lectures: in relation to our fellow men, the defects that we carry hidden spring forth spontaneously and if we are alert and vigilant like a sentry in times of war, then we discover them. In every self-discovery there is also self-revelation. A discovered defect must be rigorously analyzed, studied in all the levels of the mind and integrally comprehended through the diverse processes of profound inner meditation.

A little later on and once the defect that we have analyzed has been integrally understood, come the supplications to Devi-Kundalini, our particular Divine Cosmic Mother, with the objective that She eliminates and disintegrates the defect in question.

The work is very profound, my esteemed brothers, frightfully serious, indeed extremely profound.

Only in this manner is it possible to extirpate, to eradicate from our psyche many undesirable, infra-human, tenebrous elements within which the Essence finds itself imprisoned.

As the Consciousness awakens, the possibilities of direct experience become successively more lucid and continuous. First of all, my dear friends, I want you to learn how to practically manage the diverse sparks of an awakened Consciousness.

In practical life we can carefully detect the concrete fact that all people live with their Consciousness asleep.

In these moments, something remarkable comes to mind. Some seventeen or eighteen years ago, as I found myself in a market in the Federal District with my priestess-wife Litelantes and as we were picking up a watch that she had sent to be repaired in a watchmaking store, we were suddenly shaken by violent dynamite explosion.

Litelantes, horrified, asked me that we return home immediately. It is obvious that my answer was frankly no, by no means did I want to expose our lives to a second explosion that I knew had to occur. Her pleading was in vain... In those moments the sirens and bells of the "smoke-eaters" or firemen resounded.

Those humble and martyr servants of humanity hurried towards the scene of the explosions... "Of all those firemen who have just entered the theatre of the events, not one will be saved; they will die!" Those were my words.

Horrified, Litelantes kept silent. Instants later, a second explosion shook Mexico City in a terrible way...

The result was death for all those humble servants. They were automatically disintegrated since not even the corpses were found; the only thing that could be found was a sergeant's boot.

Frankly, I was astounded by the degree of unconsciousness that those firemen were in. If they had been awake, they would not have perished at all.

I still remember the weeping of the women who fled from that market, and of the children who, horrified, grabbed the skirts of their mothers.

If I had not been awake, obviously I would have perished, because at the place where I had to board the bus, so indispensable for returning home, hundreds of people died.

I have not yet been able to forget so many corpses that, thrown on the edge of the sidewalk of the street, laid there covered with newspapers. Unquestionably, those victims were due to curiosity...

They were curious, unconscious people, asleep, who after the first explosion had rushed to the place of the events in order to contemplate the spectacle.

If those people had been awake, they would never have rushed curiously to the place of the events. Regrettably, they were sleeping profoundly; this is how they encountered death.

When we returned to our home, located in the Caracol neighborhood, our neighbors were alarmed; they supposed that we had died.

They were indeed astounded that, despite being so close to the place of the catastrophe, we were still able to return home alive; see here the advantage of being awake.

One has to awaken, friends, and to learn to live alert from moment to moment, from instant to instant. It is unpostponable to always divide our attention into three parts:

1. Subject.

2. Object.

3. Location.

Subject: Never forgetting oneself, watching ourselves every second, every moment. This implies a state of alertness in relation to our thoughts, gestures, actions, emotions, habits, words, etc., etc., etc.

Object: Detailed observation of all those objects or representations that reach the mind through our senses. Never identify ourselves with things, because this is how one falls into fascination and into the sleep of the Consciousness.

Location: Daily observation of our home, our bedroom, as if it was something new; asking oneself daily: Why did I come here, to this place, to this market, to this office, to this temple, etc.?

These three aspects of the division of attention by no means constitute a chapter apart or something different from the process of the dissolution of the "I".

We indisputably need to self-study ourselves, to self-observe ourselves from moment to moment, if we really want to discover our own psychological defects, since as we have already said, in relation to our fellow beings the hidden defects spring forth spontaneously, naturally.

It is not merely about self-observing the steps that we take, nor the positions of the body, etc.

Vigilance upon oneself implies a silent and serene study of all our intimate psychological processes: emotions, passions, thoughts, words, etc., etc., etc.

The observation of things without identification will allow us to know the processes of covetousness, attachment, ambition, etc., etc., etc. It is irrefutable that a covetous person will struggle greatly in order not to identify with a diamond ring or with some banknotes, etc., etc.

The observation of the locations will allow us to know how far our attachments and fascinations go in relation to diverse places.

This triple set of attention is therefore a complete exercise in order to discover ourselves and to awaken Consciousness...

I was still very young, a tender adolescent, when I instinctively practiced this marvelous exercise mentioned here.

In the instants when I tell you this, two special cases come to mind, which I will narrate...

First: One of many nights, I entered through the doors of a marvelous mansion; silently, I passed through a beautiful garden until arriving a luxurious hall. Moved by an inner impulse, I walked a little further and fearlessly entered an attorney's office.

Seated at the desk, I found a lady of average height, with gray hair, pale face, thin lips, and small pointed nose.

That lady had a respectable appearance and was of medium height. Her body was not very thin, yet it was not too fat either. Her gaze was somewhat melancholic and serene.

Then, with a sweet and quiet voice, the lady invited me to sit in front of the desk. In those instants something unexpected happens: I see on top of the desk two glass butterflies that were alive, they moved their wings, breathed, looked around, etc., etc., etc. I indeed found the case all too exotic and odd: two glass butterflies and they were alive?

As I was accustomed to dividing my attention into three parts, first of all I did not forget myself; secondly, I did not identify with those glass butterflies; thirdly, I observed the place carefully.

When contemplating those glass animals, I told myself: This cannot be a phenomenon of the physical world, because in the tri-dimensional region of Euclid, I have never known glass butterflies with a life of their own; this can unquestionably be a phenomenon of the Astral World.

I then looked around and asked myself the following questions: Why am I in this place? Why did I come here? What am I doing here?

I then addressed the lady, I spoke to her in the following manner:

"Madam, allow me to go out to the garden for a moment, I will soon return. The lady nodded her head in agreement and I left the office for a moment."

Once outside, in the garden, I made a long jump with the intention of floating in the surrounding environment; great was my astonishment when I verified for myself that I indeed found myself outside of the physical body. Then I comprehended that I was in the Astral world.

In those moments I remembered that quite a while ago, several hours, I had abandoned my physical body; that it unquestionably found itself resting in its bed now.

Once this unique verification had been made, I returned to the office where the lady awaited me. I then wanted to convince her that she was outside of the physical body.

"Madam," I said, "you and I are outside of the physical body; I want you to remember that a few hours ago you laid down to sleep in bed; now you find yourself here conversing with me outside of your physical body, since it is well known that when the body sleeps, the Consciousness, the Essence −unfortunately trapped within the Ego− wanders outside of the corporeal vehicle."

Once all these words had been said, the lady looked at me with the eyes of a somnambulist, but she did not understand; I comprehended that that lady's Consciousness was asleep...

Not wanting to insist anymore, I bade her farewell and left the place. Thereafter, I headed towards California, with the purpose of carrying out certain important investigations...

On the way I met a deceased person who in life had been a carrier of heavy bundles in public markets; the unhappy man, carrying an enormous burden on his back, seemed to suffer the unspeakable... Approaching the defunct, I told him:

"My friend, what is the matter? Why are you carrying such a heavy burden upon your aching shoulders?"

The wretched looking at me with the eyes of a somnambulist, answered me:

"I am working."

"But sir," I insisted, "you died a long time ago already; that weight you are carrying upon your shoulders is nothing more than a mental form; abandon that..."

Everything was to no avail; that poor dead man did not understand me; his Consciousness was all too asleep...

Wanting to help him, I floated around him in the surrounding environment with the purpose of alarming him, of making him understand that something odd was happening in his existence, to make him realize in some way that he was dead, etc., etc., but everything was useless.

Afterwards, once the required investigations had been done, I returned to my physical vehicle that lay sleeping in bed.

Question: Master, do you mean to say that there is no possibility of a direct experience, as you have explained it in your lectures, without the dissolution of the psychological defects?

Answer: I will thoroughly answer this question coming from the audience... Gentleman, friends, ladies who are listening to me, direct experience is associated with the percentages of awakened Consciousness.

Normally people only possess 3% of awakened Consciousness and 97% sub-consciousness or sleeping Consciousness.

Unquestionably, when one reaches 4 or 5% of awakened Consciousness, the first sparks of direct experience begin.

Make a distinction between sparks and total plentitude, which are different.

Someone who possesses, for example, 10% of awakened Consciousness will thus have a greater percentage of lucidity than those who possess 4 or 5%.

In any case, as the Essence liberates itself, as the Ego starts to dissolve, the capacity for direct investigation will also increase in a progressive and orderly manner.

The exercise of dividing the attention into three parts, as we have already explained in this lecture, will allow us to witness the acquired degree of Consciousness endlessly.

I have taught here, well, doctrine and procedures to awaken Consciousness. I have given the system which is effective so as to intelligently use the percentages of acquired Consciousness.

When the Ego has been radically annihilated, the Consciousness is totally awakened; in those circumstances we can descend at will into the Infernal Worlds, with the purpose of seeing, hearing, touching and experiencing the crude reality of those submerged regions.

Because these types of investigations are so advanced that they can only be performed satisfactorily with an absolutely awakened Consciousness.

Question: Master, you mentioned two advantages that derive from the Essence: the first being that it guides us in order to live adequately and the second which grants us direct experience. In the experience that you had in the Federal District market, due to a tremendous explosion, which of the two faculties of the Essence allowed you to save your life?

Answer: Noble sir, allow me to tell you that the second of those qualities of the Consciousness, that of direct experience, allowed me to know about the event that was going to occur beforehand, which was the death of those firemen.

Question: Master, could you explain to us the difference between projections of the mind and real experiences?

Answer: I will gladly answer this new question from the audience... Allow me to tell you, ladies and gentlemen, that mental projections are of a completely subjective nature, indeed very different from real experiences which are of an objective kind.

In the first case, the mind projects what it has elaborated subconsciously and identified with those projections, falls into fascination and into the typical dreams of the un-consciousness.

In the second case, the mind has exhausted the process of thinking, it does not project, it is open to the new, it receives without identification and in the absence of all fascination and all dreamlike process.

I will illustrate this answer with a kind of supersensitive story: finding myself outside of my physical body, in the moments when it was profoundly sleeping in bed, I invoked a certain deceased who in life had been a truly close relative of my family.

The defunct presented himself dressed in a certain gray suit that he wore in life; he was laughing to himself, he truly seemed to be a somnambulist, he spoke nonsense —something that he heard from someone-... Useless were my efforts in order to make him recognize me: the wretched slept profoundly... He certainly did not see me; deep down, truly, he only perceived his own mental forms, and he laughed like a raving lunatic, like an idiot.

There are two aspects here which clarify, well, the question at hand. The defunct projected his own mental forms, he dreamed with them, he was absolutely fascinated by them, and he did not even perceive me.

In the second case I was completely conscious, awake, I knew that my physical body had remained asleep in bed, I was not projecting, I had exhausted the thinking process, I was opening to the new, I received the deceased, I investigated him, I became aware of the deplorable state he found himself in...

Thus, with this narrative I have illustrated the question that has come from the audience.

Question: Venerable Master, regarding the exercise of the division of the attention into three parts that is done here in this physical world, how is it that it can have a repercussion in the Astral World, if they are two completely different worlds?

Answer: My friends, if we observe life within normal, common and ordinary dreams we will be able to see the concrete fact that many scenes of the dream correspond to the occurrences of daily life, to the occurrences of each moment that we have lived right here in the physical world, to the actions of every moment.

As a direct consequence of what we are affirming, we can emphasize the information that the exercise of the division of the attention into three parts, will also be repeated during our dreams, during those hours when the Essence, bottled up within the Ego, is found outside of the physical body.

I think that you do not ignore the fact that when the body sleeps, the Essence, bottled up within the Myself, leaves the physical body.

Therefore, if we get used to practicing this exercise here in the physical world, from instant to instant and from moment to moment, we will then instinctively repeat it during the hours of sleep and the result will be the Awakening of the Consciousness. Then we will be able to see, hear, touch and experience all of what we have been saying in these lectures in relation to Hell, the Devil and Karma.

As the Ego is dissolving, the Consciousness awakens more and more, and we will be able to verify this by means of the exercise of the division of attention into three parts.

Once the Ego is absolutely dissolved, the exercise taught here will allow us to use the Consciousness in a voluntary way in order to investigate the great realities.

Question: Master, how can the difference between what is real and what is unreal, what is illusory from what is true, the objective from the subjective, be made accessible to the comprehension of the profane?

Answer: A very interesting question has surged from the audience, and it is clear that I hasten to answer it.

Friends of mine, some nights ago we were watching certain scientific news on television...

By means of diverse representations on the screen, the public was informed about experiments that today's men of science are performing on the brain.

By connecting certain nodules to the brain, men of science can control the different sections of the same. Under these conditions the Human Machine can be controlled by means of waves, and this has already been absolutely demonstrated.

Likewise, experiments were performed in the bullfighting arena. A scientist could, by means of such a system, stop the bull, make it desist from attacking in precisely the moments when it was about to try its luck with the cape.

With this it has been perfectly demonstrated that every organism is a machine that is susceptible of being controlled like any other.

In the case of the humanoid machine, it is obvious that the diverse psychic inhumane aggregates, taking turns one after another, control the varied cerebral zones at different times. They integrally replace the cerebral nodules, the waves and the automatic machines by means of which scientists can control brains.

In other words, we would say that the scientists in given moments, by means of their electrical systems, play the same role as the psychic aggregates, that is to say, they demonstrate the reality of such aggregates by means of the role they play.

Someone has to control the brain in order to perform acts. It is either controlled by the psychic aggregates or by the scientists through special electrical systems.

In any case, the investigations totally confirm what we are saying: the intellectual humanoid is an unconscious, automatic, subconscious machine.

How could an unconscious machine accept that it is asleep? How could such a machine affirm that the world is Maya, illusion, etc.?

The humanoid machine —because of the very fact that it is a machine, dreams, but it ignores that it dreams, it denies that it dreams, it firmly believes that it is awake and would never accept the thesis that it is asleep. The automatic and mechanized humanoid is not capable of differentiating the objective from the subjective, because of the very fact of being mechanized, and it perceives as subjective what is objective and vice-versa.

The sleeping machine, the humanoid automaton is very far from being able to comprehend the difference between Objective Consciousness and Subjective Consciousness; the machine has its own theses that are precisely based on the profound sleep of the Consciousness. It is by no means possible to make a profane and sleeping person comprehend the difference between Consciousness and sub-consciousness, between objectivity and subjectivity, between sleep and vigil, etc., etc., etc. Only by awakening Consciousness is it possible to accept those differences.

Regrettably, the profane person believes he is awake and he is even offended when someone tells him that his Consciousness is asleep. Talking in Socratic language we would say that the learned ignoramus, the asleep profane person, the unconscious machine, not only ignores but also ignores that he ignores; not only does he not know, but moreover –and what is worse– he does not know that he does not know.

My friends, it is necessary to stop being machines; when someone accepts that he is a machine, he begins to stop being one; a little bit later on, the veil of illusions is torn to pieces.

We need to transform ourselves into human beings and this is only possible by destroying, annihilating the psychic aggregates that incessantly alternate among themselves in order to control the organic machine.

It is indispensable to acquire reality, to stop being mere automatons moved by waves or by aggregates, which is the same, and to transform ourselves into responsible, conscious and true individuals.

Question: Master, what is the difference between the exercise of dividing the attention in three parts and the dissolution of the Ego in order to awaken Consciousness?

Answer: Ladies and gentlemen, throughout all of these lectures we have been especially interested in the dissolution of the Ego, in the complete destruction of all those psychic aggregates within which the Consciousness is caught, bottled up.

I find that that we have spoken very clearly, that we have given a perfect didactic for the absolute annihilation of the Myself, the Oneself.

We have explained ad nauseum that only by means of the radical annihilation of the inhumane elements that we carry within can we liberate the Essence, awaken it.

In today's lecture, we gave you a specific, explicit exercise. We spoke about the division of attention into three parts, with the purpose of utilizing —in an increasingly perfect way— the diverse percentages of awakened Consciousness that we are attaining by means of the death of the Myself.

In the first case, there is a complete doctrine related with the annihilation of the Oneself. In the second case, there is a marvelous exercise, a practice that will allow us to use the Consciousness that we will be attaining in a perfect, clear and precise way.

In any case, it is necessary that we truly transform into competent investigators of esotericism and of pure occultism. This is what we want and with these intentions we have given, through these lectures, the indispensable doctrine.

CONTENTS

"No one would be able to ascend without having previously taken the trouble to descend. Each exaltation is preceded by a terrible and frightful humiliation."

Samael Aun Weor

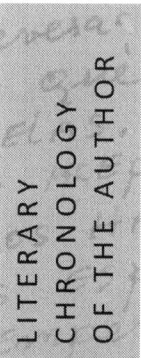

1950 ENTRY GATE TO THE INITIATION
(Later, Master Samael augmented and corrected
this work, baptizing it with the name of
"THE PERFECT MATRIMONY")
THE REVOLUTION OF BEL

1952 ZODIACAL COURSE
CHRIST CONSCIOUSNESS
TREATISE OF OCCULT MEDICINE
AND PRACTICAL MAGIC (first publication)
THE BOOK OF THE VIRGIN OF CARMEL
GNOSTIC CATECHISM
THE POWER IS IN THE CROSS
CHRISTMAS MESSAGE 1952-53

1953 THE SEVEN WORDS
IGNEOUS ROSE
CHRIST WILL
TREATISE OF SEXUAL ALCHEMY
MANUAL OF PRACTICAL MAGIC
CHRISTMAS MESSAGE 1953-54

1954 CHRISTMAS MESSAGE 1954-55

1955 CHRISTMAS MESSAGE 1955-56

1956 MAJOR MYSTERIES
CHRISTMAS MESSAGE 1956-57

1957 FUNDAMENTAL NOTIONS OF ENDOCRINOLOGY
AND CRIMINOLOGY
CHRISTMAS MESSAGE 1957-58

1958  ESOTERIC TREATISE OF THEURGY
CHRISTMAS MESSAGE 1958-59

1959  THE MOUNTAIN OF THE JURATENA
LOGOS, MANTRA, THEURGY
THE YELLOW BOOK
CHRISTMAS MESSAGE 1959-60

1960  MESSAGE OF AQUARIUS
CHRISTMAS MESSAGE 1960-61

1961  CHRISTMAS MESSAGE 1961-62

1962 AZTEC CHRISTIC MAGIC
 THE BOOK OF THE DEAD
THE MYSTERIES OF LIFE AND DEATH
THE MYSTERIES OF FIRE
CHRISTMAS MESSAGE 1962-63

1963  THE PERFECT MATRIMONY (augmented and corrected
publication)
CHRISTMAS MESSAGE 1963-64 (also called
   "TECHNIQUE FOR THE DISSOLUTION OF THE I")

1964 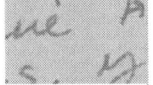 THE COSMIC SHIPS
TOWARD GNOSIS (CHRISTMAS MESSAGE 1964-65)

1965  TRANSCENDENTAL OCCULTISM
         (CHRISTMAS MESSAGE 1965-66)

1966 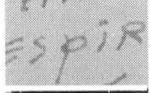 FUNDAMENTAL EDUCATION.
THE BUDDHA'S NECKLACE (CHRISTMAS MESSAGE 1966-67)

1967  ESOTERIC TREATISE OF HERMETIC ASTROLOGY
THE FLYING SAUCERS
REVELATIONS OF AN AVATAR
         (CHRISTMAS MESSAGE 1967-68)

1968  ESOTERIC TREATISE OF RUNIC MAGIC
         (CHRISTMAS MESSAGE 1968-69)

1969   ESOTERIC COURSE OF KABBALAH
             MY RETURN TO TIBET (CHRISTMAS MESSAGE 1969-70)

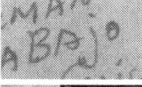

1970   BEYOND DEATH
             PARSIFAL UNVEILED (CHRISTMAS MESSAGE 1970-71)

1971   THE MYSTERY OF THE GOLDEN BLOSSOM
                 (CHRISTMAS MESSAGE 1971-72)

1972   GAZING AT THE MYSTERY
             THE THREE MOUNTAINS (CHRISTMAS MESSAGE 1972-73)

1973   REVOLUTIONARY PSYCHOLOGY
             YES THERE IS HELL, YES THERE IS DEVIL,
                 YES THERE IS KARMA (CHRISTMAS MESSAGE 1973-74)

1974   THE GREAT REBELLION
             THE SECRET DOCTRINE OF ANAHUAC
                 (CHRISTMAS MESSAGE 1974-75)

1976   TAROT AND KABBALAH

1977   TREATISE OF OCCULT MEDICINE AND PRACTICAL MAGIC
             (augmented and corrected publication)
             ESOTERIC COURSE OF THEURGY
             MAYAN MYSTERIES
             THE REVOLUTION OF THE DIALECTIC
                 (compilation of the V.M. Samael's teachings)
             FOR THE FEW
             GNOSTIC ANTHROPOLOGY
             PISTIS SOPHIA UNVEILED

2000   THE FIFTH GOSPEL
                 (compilation of all the conferences dictated
                 by the V.M. Samael)

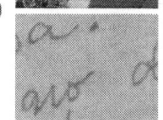

2003   GNOSTIC PRAISE OF THE ETERNAL FEMININE
                 (compilation of the V.M. Samael's teachings
                 related to this theme)

2011   GNOSTIC ETHICS AND SOCIOLOGY
                 (compilation of the V.M. Samael's teachings)

"the power of knowledge"

info@ageac.org

www.ageac.org · www.samael.org
www.vopus.org · www.radiomaitreya.org

Manufactured by Amazon.ca
Bolton, ON